Goa's Foremost Nationalist:
JOSÉ INÁCIO CANDIDO DE LOYOLA

Xavier Centre of Historical Research (XCHR) Studies Series

No. 1 : João de Barros: Portuguese Humanist and Historian of Asia by *C.R. Boxer* Rs. 120

No. 2 : Coastal Western India: Studies from the Portuguese Records by *M.N. Pearson* Rs. 100

No. 3 : Black Legend of Portuguese India (The): Diago do Couto, His Contemporaries and the Soldado Prático–A Contribution to the Study of Political Corruption in the Empires of Early Modern Europe/*George Davison Winius* Rs. 125

No. 4 : Health and Hygiene in Colonial Goa (1510-1961) by *Fátima da Silva Gracias* Rs. 450

No. 5 : Trade and Finance in Portuguese India: A Study of the Portuguese Country-Trade, 1770-1840 by *Celsa Pinto* Rs. 450

No. 6 : Goa and the Revolt of 1787/ *Charles J. Borges* (ed). Rs. 400

No. 7 : Goa and Portugal: Their Cultural Links/*Charles J. Borges* and *Helmut Feldmann* (eds.) Rs. 450

No. 8 : Goa-Kanara Portuguese Relations 1498-1763 by *B.S. Shastry* /and *Charles J. Borges* (ed.)

No. 9 : Goa's Foremost Nationalist: José Inácio Candido de Loyola (The Man and His Writings) by Charles J. Borges (ed).

No.10 : Goa and Portugal: History and Development / *Charles J. Borges*/ *Óscar G. Pereira* and *Hannes Stubbe* (eds).

About the Editor

Charles J. Borges, S.J. is Director, Xavier Centre of Historical Research, Alto Porvorim, Goa. He has been a Jesuit since 1967 and after his training in philosophy and theology, did his M.A. and Ph.D. in history from the Bombay University. He is author of *The Economics of the Goa Jesuits 1542-1759* and had edited or co-edited a number of other books including *Goa and the Revolt of 1787, Goa and Portugal: Their cultural links,* and *Jesuits in India: In historical perspective.* He has many published articles to his credit and has also lectured in India and abroad.

About the Translator

Lino Leitão was born at Varca, Goa. He studied in Portuguese and English schools and attended the Karnataka University in India and the Concordia University in Montreal, Quebec, Canada. He is the author of *Collected Short Stories, Goan Tales and Six Tales.* His short stories have been published in *Goa Today, Gulab, Gomantak Times* (Goa), *Afro-Asian Quarterly, Journal of Asian Literature* and many journals.

XCHR Studies Series No. 9

Goa's Foremost Nationalist:
JOSÉ INÁCIO CANDIDO DE LOYOLA
(THE MAN AND HIS WRITINGS)

Edited by

Charles J. Borges

Translated by

Lino Leitão

CONCEPT PUBLISHING COMPANY, NEW DELHI-110059

ISBN 81-7022-868-9

First Published 2000

Printed and Published by
Ashok Kumar Mittal
Concept Publishing Company
A/15-16, Commercial Block, Mohan Garden
New Delhi-110059 (India)

Phones: 5648039, 5649024
Fax: 091–(11)–5648053
Email: publishing@conceptpub.com

CONTENTS

PART III

PREFACE

The Xavier Centre of Historical Research is pleased to have the present publication *Goa's Foremost Nationalist: José Inácio Candido de Loyola (The Man and His Writings)* as no. 9 in its Studies Series. Mrs. Yona Loyola-Nazareth living in Canada for the last 29 years had been keen on publishing the selected writings of her late father. According to her, efforts to trace most of Loyola's books and important articles have proved futile. Except for *Panoramas Económicas e Sociais da India Portuguesa*, the rest appear to have vanished. Loyola had written "*Collar das Perolas*" during the governorship of Craveiro Lopes and in it he had accused the Governor of smuggling a string of pearls for his mistress. A warrant was issued for Loyola's arrest but Sapateiro D'Mello helped him escape to Bombay, from where he then proceeded to Lisbon. The case was settled and Loyola returned, triumphant, as Inspector of *Comunidades*.

I have included four sketches of Goa's foremost nationalist which give the reader a deeper insight into Loyola's varied personality which he put to optimum use to win Goa's freedom. His writings themselves have been grouped into three parts and the Portuguese versions of a few of them have also been included to give the reader Loyola's use of the Portuguese language to fight his cause.

As the sketches show, Loyola was no armchair thinker but one who backed his arguments with sound statistics. His articles reveal his love for Goa and the personal difficulties he went through to free Goa from Portuguese rule. True there were other nationalists and freedom fighters in Goa, but Loyola stood out by virtue of his prolific writing, his eruditeness, his outspokenness and his love for the downtrodden of Goa.

I wish to thank Mr. Lino Leitão for translating the many articles included in this volume from the Portuguese and for his introduction and sketch of Loyola, all of which show his immense dedication to his task. Dr. Carmo D'Souza has been a silent worker gathering the original articles from various archives to make this present publication possible. He has an interesting sketch too on Loyola as does the late Joseph Barros who in his inimitable style weaves anew the personality of Goa's foremost nationalist.

The work may not have been possible without the personal interest of Mrs. Yona Loyola-Nazareth who helped the present publication financially and who has also written an affectionate account of her late father. My sincere thanks also to Ms. Ernesta Bhobe for typing the texts and tables anew for publication.

November 4, 1999

Dr. Charles J. Borges, S.J.
Director, XCHR

Adv. José Inácio de Loyola

Amy Souza Loyola
Wife of José Inácio

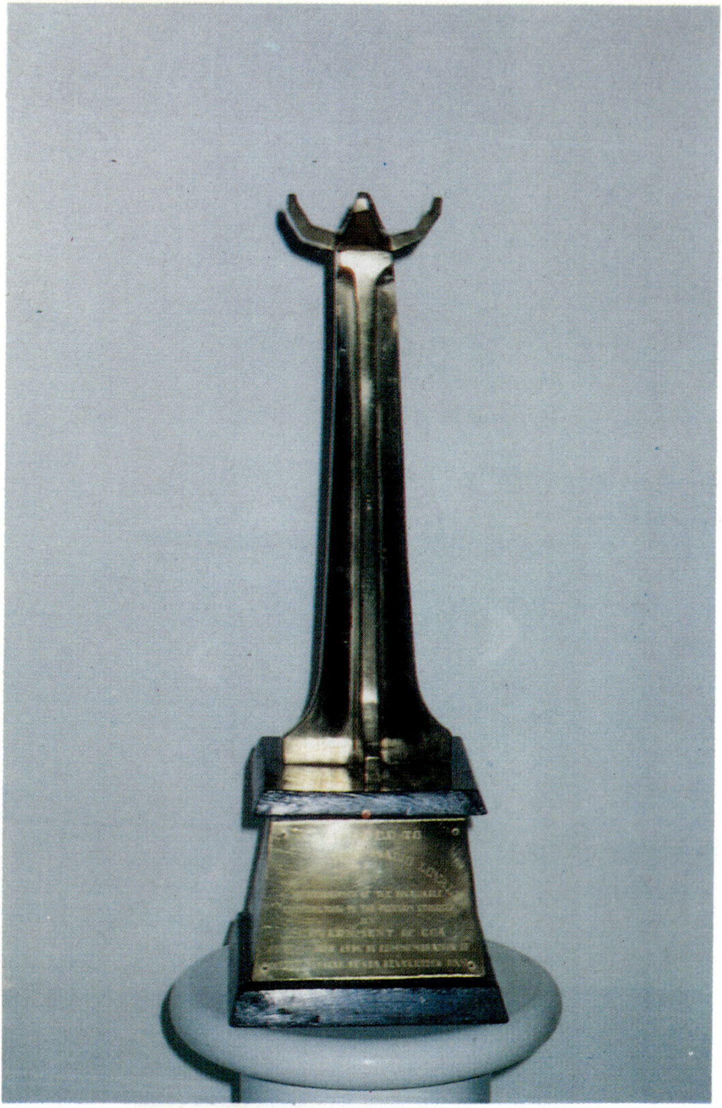

Adv. José Inácio de Loyola honoured by the Govt. of Goa on the occassion of Goa Revolution Day, 18 June 1996

Interior of The Loyola Chapel

The Loyola Home and Chapel

INTRODUCTION

During my student days in Belgaum in the 1950s and my involvement in Goa's liberation movement, I had heard of Fanchu, as he was popularly known then but I never had the opportunity to read anything written about him nor anything written by him.

In 1986, when I was in Goa, Felicio Cardozo, a well-known Konkani writer and freedom fighter, presented me with *Goa's Awakening* by Evagrio Jorge, a prominent Konkani journalist and freedom fighter. In the chapter entitled, "The Arrest of J.I. de Loyola", Jorge reflects upon Fanchu's political thoughts and his contribution to Goa's awakening from colonial slumber.

Jorge's chapter on Fanchu's writing awakened my interest in him. That same year, I visited the Menezes Braganza Institute in Panaji and discovered *Portugal e Colonias*, a newspaper edited by Fanchu while he was in exile in Bombay in the 1930s. I also read many articles by him in other Goan newspapers. But some of his articles, journals and the books that he had published, were not to be found in that Institute.

Dr. Carmo D'Souza, a Goan scholar and author of *Legal System in Goa*, involved in this project as a researcher, later mailed me photocopied articles written by J.I. de Loyola, which had been published in *India Portuguesa*, another newspaper that Fanchu had edited in Goa. These articles came from the private collection of Prof. Michael Martins, Orlim, Salcete.

What attracted me to Fanchu were his thoughts. He was a practical thinker, a Goan nationalist, who was at war with dictatorship and the high-handedness of the Portuguese Governors of the colony. He devoted his lifetime to propagating the concept of democracy among his people.

When I visited Goa again in 1992, I came across a book of Fanchu's, entitled, *Panoramas Económicas e Sociais da India Portuguesa* (Bombay: *Portugal e Colonias*, 1938). This book which was in the possession of Mr. José Alvito Menezes from Agassaim, is now with Mrs. Yona Loyola-Nazareth, the daughter of Fanchu Loyola. I translated the book under the title: *Economic and Social Views of Portuguese India.* I also translated Fanchu's articles.

We decided to publish the translated manuscript under the tentative title of *Fanchu's Thoughts on Democracy, Politics, Economics and the Social Issues of his Times.* And we went looking for a publisher. Fortunately, the idea of editing and publishing the manuscript was accepted by the Xavier Centre of Historical Research, Goa.

Many have contributed to bringing this book about. Dr. Carmo D'Souza helped me with the research. My wife, Mrs. Olga Leitão put the first draft of the manuscript on the word processor, correcting my spelling and other errors. Ms. Pavitra Elliot, a student in literature at the University of Toronto, read the first draft of the manuscript, making worthwhile suggestions. The second reading of the manuscript was done by Ms. Rosemary Leaver, a free-lance editor, who polished the text and prepared the second draft. The final editing of the manuscript was done by Dr. Charles J. Borges, S.J. who also prepared the glossary. I owe my thanks to them all.

But if Felicio Cardozo had not presented me with *Goa's Awakening* by Evagrio Jorge, my interest in Fanchu Loyola's contribution to Goa's political thought would not have been aroused. And Dr. Alvaro da Costa brought to my attention the book, *Panoramas Ecónomicas e Sociais da India Portuguesa* and informed me that I could get it from Mr. José Alvito Menezes of Agassaim. Though this gentleman loaned me the book, he did not give me permission to take the book back with me to Canada. Mr. Paul Leitão and the late Mr. Januário Coutinho photocopied the book for me. I took the photocopied pages with me to Canada where I translated them at my leisure. Prof. Michael Martins of Orlim, whom I had the pleasure of meeting during my recent visit to Goa in 1998, handed me the original issues of *India Portuguesa.* All these individuals helped me to germinate the idea of a translation of Fanchu's works. I owe my thanks to them.

May 27, 1998

Lino Leitão
Dorval, Québec,
Canada

J. I. DE LOYOLA
A Born Democrat

Lino Leitão

José Inãcio Francisco Xavier Candido de Loyola, affectionately known as Fanchu, had his own vision of *Estado da India,* and Goa, in particular. It was a vision based on the intimate aspirations of Goan society of his times. With clarity, he boldly articulated the aspirations of his people in his writings, speeches and press interviews. He would lash out at the colonial authorities when they brought in legislation detrimental to the Goan community. His mode of expression was in Portuguese, the official language of *Estado da India.*

In this work, a collection of some of his writings, speeches and press interviews, translated into English, are presented as an anthology. It is hoped that the present generation in the State of Goa by going through the selection of writings presented here, will come to know the man and get acquainted with his contributions to Goan political thought. Fanchu's writings are part of the Goan heritage and history.

Trying to understand Fanchu's intellectual and political input, the reader will notice that the ideas in his writings, which he expressed with such passion and such clarity, were aimed at securing the future of Goa for posterity. His voice was the voice of Goa's future. And his ideas were indeed like, as he believed, seeds.

All his life, Fanchu wrestled to plant the seeds of his vision, which was also the vision of the oppressed and voiceless downtrodden people of Goa. To bring people's attention to his ideas, he founded a number of newspapers. But his newspapers were suspended and the presses on which the papers were printed were often destroyed. In one case, for instance, Francisco Manuel Couçeiro da Costa who was the Governor of Goa, Daman and Diu from 1910 to 1917, suspended the *Jornal da India*, a newspaper edited by Fanchu, in 1913. The reason given by him for its suspension was that the newspaper disturbed the public order and peace, the very security of the State. Fanchu was only twenty-two years old at the time and he refused to take the insult to his newspaper lying down. With the courage of his convictions, he wrote a letter entitled *Carta Política* and addressed it to the Governor. In it, he courageously pointed out: "When the government governs as it ought to, then there isn't any problem. Your vigorous opposition makes your government unfit to govern."

Fanchu was never afraid of speaking his mind before higher authorities and he would never beat about the bush. When he was a young man, he was once brought into the hall of the Military Library at Panaji and was given a dozen strokes by Captain Almeida Eça for the press statement that he had given in British India, complaining about the lack of freedom of the Press in Portuguese India (Letter of September 28, 1946, addressed by captain Furtunando Miranda to the director of Civil Administration, Goa).

On October 11, 1946 Fanchu was arrested and deported to Fort Peniche in Portugal and he was also stripped of his political rights for 15 years. All this was because he gave a statement to the *Free Press Journal* from Bombay, disclosing the undemocratic policies of the colonial government in Goa, Daman and Diu. Though he knew what the consequences would be, it never prevented him from speaking his mind. This is one of the traits that the reader will notice in his writings and speeches. His courageous tendency to maintain his integrity in spite of the consequences he might suffer, was what created the charisma that attracted the ordinary Goan. It was for this reason that he was feared and hated by individuals in high places and by the Goan oligarchy.

He also took part in many elections to usher in societal change based on the aspirations of the people. But the elections in which he took part were tampered with and voters intimidated. In one instance, the election officers were attacked and the ballot boxes were broken. All this because one of the main principles he stood for was the cohesion of Goan society. To him this was of crucial importance if the Goans were to recognize that their duties and obligations ought to be directed towards society as a whole and not simply towards their own individual concerns.

But the inequities of the caste system with its strains of traditionalism and feudalism which had come down into Goan society from pre-conquest times, ran very deep in the consciousness of the Goan population and they permeated into every aspect of Goan life. The higher castes, conscious of their status in society, saw Fańchu as a threat to their respectability. They accused him of many things because they did not want to open the door to societal changes based on equity and respect.

If solutions were to be found, Fanchu understood that Goans of all classes had to address the problems that faced their society, or be doomed. Having faith in what he believed, he had the courage to raise and answer the painful question that plagued the Catholic sector of the Goan population. Despite their conversion to Catholicism, the Catholic Goans had rooted caste rigidities into the Church by creating religious solidarities, known as *confrarias*. In an article entitled "*Confrarias do Santíssimo*" (*Portugal e Colonias*, October 30, 1937), Fanchu wrote:

> "God created all men equal. They all have a common ancestry. In the end, we all end up being food for the earthworms. Are we not all brothers in faith? If we are, we would not humiliate our own brothers. But the *gauncares*, monopolising the brotherhood of the Blessed Sacrament, display their incompatible vanity which does not go well in the house of worship. Worse still, *gauncares* take pleasure in displaying their limitless egotism!"

The consolidation of the Goan community being dear to him, he would think about it often and sometimes, he would rise to the heights of poetry. In an article "*No Limar do Novo Ano* (At the Dawning of the New Year)" (*Portugal e Colonias*, January 1, 1937), he writes:

> "To exist is not living. Living is to cultivate the garden of your imagination and work passionately day in and day out to sow the seeds of solidarity among the human species. It is also to strive to keep the window panes of your intelligence clean and clear at all times from dust and cobwebs".

But the oppressed who had grown up from generation to generation with servitude ingrained in their minds, were passive people. Even if they had understood the political and moral injustices that Fanchu condemned as wrong, they lacked the strength and means to get rid of that offal. But some among the higher castes would respond to his arguments with distorted logic and sometimes with hostility and hatred. If one were to go through *Portugal e Colonias*, one would come across rebuttals to his ideas and perceive how entrenched in casteism were the minds at the time.

Aside from caste hierarchies, incorporated into the system was another structure, that of *contucares* (the village servants), which had overtones of apartheid and segregation. This too had come down into Goan society from pre-conquest times. Fanchu writes about this system under the title "*Namoxins*" (*Portugal e Colonias*, July 25, 1937):

> "Indignities and injustices persisted in all other institutions, subjecting the lower castes and outcastes to a lifetime of discrimination and robbing them of their human dignity. Like animals put into cages, Goans were put into the confines of the caste system. That made them timid social conformists."

A further dimension was implanted into Goan feudalism as it was emerging during the colonial era. The higher castes, who owned large estates, had acquired prestige and status in society.

They were *fidalgos*, noblemen or rather, effigies of European noblemen. In Goa, they came to be known as *bhatkars* and on their lands lived their serfs, the *mundkars*. The *bhatkar* with his *casa grande* with a gateway and opulent lifestyle, was the *mundkars'* divine lord and the *mundkars* never addressed the *bhatkar* and his wife by their names but with honorifics. The village people and the *mundkars* identified with the *bhatkar* to the point where even his glories were their glories. This unique feudal system of the *Estado da India* provided the landlords with cheap and guaranteed labour. It also gave *bhatkars* a hold over *mundkars*, making *mundkars* and village people psychologically dependent on the *bhatkars*.

In "*Batcares-Mudcares*" (*Portugal e Colonias*, September 11, 1937), elucidating article no. 2,309 from *Codigo Civil*, Fanchu sheds light on the governing relationship between *bhatkars* and *mundkars*. Though there was legislation protecting the rights of the *mundkar*, he, illiterate and dominated by the *bhatkar*, was too frightened a creature to take advantage of the legislation. This unique feudal system denied the *mundkar* even his own dignity as a human being. It gave him nothing, only a few *tangas*, says Fanchu, in "The Emigration Problem."

This deplorable feudalism based on subsistence farming offered no solutions towards the economic and social problems that the *Estado da India* faced. It kept the peasants in their place by giving them no access to education and without a strong and prosperous peasantry, the *Estado da India* was not in a position to stimulate economic development. The administrative jobs and professional positions went to the sons and daughters of the upper caste elites, as the educational system was geared towards their benefit alone.

The Goan peasant being a social conformist, could not bring about a peasant revolution in Goa. The lower castes and the middle classes with no employment opportunities were forced to emigrate. With the massive emigration of the disposed peasantry, the feudal lords who depended on the wretchedness of the *mundkars*, found it difficult to get a *mundkar* woman to grind masala for their curry or a *mundkar* child to look after their goats or to do any other odd jobs for them. Thus labour costs went up. The enraged feudal lords clamoured to bring in legislative means to stop emigration of the poor on the grounds that it was draining the country's economy. But this was no more than hypocrisy on the part of the feudal upper classes. The emigration of the poor affected their own pockets, since labour costs went up, and not in the least the economy of the whole country. As Fanchu pointed out in his stinging critique on the claims of the feudal lords, far from being a drain on the country's finances, the emigrants contributed towards the economy of the *Estado da India* by sending monetary remittances to their dependents. "The sons and daughters of emigrants", he wrote, "got better education and better job-training which they could never even dream of if they had remained in Goa" (See "The Emigration Problem" and "A Reply to Heliodorio").

Fanchu once wrote that to govern is to look ahead into the future. Looking at the *Estado da India*, he saw no economic base. If the future of Goa had to be secured for the grandchildren, he knew that his generation had to lay the kind of foundation which stimulated economic growth, so that Goa could free itself from economic dependency on British India. Goans not only migrated to British Indian cities to look for employment, but Goa depended on agricultural and on many other imports from British India. Without economic control in the hands of the people, Fanchu had the savvy to understand that political freedom was a myth.

Fanchu was in exile in British India, in Bombay, at that time. As he started diagnosing the economic growth of British India, it pained him to note the zero economic growth in the *Estado da India*. He understood the reasons behind this disparity. Though all the economic structures were in place in Goa, these economic activities were not commercially oriented and the feudal lords with their rigid patriarchal attitudes of elitism did not have the intellectual foresight to adapt to the emerging economic ideas. They were non-entrepreneurial, without any ability in risk-taking and with no desire to increase their capital.

Fanchu, who had the ability to see into the future, completely understood that if the Goan feudal lords did not initiate economic changes, they themselves would be ruined for good and with them, they would bring down the rest of the Goans. With this view in mind, he wrote a book, *Panoramas Económicas e Sociais da India Portuguesa.* These are letters to a fictional character, Luis Maria, a feudal lord. Replete with economic examples from British India and quotations from the economists of his times, he asked the feudal lords to break out of the prison of outmoded feudalism and step into a much more current economic mode, namely, cottage and small-scale industries.

Knowing that the *Estado da India* had the potential to increase its agricultural production, he advocated that the agricultural sector be invigorated so as to cut out the dependency on agricultural imports from British India. The reader may not agree with all the proposals he puts forward in his work. Nevertheless the argument he offers towards laying an economic base in *Estado da India*, is thought-provoking. He saw that without such a base, posterity would enjoy no secure future. He expounded his economic vision in profound terms:

> "But a country with a vision for the future, will not wait for the economic laws to fall into place. A country with a vision will not tarry to bring in the necessary measures to give an impetus to a certain number of industries within the country because the growth of population and the growth of industries should go hand in hand, like parallel lines. To hope that industrial growth will come due to the pressure of economic laws, to hope that industrial growth will come by itself with the automatic growth of the population, is to abdicate the responsibilities of governance".

Portugal, once a maritime power, was an industrially under-developed nation in Europe. It suffered from excessive illiteracy and poverty and an elitism, that was engendered by a class hierarchy not very different from the caste hierarchy of the *Estado da India*. Its social backwardness was not much different from that of Goa. Although Goa had been an important commercial centre at one time, the trade between Goa and Portugal was insignificant and in any event, Goa exported very little to Portugal. So Portugal had nothing to gain by laying an economic base in its *Estado da India*. In fact, it had abdicated its responsibility of governance. Knowing the dilemma in which Goa found itself, Fanchu made a famous plea for collective and social responsibility just like John F. Kennedy did. He writes:

> "If we want our communities to succeed, we must ask little from the State or the municipalities, but we must ask ourselves what we can do, that we are not presently doing, to better our communities".

Sound political institutions evolve only when the individuals in the society realise that the process of political decision-making is a shared responsibility and act accordingly. Fanchu, who understood this working principle of democracy, worked hard to accentuate the moral and ethical dimensions of decision-making in the flawed "autonomy" which was implemented by decree no. 7008 of October 9, 1920, during the governorship of Jaime Alberto de Castro Morais (1919-25).

His articles on autonomy show very clearly the priorities that he held dear, self-government has to work for the benefit of the people. He wrote:

> "We might have learned people, but what is important is the right selection of the competent candidates, with the integrity of character to lay a foundation for self-government in the society, educating all segments of the people in their civic duties. Without this, self-government will be a failure."

Or again,

> "Among the cream of intellectuals and public men in our country, who are expected to give an example of

independence and moral integrity, shameful betrayals and defections abound. Before everything else, the moral and civic preparedness of the people is the basic need for the functioning of autonomy. How can we say that we are politically mature, when the leaders of the people, ignorant of the principle of patriotic solidarity, have not even once put the public interest first, before their own interests?"

He also lays down the solemn duty of the elected members:

"At any given critical moment, the elected members have to demonstrate in solidarity their capability to uphold the electorate's aspirations up to the very end."

Without moral integrity and civic preparedness, autonomy had become a windfall for the Governor and the elected representatives of the people. Many elites supported this flawed autonomy because they profited from it and it protected their interests. Fanchu, however, having seen through the Governor's tactics, exposed his taxation policies as those which overtaxed the small farmers. In a tone dripping with contempt, he referred to the Governor as a *raja* of India with absolute powers over his subjects and, equally contemptuous of the elected elite, he makes this observation:

"It showed that we are a people without courage; it showed that we are a people without the strength to oppose the government; and above all, it showed that we are weaklings and cowards and that we can be easily bought or corrupted. That is the truth and the rest is strategy!"

And, being a democrat, he spelled out one of the principles of democracy:

"It is natural for the people's representatives to have divergent opinions in matters of approach to tackling administrative problems. But what is not permitted whatsoever, is to use their mandate to spit in the faces of the very people who elected them."

Though Fanchu was raised a Catholic, he was a secular humanist. To him religion was a private matter. With regard to Pope Leo XIII's encyclical, *Immortale Dei*, published in November 1885, which advocated that the head of a Catholic nation should be a practising Catholic, Fanchu made this point:

> "The Church should be considered separate from the State. The Church's mission is celestial. For this reason, the Church is an organisation different from the State. Church and State are independent and sovereign entities. Each exercise their power within their defined jurisdictions, one is ecclesiastical and the other is civic" (*Portugal e Colonias*, October 30, 1937).

As a secular humanist, unity among all religious sectors, particularly between Hindus and Catholics, the two main sectors of the Goan population, was very dear to him. Readers will come across several references made to this subject in his articles. But, he expressed his secular notions most clearly after the liberation of Goa. Thus from Lisbon, he wrote:

> " ... cleansing oneself of racial and caste prejudices, let the people of Goa from all villages, both Christians and Hindus, stand before the flag of the Nation, as one people, in solidarity with their desires and aspirations" (F.X. Gomes-Catão, *Esboço Histórico Arqueológico, Freguesia de Orlim, Centenário da sua Igreja 8-5-1568 — 8-5-1968*, no. 4, p. 26, 1968).

After ousting the monarchy in 1910, Portugal went through a period of political turmoil. But when General Oscar Carmona became President of Portugal in 1928, the country settled down. It gave Portugal a stable government. At the same time, Oliveira Salazar, who was brought in as Prime Minister of Portugal, turned out to be a dictator. In 1930, he introduced the *Acto Colonial* which humiliated the peoples of the colonies. For instance, article no. 2 of the *Acto Colonial* stated that:

> "It was part of the organic essence of the Portuguese nation to perform the historical function of possessing and colonizing the overseas dominions and civilizing the indigenous populations" (João António J. da Costa, *A History of Goa*, 1982, p. 279).

Fanchu, in a speech given on November 25, 1932, the anniversary of Goa's conquest by Afonso de Albuquerque, strongly objected to the imperious tone of the *Acto Colonial* which humiliated the people. He said:

> "Let us take a pledge not to give in to these repugnant ideas, and let us take a pledge not to spite each other. These fissiparous ideas are like the welts of lashes given across the faces of some us. They have taken away all our rights in favour of others. Such ideas in the end, create two distinct classes: first class and second class citizens though all of us are the citizens of one country."

Fanchu, went on to point out in the same speech that India's civilisation was in fact very ancient, advanced and developed, and the idea of Portugal's mission to "civilise the indigenous population" of the *Estado da India* was ridiculous. Coming down hard upon the colonial establishment in the *Estado da India*, he predicted that because of its domineering policies, the Portuguese empire would eventually collapse.

Fanchu wanted political and social institutions to evolve within the country so as to accentuate the ethical dimensions of decision-making. For this reason, civil liberties had always been his first priority. He wanted the people to be conscious of their rights, controlling their own political and economic destiny; and then they could bequeath the land to their grandchildren.

A born democrat, Fanchu left a statement on civil rights to Goan posterity, which would make any Goan anywhere, proud to be a Goan. He was an intellectual who supported his ideas with action, and if humanity and sacrifice distinguishes greatness, Fanchu was a great Goan.

J.I. DE LOYOLA
The Man With a Futuristic Vision

Carmo D'Souza

José Inácio Francisco Candido de Loyola (1891-1973), affectionately called Fanchu Loyola was born in the village of Orlim in Salcete, Goa on March 11, 1891. He was the son of Avertano Loyola and Maria Angelica Conceição Gomes. The Loyola family had at that time established itself on Goa's political scene. It was instrumental in running the *Partido Indiano*. The party's views were voiced in the newspaper *India Portuguesa*. A story goes round that Fanchu's grandmother claimed that she had dedicated her three sons to the three important professions then in Goa: a priest to God, a doctor to the society and a lawyer to the devil. The lawyer, José Loyola (senior) was a political giant that Goa produced in the 19th century. He carved a name for himself in Goa's electoral history. He was the central figure in the political events of 1890s. As a consequence of this upheaval he was forced together with his four accomplices to take refuge in British India. The Governor-General of Goa demanded the extradition of José Loyola (senior) and his four accomplices. This demand led to a series of correspondence between the Portuguese and the British governments and also inter-departmental correspondence among British officials, today labelled as the *Foreign Department 1891*, at numbers 126-132 and housed at the National Archives of India, New Delhi. The accused were charged with sedition, disobedience, crimes against the exercise of political rights, and homicide among others. The question before the British was whether they had to surrender the accused if the demand was with a view to furnish them for offences of political nature.

Fanchu Loyola was initiated into politics right from the cradle. In his early twenties he showed signs of political maturity normally found in veteran politicians. At that stage he was editing *Jornal da India.* Governor F. M. Couçeiro da Costa ordered its suspension on the grounds of the security of state, public order and peace. Loyola retaliated by publishing a small pamphlet entitled *Carta Politíca* addressed to the Governor. While he agreed to comply with the suspension order he clarified that he would continue to fight against the arbitrary regime whenever it interfered with his freedom of expression. He vowed to come out with another publication to replace *Jornal da India* in case remedial steps were not taken and promised to bring out series of publications, one to replace another whenever the government suspended his papers and interfered with his freedom of expression. He carried out his threat by publishing *Rebate. Carta Política* is an example of Loyola's undaunted spirit that refused to be trampled and cowed down by the use of the government's arbitrary powers.

The twenties of this century saw Loyola, in full cry against the so-called Provincial Autonomy declared by the Portuguese government for the State of India. Surprisingly, a democrat like Loyola found flaws with that autonomy, which many other politicians considered as an initial experience to a more liberal democratic system. However if one closely follows the fine line of arguments advanced by Loyola in a series of articles in *India Portuguesa* one can understand his pain at the political events that followed as a consequence of that autonomy. The Legislative Council of the State of India as described by Loyola's vivid pen witnessed shameful proceedings in which the Governor manipulated people's representatives and carried out his designs under the label of autonomy. Loyola's analysis of the composition of the Legislative Council proved how autonomy was flawed and hence bound to fail as an exercise in democracy. He openly attacked Governor-General Jaime de Morais for his role in manipulating the Legislative Council and took the representatives to task for their irresponsible conduct. As per Loyola's view, the Council indulged in the wasting of time and revenue. Those series of articles from Loyola's pen are a valuable material for research scholars in order to understand the political undercurrents in Goa during that period.

Loyola was at the fore again on the Goan scene in the elections of 1926 to elect representative to the Superior Council of Colonies. The controversial ballot created a stir especially at the polling booth at Calangute. The two rival candidates were Prazeres da Costa supported by *O Heraldo* and Mariano Martins supported by *Heraldo*. Allegations and counter-allegations of rigging appeared on the pages of the two major dailies of Goa, with the election at Calangute continuing for a week while the rest of Goa waited in suspended animation. Loyola was the election strategist behind the Prazeres victory. *O Heraldo* of November 13, 1926 reporting the victory celebration refers to the popular fiesta that followed the declaration of results.

Loyola believed in the development of agriculture as the base for the economic advancement of Goa. It is interesting to note his agricultural experiment undertaken in 1927 in the rice-fields of Carambolim. At this stage he occupied the prestigious position of inspector of village communities. The object of that intended green revolution was to attempt three rice crops instead of the traditional two during a year. The scheme was launched with much fanfare under the patronage of the Governor's wife, Julia Craveiro Lopes and accompanied with a twenty-one gun salute. Unfortunately, the scheme did not succeed due to various factors. Dr. Joseph Barros in one of his speeches held in Menezes Braganza Hall gave a vivid description of that experiment. The incident reveals Loyola's deep interest in Goan agriculture which was dear to his heart. In fact he devoted some of his writings to the economic aspects of Goa.

Loyola's "*Basta*" (Enough is Enough) reverberated throughout the length and breadth of the State of India on November 25, 1932. The simple expression turned into a sublime political slogan which expressed an indomitable spirit that refused to bow down to the arbitrary executive power. The speech was discussed for several years later and assumed legendary proportions during the Portuguese rule. The Governor-General had conferred on Loyola the privilege of addressing a distinguished gathering in front of the statue of Afonso de Albuquerque. The occasion was the commemoration of the reconquest of Goa by Albuquerque. Loyola extracted the final words of Albuquerque's last letter to King Manuel of Portugal to build up the special case of Goa. "India will speak out for herself and for me," he said quoting the famous lines from Albuquerque's letters. He traced the historical development of the policies followed by Albuquerque. In his inimitable style, Loyola put life in the statute of the Conqueror and inferred that India had spoken out and continued to speak constantly for herself and for Albuquerque. He warned the Portuguese authorities of possible grave consequences if they diverted from the old policy formulated towards Goa by Albuquerque. He referred to the possibility of revolt in the near future if corrective measures were not taken and the possible danger of the Portuguese overseas empire going into flames due to the growing hostility to the Portuguese dominion.

The legendary speech resounded throughout the length and breadth of Goa. A debate arose as to the contents of the speech and whether it was a sign to revolt. It is interesting to note that the same text was published again a decade later. The circumstances in which the speech was delivered enhanced the value of the words uttered on the occasion. It is claimed that the distinguished audience consisting of the upper layer of the government officials, justices and others applauded at the end of the speech. Few in the audience were able to gauge the subtle attack mounted on the oppressive regime. A person who was part of that audience claimed that after the speech Loyola drove away in the car waving to the crowd and went underground to surface again in British India. The daring speech and the escapade was a blow to the Portuguese administration. Such feats kept the morale of the Goan people high during the colonial era. His slogan "Enough is Enough" created a flutter as the speech was reported in the press the following day. Every year the feast of St. Catherine reminded the Goans of that historic speech. Perhaps the speech was one of Loyola's greatest contributions to political history of Goa. It is to be noted that he carried out his relentless fight from Bombay where he edited *Portugal e Colonias.*

Throughout his career, Loyola displayed a remarkable independence of thought and did not fear even the mighty rulers such as Governors. In his early twenties, he fired his first salvo in his *Carta Política* against Governor F. M. Couçeiro da Costa. During the so-called autonomy in the twenties of this century, he wrote a series of articles bluntly attacking Governor-General Jaime de Morais. He wrote, for instance:

> "Mr. Jaime de Morais who always had his way without any obstacles, thinks that he is an authentic *raja* of India with absolute powers over his subjects".

In another place referring to his arrogant conduct, he wrote:

> "I can almost hear him, shouting in the belief that he is exercising his sovereign will: *I want, I can, I will*! But his kingdom autonomy, upon which he stands, has turned out to be a heap of garbage."

In 1946 Loyola sent Goa's heart pounding as he faced trial by the military court, an aftermath of the Lohia movement. He was accused of crimes against the security of the State by his statements that appeared in the *Free Press Journal*, Bombay, under the title "The Coming Struggle in Goa" The statements were about the Lohia movement for restoration of civil liberties in Goa and about the intolerable regime prevailing there. He claimed that the civil rights were enjoyed in Goa during the earlier period. He contended that civil liberties were the essence of human nature and that they were guaranteed by the Portuguese Constitution, but suspended by the discordant laws made by the executive wing.

Loyola was a human rights activist in Goa, who opined that civil liberties did not have a national character but belonged to the people of the world at large. He considered any restriction on individual liberties as intolerable and was of the opinion that individual liberties were prior and superior to the Constitution, being the very essence of man by birth. Loyola belonged to the school of thought that believed that individual liberties should not even be consigned to the Constitution. The military court on November 11, 1946 sentenced him to four years' rigorous imprisonment coupled with a fifteen year suspension of political rights. He was deported to Portugal and imprisoned at the Peniche jail. He was set free under conditional liberty on January 12, 1947 in Lisbon.

I have decided to include in this biographical sketch some oral evidence collected by me from some close associates of Loyola. He possessed a magnetic personality which cast a spell on his supporters who were not merely sympathizers but identified their cause with that of Loyola. They subscribed and read his newspapers because he expressed in his articles their own views presented in a systematic and refined manner. They took a partisan stand to Loyola's writings with boastful expressions in Konkani such as "*Loyolan borench dillem*" implying that Loyola had made a sound attack or presented a fine response to the opponent's attack. It is evident from this that Loyola had certain charisma over the part of the intellectual section of those days.

The support from his fans and admirers was not merely through words. They showed their faith in him by backing him to the hilt. He was their worthy leader who spoke out with courage and moral authority. The late Dr. Álvaro da Costa, a close associate of Loyola, speaking to me recalled that when on one occasion Loyola was facing imminent arrest due to a particular write-up against government authorities, a section of the Margao business community, collected money late in the evening and packed Loyola across the Goa border. They could not let their leader fall into the unfriendly chains of the government authorities in Goa.

Loyola's magnetic influence on his supporters is evident from another incident narrated by the late Dr. Álvaro da Costa. Party politics often required financial assistance from the wealthy friends and associates. Loyola requested Dr. da Costa to go on his behalf to the house of a particular landlord with a request for a sum of money. Dr. da Costa was very doubtful about the success of the mission, knowing well the miserly disposition of the landlord. He set out for the village a few kilometres away from Margao and reached there at dusk. As he approached the huge mansion he saw inside a flicker of light from a kerosene lamp, which confirmed the miserly nature of the landlord. The doctor with a heart as heavy as lead delivered the letter. The miser disappeared inside one of those dark rooms and emerged out with a thick envelope half an hour later. The miser did not show any traditional Goan hospitality to the doctor. On accepting the envelope the doctor thanked the landlord, sure that it contained the desired amount. When the envelope reached Loyola's hand, he opened it with a laugh displaying the money.

Loyola when in need got the financial support from his associates without whose assistance it would not have been possible to wage the election battles and carry on his journalistic activity. It is said that Loyola's supporters never denied him money whenever he requested for some amount. There were some landlords who considered it a privilege to entertain Loyola and his political disciples at their homes. Many rich people threw their doors open extending the traditional Goan hospitality whenever he happened to be in the village. It may surprise many historians why Loyola's supporters relied entirely on him their leader as they could not expect economic gains from the politic al moves. Often the moves were anti-establishment. Perhaps they found in some of Loyola's political maneuvers, the preservation of their Goa dignity and honour.

Often controversies surrounded Loyola's political moves. In fact he was a controversial giant that Goa produced in this century. To call him uncontroversial or a cautious politician who engineered his moves diplomatically, is the greatest insult and injury to his memory. He never feared controversies. It was his unique, distinctive approach to problems that made him so controversial. It is to his credit that he made his stand clear irrespective of the stature of his opponents. Thus we find him pitched against some of the Governors of Portuguese India.

When he took sides on controversial issues against the establishment, Loyola took great pains to explain his position. It is these explanations and reasons that give an insight today into his personality as well as into the problems and issues of the day. His writings, today, form a rich source for research material.

Loyola's controversial approach to issues can be seen in his battle against the so-called autonomy, in the various electoral battles as well as in the movement of the restoration of civil liberties in 1946. Though he was jailed as a follow-up of political events in 1946, his trial shows a unique stand which can be differentiated from that of another political leader, Tristão Bragança Cunha. Loyola often strode a unique path, a new path which left distinctive footprints in the Goan history. He did not walk his unique path alone. He had a large number of supporters and admirers. He understood their feelings, their sentiments, their aspirations in clear political concepts. It is this characteristic of identification with his class of supporters, that gave moral authority to his writings.

Loyola was a man of his times and hence can be placed in a particular historical time-frame. In his writings it is possible to identity concepts and language expressions in vogue in those times. Hence his writings are a valuable material and give an insight into the society of that time. However his greatness lay in being able to raise up certain issues like a skylark and break the time-concept frame and view the world with a futuristic vision. Many of his political writings contain the seeds for an effective government which are relevant even in modern times. His writings on autonomy are a rich source to understand the conflicts between the theory and practice of self-government. The world today is struggling with the theoretical concept of democracy and its practice as evidenced in the Afro-Asian experience. However, one of Loyola's greatest contribution is his thought on civil liberties as expressed in his 1932 speech and in the trial in 1946, respectively. He was one of Goa's finest human rights activist in the first half of this century.

Loyola returned to India in 1958 but went back to Portugal after the liberation of Goa. He passed away there in 1973. He died a dreamer always loving the land of his birth.

LOYOLA
A Man of Honour

Yona Loyola-Nazareth

Fanchu Loyola was born at the home of his maternal grandparents on March 11, 1891. At the time, his father Avertano de Loyola and his uncle Dr. José Inácio de Loyola were both in exile in British India, in the aftermath of the September 21, 1890 political skirmish at Margao, during which 21 citizens had lost their lives. The two brothers returned in September of 1891 to Goa. It was then that the family returned to Orlim and the baptism of Fanchu took place. It is rather uncanny that when my mother was expecting my youngest sister Elaine, my father had to flee the country to avoid imminent arrest as a result of a vitriolic article he had published. He returned sometime in September-October 1929, when my sister was ten months old.

My mother did her utmost to discourage my father's political entanglements and to concentrate on his practice. It was futile. Ultimately she gave up. She remarked, one day, "After all politics is in his blood! Money means nothing to him!" My cousin Lolita Loyola Furtado Fernandes once mentioned to me that if "only Uncle Fanchu had concentrated on his legal practice he would have been a millionaire". After all, he was the only lawyer in Goa at that time to be well-versed in English. Indeed he had been retained by British clients from Bombay to resolve legal matters pertaining to the railways. I remember well these distinguished gentlemen calling on my father. Shortly thereafter he was arrested.

My mother would often remark that my father was irresponsible. It was only after I requested the late Dr. Joseph

Barros to do a little research on my father's background that I learnt that he had lost his mother when he was six years old. Thereafter, he and his younger siblings were looked after by their cousins, daughters of Dr. José Inácio de Loyola. His father and uncle were lost in the world of politics. How and from whom was my father supposed to learn about "responsibility?" By the age of 21 his father died, leaving him with the responsibility of looking after his two younger sisters.

I never comprehended the depth of his love for Goa till he returned to Bombay in 1958. He returned from a visit to Jawaharlal Nehru in Delhi quite defeated and disconsolate. I could not fathom his distress. He paced restlessly up and down the hallway, sighing until I could bear it no longer. I questioned him. His answer puzzled me, at the time. "My child, we have lost Goa. You and I have lost Goa". Lost Goa? In 1958? He then proceeded to tell me that although he had done his utmost to persuade Nehru to conduct a plebiscite in Goa, he was convinced that with Krishna Menon at the helm, a 'military take-over' of Goa was imminent. Little wonder he was called a man of 'vision'.

In the course of the last few decades, as the prevalent political scenario in Goa emerged, I finally understood. Determined to visit his beloved homeland for one last time, he returned to Goa. But volatile circumstances prompted by his many political enemies, compelled him to leave to avert the possibility of his being arrested again. Disillusioned and too old to take up the fight, he returned to Lisbon to live in isolation and mourn the loss of his beloved Goa. He was adamant in his refusal to join my elder sister and her family in Uganda, or my younger sister and her family, residing in Rome at the time, where he could have lived in luxury. My pleas to join me and the family in Bombay fell on deaf ears. Was he punishing himself for 'failing' his country? "Goa for the Goans?" An impossible dream! And thus, he chose to die in voluntary exile.

My father always empathised with the Portuguese people. He pitied them and mocked them for being mere 'puppets' in the hands of a vile dictator. His attacks were directed at the servile officials carrying out the suppressive and oppressive measures imposed by António Salazar. An insightful article of his was published in the *O Heraldo* in the late 1960s, exhorting the people of Goa to extend the hand of friendship to Portugal. As was to be expected, a certain segment was outraged. And, yet, years later, this proposition was endorsed.

My father had married Amy Amelia D'Souza, daughter of Thomas D'Souza of Tivim in 1917 at Orlim. Born and bred in Karachi she was a talented pianist, had a teacher's diploma and taught at St. Patrick's School, Karachi where she had the privilege of teaching the late Cardinal Valerian Gracias of Bombay. Accustomed as she was to modern amenities in British India and unable to speak either Konkani or Portuguese, it is amazing how she adapted herself to the living conditions in a Goan village. She gave birth to four children, three girls and a boy. Appalled at the education system, she determined to have us educated in Bombay, and thus my father supported us paying heavy fees to the best English convent school for girls and to the Jesuit Boy's Academy for my brother. My father had clients at Daman and Diu and on occasion when he had to attend a court case there, he would pay us a visit which we much cherished.

Tragedy struck our family on October 17, 1937. My father was on his way to Daman and as my brother Avertano was on holiday, my mother persuaded my father to take him along. As my father had quite a few friends at Daman, it was arranged that my brother would spend a fortnight with two elderly women. My father visited us again on his way to Goa when on the fateful Sunday afternoon, as we sat for lunch, the front doorbell rang. My elder sister came in with a telegram for my father. He opened it. Silent for a second, he then, very calmly asked my mother to pack. They were to leave for Daman by the afternoon train. My brother had drowned. My mother was shocked and packed a few things. The pain and anguish was too much for her. My father did his utmost to console her. I recall him cradling her in his arms and pacing up and down the bedroom with her.

After my brother's death, my mother wanted to return to Goa and so we returned to Margao the following year. It was there that for the first time, we as teenagers saw and savoured the *joie de vivre* that my father exuded, his keen sense of humour, his wonderful smile, and his tender love.

LOYOLA

Goa's Political Enfant Terrible

Joseph Barros

Although young Fanchu Loyola was born in the lap of luxury and with a silver spoon in his mouth, his tender infancy does not seem to have been all that happy and gay. Like Prince Siddharta he saw face-to-face and at very close quarters tears and tragedies all around his palatial house. The village folk lived a hand-to-mouth existence.

At the early age of five, Fanchu saw the sudden demise of his paternal uncle Msgr. Francisco Xavier de Loyola, then two years later that of his dear mother Maria Angelica, and four years later that of his godfather and uncle José Inácio de Loyola. We can well imagine the psychological trauma, the mental shock and the bewildering consternation in which young Fanchu then found himself.

His early education revolved around his own house which was like a spacious educational complex because of the large number of cupboards full of books and papers, which adorned the main hall. He did his Portuguese primary education in his own village of Orlim and later studied English at Karwar. He then took up law.

At the age of twenty-six, he married on January 27, 1918 Monica alias Amelia Souza, the eldest daughter of Tomas Cesar de Souza and Especiosa de Souza from Tivim. Their first child was Elma Maria, born in 1919. Their only son Avertano born on March 23, 1923 was accidentally drowned at Daman on October 17, 1937. Their daughter, Yona was born on February 2, 1925 and their last daughter Elaine was born on December 3, 1928.

The house of the Loyolas is very palatial and surrounded by tall coconut trees said to have been planted by Fanchu's uncle José Inácio who besides being an excellent physician was a very practical agricultural man and printed in his own press at Orlim in 1912 the remarkable botanical manual *A Arte Palmarica*. It appears that Fanchu inherited from this famous uncle a love and passion for gardening and horticulture, which stood him in good stead during his term as Inspector of *Comunidades*.

The house of the Loyolas at Orlim was in the past the rendezvous of eminent Goans, be they lawyers, journalists, politicians or landlords who thronged there to deliberate on the public issues concerning the Goan people. The historic and ancestral family of Fanchu Loyola's forefathers, hails from the time of the Hindu conversions to Roman Catholicism by the Portuguese missionaries in Orlim in 1568, when St. Michael's Church was built.

Fanchu's mind and heart always pined for politics and journalism which were two very effective and long range weapons which he carried in his armoury. He published during his dynamic political career both in Portuguese India as well as during his exile in British India, several newspapers which can be studied for an in-depth study of his personality and political ideology, for which he had to suffer trials and tribulations very often.

As a journalist, Fanchu had a very dazzling, quick and facile pen, which made him an excellent and a resourceful journalist and fiercely polemical. In the early stage of his journalistic life and career, he helped his father Avertano in editing their family paper *A India Portuguesa*. He also founded later on several other newspapers in Portuguese such as the *Opinião*, *Lanterna*, *Rebate* and *Jornal da India*, which were published in his village of Orlim, but which had a rather short duration as compared to other papers like *Ultramar* or *O Heraldo*, started at Panjim by Prof. Messias Gomes, a relation of Fanchu himself. He also published newspapers like *India Portuguesa* from Margao and Panjim and *Oriente* and *Portugal e Colonias* from Bombay where he was in political exile for some time. No Goan ever published so many papers as he did.

The newspapers which Fanchu started during the course of his political life with a view to debate, discuss and propagate his opinions and also to shed light on the vital issues concerning the Goan society, were a great financial burden on him. He, single-handedly could not face all the burdens of sustaining them which he started in the midst of political controversies. He had either to borrow or tighten his own belt. He did both these to keep the publications going without which he would have felt himself a fish out of water.

Among the several newspapers which Fanchu edited, the *Opinião* published by him in 1917 at Orlim was a very balanced paper emitting his profound and elaborate views and opinions on the intricate issues affecting the Goan public. A deep thinker and a practical-minded politician that he was, his considered opinions were highly respected and much sought after by his contemporaries in Goa and in Lisbon.

Advocate Fanchu came into the lime-light of the public at Goa and in Lisbon early in life because of his personal merits, charismatic personality and his high family connections respectively. Whenever any social function was held in his village or in its surroundings, he was invariably invited either to raise the toast or act as master of ceremonies. Nothing could happen in some of the aristocratic houses at Ul-Dando and other places without his charming presence. A meticulous survey of some of the important newspapers and news items of his day will amply bear evidence to this fact. If there had been an opinion poll in those days, he would have surely have ranked as the topmost charismatic personality of Portuguese Goa. No wonder the clairvoyant prophecy made by his uncle José Inácio de Loyola on March 11, 1891, at the time of Fanchu's birth that he would be a great man *(um grande homem)* was coming true very remarkably.

Fanchu never ran after publicity, but publicity came to him with such a whirlwind impact that his name and fame invariably hit the headlines of the Goan and Lisbon presses in spite of the machinations of his political rivals who regarded him as a thorn in their flesh. The Goans were much interested in his whereabouts that even a visit of his to Panjim, was always reported by the leading dailies of the city. Such was the fame and social prestige of this celebrated popular leader of the Goan masses, who looked upon him as a kind of a Messiah to lead his followers to prosperity and social security. That was the popular mythical aura created around his name. He himself never believed in it. Such was his innate modesty and the simplicity of his life and actions.

As a politician and journalist he had to face the wrath of the local administrators and government functionaries on several occasions due to his political outbursts and impetuosity which often drove him into many tight corners. But smart and sharp as he always was, he often escaped dramatically.

Another political tussle in which he found himself on account of his liberal views and democratic ideals, was when he delivered a fiery speech at a public function on November 25, 1932, the historic date of the take-over of Goa by Afonso de Albuquerque in 1510 from the hands of the Adil Shah. In this open and frank speech, delivered before a large crowd which included officers, academicians, civil and ecclesiastic personalities, Fanchu Loyola chastised the incompetent officials as unfit and incapable of administering the territory. It must be stated in all fairness, that Fanchu did not strike at the Portuguese sovereignty of Goa, but only took to task the misdeeds of the colonial administration. Democrat that he was, he wanted to clear and clean the Augean stables.

This sensational speech which was largely publicised and eulogised by some staunch Goan democrats, raised a hornet's nest around Fanchu, who in order to escape from the clutches of the law, had to seek refuge in British India, which he luckily succeeded in doing. He made Bombay his temporary abode and from there he conducted his legal activities to earn his living, for he usually always was short of cash. In Bombay he was known among the British as *Loyola, the Portuguese lawyer*. By and large, his frank and outspoken speech was largely appreciated by the Goans and by the local politicians. This incident however did not affect nor influence his normal legal practice, in Goa nor in Daman.

Another event connected with the life of Fanchu was the unique agricultural experiment conducted for the first time in Goa, in the rice fields of the *Comunidade* of Carambolim, in December 1929, during the governorship of General João Carlos Craveiro Lopes, when Fanchu was the Inspector of *Comunidades* of Portuguese India. To encourage the farmers of Goa and to make Goa agriculturally self-sufficient, he decided with the help of the directorate of Agriculture to experiment on the introduction of a triple cultivation of rice in Goa. Besides the usual regular *vaigan*, another cultivation was planned, so that Goa could produce rice all the year round. As it was an ambitious scheme, the first experiment took place amidst great expectations at Carambolim in a rice plot called *Savota* belonging to the *comunidade* on December 15, 1929, under the patronage of Madame Julia Craveiro Lopes, the wife of the Governor, who was known as the godmother of the rice campaign. With her own hands she sowed the plot and the bishop of Cochin blessed the ceremony marked by pompous speeches. A 21 gun salute was accorded on this unique historic occasion.

As an experiment, it appeared to be a very fine and enthusiastic effort by all concerned to turn the agricultural deficit of Goa, into a surplus production. But unfortunately there was no follow-up policy, the enthusiasm was very short-lived and the agricultural deficit continued as usual. This experiment was nicknamed by its detractors as *Loyola's third seed.*

The failure of the experiment cannot be attributed to the Inspector of *Comunidades* alone, for technical efficiency on the part of the directorate of Agriculture lagged far behind. It was the result of several causes, bureaucratic, technical and political.

In his private life, Fanchu suffered the terrible tragedy of the death of his only son Avertano, who died of drowning at the age of 14 at Daman on October 17, 1937. So loved was Avertano that his classmates wrote the following poem in his memory:

"A bright light from our school is gone,
A voice we loved is stilled;

A place is vacant in our hearts,
Which never can be filled."

This tragedy cast a shadow of gloom over Fanchu and his family. Though deeply brooding over his great loss, in an unprecedented gesture of sublime renunciation and humility, in eternal memory of his departed son and before the Sacred Heart of Jesus, he appealed through the pages of his weekly *Portugal e Colonias*, for public forgiveness for all his errors of omission and commission which was generously and ungrudgingly granted by all his friends and foes alike. This was to be his spiritual solace for years to come and he had recourse much more intensely than before to prayer and meditation.

Like the eminent Goan parliamentarian Francisco Luis Gomes, who was a great democrat and liberal at heart, Fanchu also in his own way attempted to take up cudgels in favour of civil rights and political liberty for the Goans. He even tried to contest for the Portuguese parliamentary elections, a thing which did not materialise due to events beyond his control.

In the meantime, the winds of change were blowing over the face of the vast Indian sub-continent and the thinking minds of Goa could not remain themselves in seclusion and socio-political isolation for a very long time. The Goan mind was pinning for new political vistas and avenues leading to the happy dawn of civil rights and liberty.

In June 1946, Fanchu who was politically and socially restless, made common cause with Ram Manohar Lohia, the Indian socialist leader, regarding the legitimate demand for civil liberties in Goa. He befriended Lohia who got himself deeply involved in the campaign for civil liberties for the Goans, issued press statements, granted interviews to the press, including *Free Press Journal* which gave excellent courage to Fanchu Loyola's political views and opinions.

But in none of his political statements, Fanchu challenged the Portuguese sovereignty over Goa, Daman and Diu. In the first instance, he only claimed vehemently civil liberties and civil rights for the local people which was, of course, a very legitimate demand, viewed from the point of international law and natural justice. In none of his political statements he gave an ultimatum to the Portuguese to quit Goa, Daman and Diu. He only aspired for economic, social and political autonomy for the Portuguese territories in India. This was the gist of his political credo.

The very fact that he wanted to make Goa agriculturally self-sufficient in *xit-kodi*, in 1929, explains the working of his fertile mind, for economic autonomy is the forerunner of socio-political maturity and emancipation. If Afonso de Albuquerque being a foreigner could envision Goa's emancipation, much more so could Fanchu, the great son of the red soil of Goa. None could deny him the legitimate freedom of his mind. His demand was within the constitutional framework of the Portuguese nation. The message was loud and clear.

But by some strange and enigmatic quirk of destiny, a very fantastic case was framed unexpectedly against Fanchu, the *enfant terrible* of the Goan socio-political stage, by an administrative bigwig of Goa. In 1946, he was prosecuted, jailed unceremoniously at the Aguada Fort, tried by the draconic Military Tribunal and exiled to far-off Portugal for four years with loss of political rights for a period of fifteen years.

Fanchu Loyola's famous political trial aptly defended by the Goan legal luminary, António Gomes Pereira which took place at the Military Tribunal in Panjim, makes very interesting reading and throws a flood of light not only on the political philosophy of Fanchu Loyola, but also on the political ideology of the fascist regime of his times.

After his release from the prison at Peniche in 1950, Fanchu shuttled between Portugal and India, but at last he chose to settle in Lisbon where he had several professional friends both in the field of law as well as in journalism. Moreover, as he was very well conversant with the Portuguese legislation and had an excellent mastery over the Portuguese language, he decided to fix his residence in Lisbon and resume his legal and journalistic practice.

PART I

1

AUTONOMY

No one, I am sure, will dare accuse a son of India of being unpatriotic, if he were to speak his mind and freely admit that his country is not ready for autonomous rule. No doubt, India compared to other Portuguese colonies, has assimilated western modes into its tradition but she does not have the basic training in civic and political skills. Hence it is difficult for her to gain from the advantages offered by self-government.

It is true enough that thousands of people were indeed in favour of autonomy for this country. Every worthy citizen ached to see self-government functioning in India. This was because of the general notion that a decentralized administrative system with direct participation by the sons of the soil would give a better government to the colony. They believed that self-government would straighten out the finances, provide moral guidelines to public services and cut down on administrative expenditure. Finally, they had hoped that such a government would accelerate the introduction of sanitary projects and would regenerate the economy. Such were their expectations.

However, it has been four years now since self-government has been put into practice and they have been four years of bitter and painful disillusionment. Because of this experience, the people now recognize and declare in one voice that direct rule from *Terreiro do Paço* was much better. For, if everything is taken into account, it can be said that self-government, instead of improving the economic situation in the colony, has worsened it. It has produced nothing of substance. Its policy papers have nothing worthwhile in them and, lastly, it has introduced unjustified new taxes and squandered public finances!

People had high expectations of self-government ushering in development, like cutting down on administrative expenditure, introducing a prudent budget, protecting industries, giving incentives to agricultural projects and providing new directions for the use of natural resources and energies, which India has in abundance. But now it is only too evident that self-government, with the sons of the soil at the helm, has had counterproductive effects. Under the umbrella of the Legislative Council, the ministers abuse the system to line their own pockets, and use the Council to act according to their whims and fancies.

The Council has never been able to maintain the dignity of its position of responsibility. Had it not been for the autonomy and new legislation introduced by the Legislative Council, the state of Portuguese India would have been much better. The introduction of new taxes has ruined the taxpayer, and the increase of administrative expenditure has brought in waste and extravagance, exerting excessive stress on the budget. No Governor would have dared to raise taxes of this nature and no minister would have approved them.

The people of India, then, who once clamoured for autonomy now unanimously recognize that it has failed them. *India Portuguesa* which is both the voice of the majority as well as the voice of a political party, has appealed to the Central government to restore the old form of government, namely, direct rule. Only through the intervention of the Central government will the damage done to this land be healed, thereby restoring the confidence and faith of its people in their future?

(*India Portuguesa*, October 1, 1923)

2. It will not be out of place to state that, though the initial intentions were noble enough, autonomy has failed disastrously in this colony. The combination of factors and circumstances which have led to its downfall need to be analyzed.

One of the main reasons for the failure of autonomy is the political incapacity of the people's representatives. Although they form the majority in the Legislative Council, they have not supported a single proposal that the people have put forward. The Press has been demanding a reduction of expenditure for a long time. It has pointed out the existing incurable maladies that infect the system, and has proposed ways to simplify public services. The public services, having degenerated a vast amount paperwork, consume rivers of money, a complete waste, since the paperwork has shown neither practical utility nor any productive purpose.

If the uproar caused by the Press is any indication of the current popular opinion then it expresses the aspirations of the Luso-Indians. They are the ones who are paying the taxes, taxes that are ultimately wasted in the employment of inglorious bureaucrats. The truth is that the Legislative Council has not passed a single bill to balance public expenditure. On the contrary, instead of simplifying the bureaucracy, the government has tended to create more services and departments and consequently increased expenditure on all sides. It has invented luxuries and wastes money as if the country were swimming in gold!

India no doubt has witnessed many ruinous and noxious governments from the Portuguese administration. It is quite true that they have squandered money on silly things, but it is also true that in some respects they have done some constructive work and have promoted the progress of the country. Not all has been a waste. They did bring in projects which helped to increase economic productivity. The same, however, cannot be said of autonomy. It has not introduced a single measure that has benefited the country, either in the present or for the future. The sad result is that the country is not able to redeem itself from the evil effects of colonial rule.

The British in neighbouring India spend lavishly and the officials are well paid. But though the bureaucracy consumes rivers of money, it also produces useful work which the people can witness and verify for themselves. With us, on the other hand, it is a different story. Here we spend tens of thousands of rupees throughout the year for the upkeep of a bureaucracy that produces nothing worthwhile. It serves no purpose. All the public offices here are in such a disorganised state that it reminds one of the Biblical chaos.

If autonomy were to demonstrate some restraint on its public expenditure then it would have the right to introduce new taxes. Since it has not done that, levying taxes is no more than extortion and so, it is not right to demand more taxes from the people of this land.

(*India Portuguesa*, October 23, 1923)

3. The four and a half years' autonomy, with its overspending of public money, has dealt a devastating blow to Portuguese India. So much so that it has plunged the country into no less than a recession. To put it any other way would be simply to blind oneself to the facts. *Est modus in rebus.* How true! Autonomy was an experiment that failed to yield the desired results. Experience has proved that it is more a utopian concept and, from a practical point of view, to be condemned categorically. But returning to old administrative formulas certainly will not remedy the harm perpetrated by autonomy. Direct rule from *Terreiro do Paço* as exercised in this country and other colonies in the East is an imperfect system containing too many flaws. I am not sure if it will serve a purpose unless it adjusts itself to meeting the real needs of the country. If it is to be of any use, it ought to be altered considerably before it can become an answer to the present economic needs of the people, people who have suffered tremendous hardship during the Great War.

There is every reason to believe that the present government will continue in this wasteful fashion. For it is common knowledge that today's Legislative Councils are symbols of destruction and Governors use them to suit their own purposes like shields to cover up their own misconduct.

Moreover, it is difficult to trust the ministers with the running of the colonies. For, in many instances, those who handle the colonial portfolio do not come forward with the necessary solutions to the problems. In the first place, the portfolio of the colonies should not have been made into a political position. But since it is, we have to recognize that it involves the risk of an inexperienced minister being given the portfolio without a thorough grounding in the essentials of administration. He is thus bound to commit blunders for lack of knowledge of colonial matters.

We believe, therefore, that the kind of administration that is needed is one in which the minister governs directly, giving his best to the country. In the unstable political climate we are in, the Governors often flirt with the opposite camp. So, in our view, the Governor of the colony should be a symbol only, a figurehead and nothing beyond. The actual business of administration, properly speaking, must be executed by the heads of departments. The administrative responsibilities should be allocated to not more than five secretaries, and each department should have its own clearly defined bye-laws, funds and budgets and given ample power to take action should the necessity arise.

In a general budget, the revenues should be distributed among the various secretaries. But a distinction must be made between the budget for the personnel department and for fund allocation. The salaries for the heads of departments should come under a special clause in the budget and in no case should the salaries of personnel exceed one-third of the allocated fund.

This even distribution of funding will help to save one major waste. There are offices and organisations which at the moment lie unproductive as they have been given no grants to make them productive. Since there is not enough money to generate work, the staff are bored and unproductive. Yet the State continues its payment to departmental heads, sub-heads, additional officers and the rest of the staff working in these offices and organisations even though it has been found that they are redundant. However, the distribution of revenue so that each of the various departments is given a certain allotted sum will remove some of the problems they now face. The departmental heads, conferred with administrative responsibilities and regulated by clear guidelines, will be more efficient and effective in their work.

We find that this is how it is conducted in neighbouring British India. In British India, unlike here, the head of any public service acts like a head of his department, independent of the Governor. With the result, the departments seem accordingly much more productive.

(*India Portuguesa*, November 22, 1923)

4. Neither brilliant rhetoric nor seductive theorizing can prevail against the overpowering evidence. Last week's political events have proved beyond a doubt that Portuguese India is not adequately prepared for self-government, despite the fact that her citizens are on the whole well-educated.

The 21st session of the Legislative Council meetings has shown that we lack the moral and civic responsibilities that would allow us to take advantage of self-government. It is worth confessing our inability to govern ourselves. This privilege has been granted to us too prematurely. Like stubborn idiots, we go on pretending that we have made some progress, but the truth is, we have not.

It appeared at first sight that the members of the Legislative Council who were united in principle greatly honoured the intellectual and moral capacities of the people by paying heed to their needs. In the 21st session, Council members presented the required ten signatures of those who would vote against the motion for additional taxes, unless the expenditures were cut down effectively. They also asked for the postponement of additional customs-duties and high taxes on *abcari* proposed by the government.

Being sure that the motion would in the end triumph, the people started applauding and cheering, and, savouring the sweetness of anticipated victory, crowned their representatives with laurels. For the first time, they saw their representatives united in a common front and true to their responsibilities. They saw them standing up for the electorate's aspirations. They saw them demanding that the government govern according to the will of the people and they saw them proclaiming loudly and firmly that they would not tolerate the orgy of waste from this squandering administration. They would not, they said, make it possible for even a cent to be taken from the people towards additional taxes, until the annual expenditures were pragmatically cut down.

The stand taken by the elected representatives would have been highly commendable had what they expressed on paper been converted into actions. Also, it would have restored some faith in autonomy, which till today has not done a thing besides fleece the taxpayer. But instead, the outcome of all this grand noise turned out to be sadly disappointing! It would not be of any comfort to the unfortunate people of this land to know that they are tortured by a merciless and cruel destiny. The motion, which to all appearances was irrevocably endorsed with ten signatures, was thrown out of the Legislative Council. And why? Because one of the signatories did not show up in the Legislative Council at the time of voting! And another one disowned his own signature at the last moment, without notifying his colleagues! Voting against his own work, he picked up his bags and crossed the floor to join the official side! The rest of the eight members walked out in disgust.

The motion was miserably defeated. The taxes were approved.

And now? The surge of enthusiasm which passed momentarily through this country has collapsed. The taxpayer who for a fleeting moment had felt relieved, as if the thorn from his flesh had been removed, is in anguish again. The dream of near-joy has become a reality of a great shame, the shame that smears all of us.

The eight members who walked out of the Council Hall saved their personal honour, at least. But, the moment the motion was defeated, the collective honour of the country went down the gutter for good. The final events of the so-called "voting" session of the 27th were despicable acts which proved ultimately Portuguese India's bankruptcy in matters, politics and moral integrity.

In no way, can we ignore the intrinsic significance of the voting on the 27th. An uncritical eye will look at this episode as no more than a fiasco. But that is not so. Because at the core of this case there lies another matter, and that matter is a complete lack of a sense of moral obligation. At any given crucial moment, the elected members have to demonstrate a solidarity in their capability to uphold the electorate's aspirations till the very end. In this instance, they failed this test and so failing, unmasked with total clarity that Portuguese India is not ready for autonomy.

(*India Portuguesa*, January 3, 1924)

5. Self-government can function well only in countries which possess a certain degree of political know-how and have a better civic sense than we do in our country. This we want to emphasise once more.

The inhabitants of a colonized country might display a kind of progressive thinking in politics because of the general high level of education they have achieved. But being highly educated does not mean much when it comes to running a country. The most important thing needed here is a strong sense of moral unity. Each citizen should be patriotic, and there should be consistency of political aspirations among educated men.

It is a serious mistake to assume that Portuguese India is ready for autonomy simply because she has an elite that shines in various intellectual fields. First of all, that elite is very small. Besides, the people of this land are divided into two sections, Catholics and Hindus. These two religious groups, whose aspirations are entirely different, create an impasse for unity. Furthermore, the people of this land are divided into castes and sub-castes, and even to this day, they do not intermingle socially. This again is a great problem, because her various leaders cannot come together under a broader political base.

The cohesiveness of a society is the most indispensable ingredient for the success of any autonomous rule. But how can a country fragmented with many different loyalties aspire for autonomy? However winsome theories and philosophical concepts of political unity may be, they are of no use if the reality of facts show the opposite. To see the extent to which this country is fragmented and disunited we need only look at the political chaos of the two previous weeks which speaks louder than anything that has happened in the past.

The two elected members of the Legislative Council, who defected and went over to the side of the government on the issue of introducing additional taxes, do no credit to the image of our leaders' political capabilities. One of them rejected his own signature for no plausible reason and without giving any justification for his act. The other simply did not turn up on the day of the voting. How else can we interpret such acts except to say that they reveal our own incompetence in the safeguarding of the rights of the majority?

Soon after, the elected members, wanting to establish a principle, rejected the motion of order by not voting on taxes without a prior cut on expenditures. They released a manifesto to the country with a view to asking the opinion of the people in this matter. They wanted the country to make a decision on how the Council members conducted themselves. They wanted the people to point out, through the organisations they belonged to, the future path for their representatives to follow. The manifesto was meant to awaken the people from their lethargy and help generate a public opinion on the political situation. If it were to reach them in time, it would have given them a chance to examine carefully the current activities of the Council, including the defection of the two members who had crossed over to the government side.

But before the manifesto could reach the people, something happened. The two members who sat as independent members in the Council, made a surprise move. They too crossed the floor to join the two defectors! Perhaps it was done in a spirit of camaraderie! With two more defections, it became possible for the Council to announce that they would be in session. They did this in spite of the fact that nine members declared that they would not show up in the Council until the country gave her verdict!

This country has not the least sense of solidarity and only here can such chaotic events take place. The individuals who participated in this political debauchery not only compromised their reputations but also jeopardized the collective pride of the people. Well, gentlemen, tell me frankly, is this country ready for autonomy?

If Portuguese India had been prepared enough in the science of politics, such shameful acts would not have taken place. Nor would the country have permitted them.

It is natural for the people's representatives to have divergent opinions in matters of approach in tackling administrative problems. But what is absolutely not permissible is to use their mandate to spit in the faces of the very people who elected them. The two independent members did just that. They shamefully betrayed the people's trust, debasing the country morally and politically.

We cheat ourselves if we do not admit our faults. Portuguese India is indeed a beautiful land with intelligent people. These people have a rare facility for assimilation but they are far from attaining political maturity. We have yet a long distance to travel, and we have to formulate a plan as to how to satisfy the rights of the majority before we can attain freedom.

We might have learned people, but what is important is the right selection of competent candidates, with the integrity of character to lay the right foundation for this society, educating all segments of the people in their civic duties. Without this, self-government will continue to be a failure.

Portuguese India adopted her autonomy prematurely. We have used the autonomy badly like a child who had been given a firearm by its thoughtless parents, thereby causing an accident. It cannot make us proud. Autonomy, more or less has brought about economic and financial disaster. It has ruined our moral and political integrity because from the very beginning, we conducted ourselves without any dignity or commitment to lofty ideals. It is from this point of view that we have to recognise the futile application of autonomy to this colony.

It is better for this reason to return to direct rule from *Terreiro do Paço* than to continue with this experiment, an experiment that is destroying Portuguese India both financially and economically.

(*India Portuguesa*, January 10, 1924)

6. *Boletim Oficial* of the 14th of this month has published new tax-guidelines for the Customs. The import and export duties on

various articles, including essential goods, have gone up. Though rice is the staple food of the local population according to geography books, it has not been spared from higher taxation. The needs of the people deserve more attention and consideration. Instead, without a second thought for the people, the government has once again behaved capriciously and has succeeded in aggravating the miserable conditions of the people of this land. And once again, autonomy has demonstrated clearly, that it did not take into account the people's hopes and needs.

The scornful indifference of the Governor-General to the boycott of the Council by the elected members, who were defeated in that unforgettable session of December 27, as a protest against raising taxes is a blatant violation of the truth. Only fools and idiots would fail to see it any other way. No other country in the world but India would have tolerated such an ugly situation. And no Legislative Council would have passed a tax bill without resolving its internal conflict with its effective members, members who absented themselves from the sessions, in order not to collaborate with the government in the increase of taxes.

Once the effective members had boycotted the sessions, the government was not within its rights to call in substitutes to guarantee the functioning of the Council. It is nothing but gross and vulgar sophism to argue otherwise. This is not to say that the government is not allowed to call in the substitutes. It is, but only when the effective members are absent because they are unable to attend a session. In this case, their absence was not for reasons of an inability to attend but a boycott, which is not the same thing. Hence, the summoning of substitutes to participate in the Council's sessions was an abuse of power.

Breaking the rules has in no way enhanced the government's reputation. It has exposed its true nature which has been so ingeniously hidden for such a long time. It proved that the government has never attached any value to public opinion.

So long as the people's representatives were prepared to make compromises with the government in order to retain authority in the carrying out of their responsibilities, the Governor-General, with a seductive smile, boasted that they could count upon him for his loyal co-operation. But when the elected members started claiming their right to independence with respect to their responsibilities and stopped being servile and subservient, he disliked it, and forgot his promise. Dr. Jaime de Morais who always has his way without any obstacles, thinks that he is an authentic raja of India with absolute power over his subjects. With a crown on his head, he thinks he is irreproachable, like a monarch in those good old days of absolutism. He acts as if he is an omnipotent king ruling over his kingdom, autonomy. I can almost hear him, shouting in the belief that he is exercising his sovereign will: I want, I can and I will order the feudal era! But his kingdom, autonomy, upon which he stands, has turned out to be but a heap of garbage.

For four and half years, the Legislative Council has ruled as if it were governing in paradise. But both the parties have been rudely awakening from this voluptuous dream. Four and a half years ago, when autonomy was first established in this country, champagne bottles popped and brilliant speeches flowed. But none saw the abyss, an abyss which went deeper and deeper everyday, bringing the country to the brink of despair. Intoxicated by autonomy we were dazed and our eyes glazed as if we had a strong dose of *bhang*.

However, when the government, which was bankrupt, wanted to squeeze more taxes out of the people to balance the budget, the Legislative Council sobered up. It was then that they saw the government for what it was. It was like a solemn restaurant waiter in a black jacket who, hiding his contempt behind a smile, presents his drunken customers with their enormous bill. Struck by the tragic truth of the situation, they resisted the demands of the government for the imposition of new taxes.

This is the first time in India that the government and the elected members have been at loggerheads in a debate, and the government does not want to get defeated. Using the same old reasoning, the government has brought in new taxes whose adverse effects upon the economy of the country will soon begin to tell.

And now? Though the tax-guidelines are already out, the recent devastating events may in fact portend a more favourable future for the elected members. For now that they have seen through the government's frame of mind, the defeated members should have learnt how to act in the future. Never again, should they renounce their mandate or desert their post. United, they should be, united as never before. Burying their differences, they should fight bravely to execute the very principles that dictated to them their motion of order. The battle lines are now clearly drawn as they were never before, and the fight must go on, not outside of the Legislative Council, but inside it.

The conflict that started on the 27th is not over, nor will it be over, nor can it be over. Frankly, it is just the beginning! This way, not only is the honour of the defeated members still intact, but the very pride of all of us is upheld by them. Until now, we have not been honest with ourselves and admitted that autonomy does not work in this country. The conduct of the elected members, depending upon the way they govern later on, will tell us if we are ready for self-government.

(*India Portuguesa*, January 17, 1924)

7. As the telegram from the Minister of Colonies that was sent to the defeated members in response to theirs indicates, self-government will never be a practical feasibility in this colony as long as the popular majority in the Legislative Assembly includes two representatives from *Praças do Norte*. The inclusion of these two diminishes the power of the people's representation in the Assembly. That is to say, aside from the political unpreparedness of the people, the Legislative Council itself, the way it is composed now, is a major obstruction to the effective rule of autonomy.

This is because, against the eleven elected members, there are six appointed local or ex-officio members in the Legislative Council, diminishing the impact of the people's representatives. Besides these six, there are two who are supposedly the people's representatives but they are not. On the other hand, they are there, in fact, to protect the government's interests. This autonomy is nothing but a vulgar farce. In this kind of game, the government keeps all the trump cards in its hands like Pilate in the Bible.

Under the circumstances, it is a huge joke to speak of the people being represented by a majority in the Legislative Council. They are not and they never have been. As recently as now, the two representatives from the *Praças do Norte* have shown themselves to be not the people's representatives at all but the government's puppets. In this kind of autonomy, only the government rules, the people's votes do not count.

As it is composed now, the Legislative Council from the point of view of representing the opinion of the majority will always be a sham. The people can only count on nine out of eleven of the elected members in fact, and the government representatives are seven. If you add two from Daman and Diu to the seven, they make nine. Besides, the government is at all times in a position of absolute superiority. For the President can exercise his deciding vote at all times in any contingency.

According to the telegram of the Minister of Colonies, the Acts of governments once voted by the majority in the Legislative Council, cannot be opposed. However, if the Governor of the colony is not an idiot, he will always manipulate the two representatives from *Praças do Norte*, and casting his deciding vote, the government will always obtain a majority. In the recent battle over the tax-guidelines, Dr. de Morais did exactly that. But then, in such instances can we really maintain that the Legislative Council voted at all, and especially a Council that was made up of a majority of elected members? How then can autonomy be possible in this colony?

Although the representative system might look just, it is unjustly lopsided. Ultimately, this system does not represent the people. And, as long as the government can manipulate the two pseudo-elected members from Daman and Diu in its favour, a motion in the Legislative Council would always be passed as approved by the majority!

The Minister of Colonies, certainly, does not understand the logistics of the Legislative Council of India. Thus when the telegram from India informed Lisbon that the majority had approved the motion in the Legislative Council, the Minister of Colonies naturally took it for granted that the motion had been voted on by elected members who were in the majority. But what he does not know is that the substitutes had been won over by the government. If he had, he would not have given the advice that he gave to the defeated members in his telegram.

Undoubtedly, this incident is an eye-opener. It shows to those who were in doubt before that it is impossible to fight against the abuses of the government, as long as this fictitious majority is kept in the Legislative Council. It weakens the Council, as we have demonstrated before, and anything that goes wrong is blamed upon the country. The country does not deserve this.

The champions of autonomy, having now realised it, complain that autonomy was instigated simply to act as a cover-up for government mismanagement. And now it is their duty to protest against the composition of the Legislative Council as it is decreed. They understand now that it was wrong to have agreed to an inclusion of seven official members and to adding the two extra members from *Praças do Norte* to the elected members. Those two members though apparently part of the elected members, are in fact official members. Besides, a mystery surrounds the ballot-boxes of *Praças do Norte*. There, the great electorate is the government. It always was, it is today, it was yesterday and it will be tomorrow.

When there was a reaction against Mr. Freitas Ribeiro's decision concerning the composition of the Legislative Council, he answered that he did not want a majority of the people's representatives in the Council in the initial stages of the new regime of autonomy. He promised that he would gradually increase the proportion of members in the Council, according to our wishes, depending upon our preparedness for autonomy.

We were deceived into accepting a Legislative Council that does not in the end at any time represent the people. *Praças do Norte* was allotted two seats when previously there had been only one in the Council. With this trick, the district of Mormugao lost its representation.

Now, we have to put up with this.

(*India Portuguesa*, February 1, 1924)

8. Truth speaks louder than hollow rhetoric. Once again, it has demonstrated in action that autonomy does not work in this colony.

On December 27, the defeated members had walked out of the Legislative Council with a leonine air. But the stand that they had taken was weakened when they were ordered to return to their seats. Ashamed and crestfallen, they returned to their seats. Such episodes of our political life and of those individuals involved may be colourful and hilarious but at the same time it also reflects that as people, we are not sufficiently united to be able to take advantage of self-government.

Anyone who wants to make a careful, unprejudiced examination of the political incidents of the last few months that took place in the Legislative Council, will definitely notice the harmful effects of these events. In case you missed them, here they are, once again:

> "The ten elected members of the Legislative Council awoke one beautiful morning with a clear conscience which urged them to take charge of their responsibilities, at least we sincerely hope that it was like that. They decided not to vote for the proposed new taxes until the government seriously considered lowering the taxes in the annual budget. And soon after, *in continenti*, they drafted a motion of order having discussed it among themselves, and all of them signed it. By signing it, they vouched their intent not to approve that even a penny should be contributed as tax, until the expenditures on public administration were cut to a minimum."

The Legislative Council of *Estado da India* is composed of eleven elected members and seven official members. Out of the eleven elected members, one was absent and did not sign the motion of order. Even if the absentee went over to the government side, the government in that case would have had only eight votes, and the elected members would have had ten votes, enough to win the motion.

However, when the motion was put to a vote, the story got interesting and this is what happened. The absentee from the eleven members voted with the government and another one from the eleven repudiated his own signature and voted with the government. And one more from the eleven did not show up for the voting! This was the voting result: "nine for the government and eight for the motion. The motion was defeated!"

The eight defeated members, astounded with the results, walked out in anger from the Council. By this gesture, they intended to deny the government the needed quorum granted by the law and thus prevent the Council from functioning. And, along with this, proud of their resolution, they dispatched a manifesto to the nation, explaining the intent behind the action that they had taken.

Unfortunately, however, the Council went on as if nothing had happened, *admiramini et obsipicite*! While the defeated, proud of their move, expected that the nation would be galvanised by their heroic feat and dreamt that a crown of laurels would be placed on their heads, the government summoned the substitutes and the Council continued to function. This wholly eliminated any effect the walk-out strike of the elected members may have had!

Among the cream of intellectuals and public men in our country, who are expected to give an example of independence and moral integrity, shameful betrayals and defections abound. So how on earth can we pretend that autonomy is workable in this country? Before anything else, the moral and civic preparedness of the people is a basic need for the functioning of autonomy. How can we say that we are politically mature, when the leaders of the people themselves are ignorant of the principle of political solidarity and have not even once put public interests ahead of their own?

But the tale is not over yet.

The defeated members, dispatched telegrams to the Minister, protesting against the arbitrary acts of the Governor of the colony, each time prouder than before, each time more defiant than before and each time more aggressive than before. They informed the Minister that the Council had been made to function forcibly by bringing in the substitutes, filibustering the stand taken by the elected members. This, they told him, was a violation of the regulations. They told him it was despotism, they told him it was an insult to the dignity of the elected members, and so on.

It was a pleasant surprise to know that finally there was an open discord between most of the elected members and their Governor!

So far so good. But then what happened? The issue remained unresolved, while the telegrams went to and fro between *Terreiro do Paço* and the Governor of the colony. The Minister appeared to be uncertain and was still attempting to make up his mind about what he should do. Then suddenly, the defeated members, exhausted by their own efforts, unable to follow the whole thing through to its end and wait for the Minister's decision, returned to their seats!

Like shadows or ghosts, with their mouths hanging open, they shuffled back into the Council Hall. Neither the country nor the Minister, nor the Governor took any notice of them!

What was the meaning of this? One might have understood, do you not think, the sudden change in their attitude, if they had returned to oppose the government because the Governor was using their absence to get his legislation passed. Since the Council was functioning with substitutes from Bardez and the Governor was hurriedly obtaining approval for this, it would have been the right move to come back to oppose the Governor's actions.

But no, sorry! The defeated members did not return with moral courage. They did not return as leaders whose dignity had been hurt. They did not return to supervise the government's actions. Instead they came back like school boys who had played hooky. They came back looking ashamed like culprits in the presence of their teacher.

The last minutes of the sessions of the Council made certain things absolutely clear. The defeated of December 27, forgetting the bitterness that had been aroused in them, forgetting the scorn with which the government had treated them, in a most despicable manner, meekly accommodated themselves to the vexations and the humiliating situation. You saw on their faces compromising smiles, as they nodded to the government. It was the same old subordination. It was the same servility as it had always been!

Frankly, are we worthy of autonomy, when such shameful episodes take place in our country? How can we pretend that we are eady for self-government when the representatives of the people are such creatures?

Autonomy has been a disgrace. It has ruined the economy and the finances of the colony. It exposed our moral bankruptcy. It has shown that we are a people without courage. It has shown that we are people with no strength to oppose the government and above all, being the weaklings and cowards that we are, it has shown that we can easily be bought or corrupted. This is the truth and the rest is all farce!

The defeated members who came back to their work did not make a sacrifice for the nation. No. They sacrificed their own dignity, leaving greater evils in their wake, which would have been fascinating even if they were not there. Everybody knows what they are.

(*India Portuguesa*, March 13, 1924)

9. By praying for the soul of autonomy, we can vote for the soul of the nation.

On February 10, the members who had been defeated in their motion on December 27, and had subsequently walked out, returned to resume their duties in the Council. On that day autonomy died. The members failed to uphold the dignity of their positions. Once again, in a servile and subservient manner, they fraternised with the government. Their sheepish attitudes made possible the episode of March 19, a fitting epilogue to the earlier events in which they heaped so much debasing shame upon themselves.

March 19 shows that autonomy, as the governing body of the nation, has failed not only politically but also, miserably, as a moral entity. It has failed morally because the representatives of autonomy remained indifferent when one of their colleagues was attacked by an official. Since an attack on a co-representative is an insult against them as well, their indifference was equivalent to not standing up for themselves.

It is no use hiding the facts. The assault on João de Figueiredo, an elected member of the Legislative Council, by the director of Revenue cannot be thought of as simply a personal matter between the two of them. It would have been so, had both the contestants been engaged in a battle of words. But there was not even a discussion between the two. The conflict between them later on developed into a scuffle.

Did João Figueiredo, the elected member, behave inappropriately in the Council? Did he come in drunk? In the first place, even if he or any other member had come in drunk, the offence would have been perpetrated against the presidency and the president of the Legislative Council is the Governor-General of *Estado da India*. Hence, it is the Governor's duty to deal with the situation. Certainly others have no right to give offenders lessons in the proper code of conduct. The director of the Revenue by taking justice into his own hands has worsened the situation.

Secondly, having taken justice into his own hands, should he have dealt with it in the manner that he did? You Sir, you thought that you were at a table in a restaurant or a café in Lisbon, did you? Or, did you not know that you were before a respected Assembly in the Legislative Council? Even if the director had the right to deal with the situation, he should look into such affairs without resorting to the kind of brutality he showed. Otherwise Sir, you act like a gendarme inside the Council.

Our intention here is not to defend the assaulted victim, albeit that he is both intelligent and sincere, with no vested interests in what he does. He has not the qualities to be in the Legislative Council, because he is not patient enough to study the problems seriously and deeply. Though impulsive, he is also naive and has been dragged into all sorts of ill-advised schemes by many crooks, who have profited thereby.

We intend simply to denounce in a spirit of solidarity the attack that was made on him, because Mr. Figueiredo's colleagues did not raise even a finger in protest against the attack. Although now, since Mr. Figueiredo made a public statement saying that he did not hear the insults hurled at him by the director of the Revenue, we have no sympathy for him. We, the people, do not deserve this.

Clearly, we cannot support those who have no pride and honour in themselves.

But in this conflict, our interest is not in the personal aspect of the case. It lies in the larger moral significance it has for the country in general. When an official member of the Council slapped an elected member on the face without being given any provocation, the people's representatives did not protest at all in solidarity and that is what concerns us.

Can we have autonomy in this land? Can the Legislative Council continue to exist after the incident of March 19? The conscience of each of us should be the judge of that! On our part, the conviction grows deeper each time we have not got the makings to benefit from self-government. We say this with regret, and not with pride.

Autonomy has left us in a state which has exposed the inferior quality of our intellectual and moral formation. It would be impossible to regain the respect we once had in the future. Day by day we fall in the scale of political dignity, showing ourselves to be braggarts and cheats with no one taking us seriously.

Today both public opinion as well as the voice of the Press have zero merit in the eyes of the government. Today the government officials are indifferent to public protests, to public meetings and to the public appeals in the newspapers. Public opinion has had no value since the rule of autonomy was established. In the Legislative Council there are eleven individuals who speak in the name of the people and these eleven accommodate easily to any humiliating arrangements. Poor people!

If the government wants more money through new taxation, they vote for it. They do not care about the hardships endured by the taxpayers. If the higher officials want pay increases, they vote for it. No matter that the coffers are empty, it is not their concern. They just go ahead and vote and approve all kinds of legislation ruinous to the people and all this, in the name of the people!

Nobody is surprised anymore at anything that goes on. After having debased ourselves so deeply during these years, the incident of March 19 was merely what followed logically from past events.

(*India Portuguesa*, April 10, 1924)

10. Recently, in the Lisbon newspapers, the colonial problems, which had been relegated to oblivion for so many years, are being discussed, once again, with keen interest. And this is encouraging. It appears that public opinion in the Metropolis has finally awakened after a long lethargic sleep, knowing that the future of the nation is inescapably dependent on the overseas provinces.

The Press stated that Mr. Vicente Ferreira, former Minister of Colonies, wants to do away with the administrative and financial autonomy that has been conceded to the colonies of the East. We believe that the statement is true, because Mr. Mariano Martins, the present Minister of Colonies, also has confirmed that there is a plan to curtail the powers of autonomy. For us, these are clear indications that *Terreiro do Paço* has already formed its opinion of the public ability in certain colonies regarding decentralisation.

Though India, among Portuguese colonies, has a higher level of civilization, the experiences of the past five years have shown that autonomy was like an exotic tree that failed to get acclimatised to this land. The finances of the colony, which were already in a bad shape due to the errors of the central administration, were further aggravated by the ineffectiveness of the first Republican government.

In the course of seven and a half years, the Republican government has not allocated a single project to improve the finances of the colony. And today, we are in the desperate situation, because we are at the mercy of this new administration. This new administration, without any consideration for the people of the country, went on spending from left to right and gave salary raises to the functionaries, increasing thereby the expenditures beyond the capacity of the annual budget.

The tragedy of all this is that not only did the deficit shoot up, but the taxpayer was left without any money to spend. By taxing all the consumer goods mercilessly, decentralisation was responsible for the rising cost of living. This resulted in a major exodus of rural workers to foreign countries!

The Legislative Council of the *Estado da India,* with its majority of elected members, disastrously ruined the public finances and the economy of the country. This being the case in India, one can imagine the effects of autonomy in other colonies, where the level of education is inferior to ours and furthermore, in those countries, it is the officials who dominate the Legislative Councils. One is not surprised therefore that *Terreiro do Paço* is concerned about the future of the colonies. They are worried that the colonies, given the way they are governed at present, will become a burden to the Metropolis.

We have talked about the administration of this colony before because its future particularly interests us and we think, it is right to talk about it, once more. We understand that the administration should be headed by the Governor-General. But he should be a direct delegate to the Minister of Colonies while the departments of administration should be distributed among five or six secretaries at most. They should be in charge of these departments with a lot of responsibilities attached to their posts. Their responsibilities should be well-defined in the regulations of each secretariat.

The State's revenue, leaving aside reserves for payments and allowances for the Governor-General, judicial magistrates, military officials, *Padroado* and other similar expenses, should be distributed proportionally between the different secretariats. Each secretariat should be allotted a certain amount of grant money and each one should draw up a separate budget, individual to its department. These budgets should be then debated in the council, (the council having the same structure as before) and approved by the Governor-General, while the general budget of the colony should be debated in the Colonial Council (for example, in Portugal) and approved by the Minister of Colonies.

The expenditures of the personnel and staff of each secretariat should never exceed one-third of the grant, and these moneys should be audited thoroughly by the Fiscal Council of the State administration, presided over by the inspector of Revenue. At the same time, the department of Revenue could be audited too.

We are of the opinion that an administrative unit based more or less on the model indicated above would ensure better public services. This way, the State's moneys would be spent more profitably.

The paperwork, besides being the cause of chaos and disorder, erodes the State's money and allows no money for any other development. It is for this reason that the paperwork should be simplified as far as possible.

The administration that we are witnessing today is anarchic and inefficient. Confusion and uproar are everywhere. Public needs are not addressed and the people are angry. The State's properties are going down progressively in value. The civil servants are shouting because they are not paid for days and the public is clamouring too, because public works are in a mess. These are the symptoms of an anarchic and deplorable government!

Autonomy has to end, because experience dictates its impracticability in this colony. But, in its place, it is necessary that the Republic give us an administrative system corresponding to the reality of our lifestyle.

(*India Portuguesa*, April 28, 1924)

2

A REPLY TO PEREIRA BATALHA

April 10, 1924

My dear Pereira Batalha:

In *Província*, no 310, dated March 24, I read your article entitled, "Deserting the grave".

In this article, you could not bury the hatred of so many years that you have been nursing against me in that diminutive heart of yours. I think it would be ungrateful on my part not to thank you for the recognition that you have granted me so generously.

You attribute to my influence the change of opinion that has recently taken place in *Terreiro do Paço*, regarding the autonomy granted to this colony. I can see that you are seriously worried about my articles against the autonomy that has been conceded to India, that have been appearing recently in the newspapers of the Metropolis.

In your opinion, these articles threaten the regime of decentralization. Even from a distance, one can sniff your political slyness like the smell of something burning. Your viewpoint makes it appear as if ministers and journalists are conspiring against the kind of autonomy you have brought into effect in India. And hence you attack me like a wild beast. You say that the resentment of the masses is because of me. You blame me for all that is happening. You accuse me of having hidden ambitions and, as a result, I am attempting to suffocate any small liberties conceded to this land.

You are a devil, a wicked one at that, my dear Pereira Batalha But I am not angry with you at all. On the contrary, I am flattered because all the noise you have created protesting my views in fact has made me an important public figure. I never thought that an unknown person like me would reach the heights of such prominence.

An article in *Diário de Lisboa* states that the autonomy brought economic and financial disaster to the people of India instead of bringing success. But, according to you, "The campaign against the autonomy that is launched from the balconies, is launched by a paper which says that it is the voice of the party, a party that stands for India. It is this paper that damages the prospects of autonomy. Not only are hard blows being aimed at the autonomy in that colony, but the Press in Lisbon also criticizes the way the autonomy is implemented in that State".

And further down, you continue,

"The penetrating writing of *India Portuguesa* of Margao, has appeared in Lisbon dailies and in other papers. It is creating a disturbance in political circles where colonial problems are discussed. And in Lisbon it is accepted as an established fact that the autonomy has contributed to the bankruptcy of public finances."

My dear Pereira Batalha, it is only because I have known you for so long and so intimately that I know that you are an intelligent man, otherwise, I would have thought that you are the greatest idiot that had been put on this planet!

I am not a discreet person by nature. I know that you detest me politically, and that you are busy gathering all your energy to destroy me. I have learned this from individuals whom I happen to know well enough.

My dear Pereira Batalha, it would be better for you to pray to St. Ugolina, the protector of poor souls, for you are a poor soul indeed! You say that it is I, and my paper, that are responsible for damaging the prospects of autonomy. But then, you yourself have proclaimed that it is the penetrating nature of my writing that has given rise to the criticism of the way autonomy has been implemented in India, in the political circles of the Metropolis where colonial problems are discussed.

And there must be some truth in this. Since, again as you yourself have pointed out, if Lisbon has accepted as an established fact that autonomy in India has contributed to the bankruptcy of public finances then it is entirely because the newspapers of the Metropolis have taken up the campaign that was launched by *India Portuguesa.*

Besides, I ask myself here, why is it that the country's other newspapers, including *Proíncia*, a paper that is directly under your competent expertise, have not made the same impression in the Metropolis? All newspapers except mine have sung the praises of autonomy and supported their views by citing facts and figures. But why is it that only *India Portuguesa,* directed by me, with its "penetrating writing," as you put it, that has been able to draw the attention of political circles where colonial problems are discussed in *Terreiro do Paço.*

All papers in this land, both important and unimportant are busy singing the praises of autonomy. All of them want autonomy, and all of them declare and confirm that autonomy has been good to India. It is I alone, you say, who oppose autonomy and Lisbon, you say, has taken up the cue by in turn declaring that it is an evident fact that the autonomy has rendered bankruptcy to the public finances. What are you driving at, my dear Pereira Batalha? Are you then suggesting that the Metropolis is deaf to the opinions of other newspapers of this land and that it only regards *India Portuguesa*'s views as true?

I do hope it is not because you are thick-headed that you suggest this. If you are, then you would be offending me personally. But perhaps you intend to praise me in all sincerity when you say it was I who was responsible for bringing about the change of opinion in Lisbon regarding the kind of autonomy granted to this country, an autonomy that did not function well. In which case, I must thank you very much indeed for bestowing upon me such prestige and honour in the political circles of the Metropolis where my paper is judged as an upholder of evident truth!

Your statement that the penetrating writing of *India Portuguesa* is being taken up by the newspapers of the Metropolis and that it is creating waves in the political circles where colonial problems are debated, is therefore music to my ears, my dear Pereira Batalha! And this gives me the right to believe that all newspapers of India, including *Provincia*, which are defending the autonomy are merely voicing the braying of donkeys which can hardly soar upwards to heaven.

The voice of *India Portuguesa* alone is heard in political circles where colonial problems are debated.

I am a young man and a novice in politics, my dear Pereira Batalha, and my opinions are listened to, dismissing the rest of you! That makes me proud. And you, Sir, wanting to reduce me to nothing, have ended up putting me on the highest pedestal. From that vantage point, I view my enemies as tiny frogs and you, Sir, among them are the tiniest, a very tiny ant and despicable. Giants like me crush them under their feet.

Today, a scornful roar of laughter is being sent to you.

Et nunc et semper

J. I. de Loyola

Bilhete Postal

To dear Pereira Batalha
Director, *Província*

(*India Portuguesa*, April 10, 1924)

RESPOSTA AO PEREIRA BATALHA

Na Província no. 310 de 24 de Março, leio o artigo "Abrindo a Gova" e conquanto V. não tenha podido represar, desta feita, o rancor que de longa data vem alimentando, contra mim, na sua alminha de pigmeu, nem por isso me julgo desobrigado de lhe agradecer a celebridade que tão generosamente me quer conferir, atribuindo-me a responsabilidade da reviravolta da opinião que presentemente se está notando no *Terreiro do Paço*, acerca da autonomia concedida a esta colónia.

Vejo que V. está sèriamente alarmado com, a propaganda que, nestes últimos tempos, se está fazendo nos jornais da Metrópole contra a autonomia concedida à India, V. sente que paira uma grande ameaça sobre o regime de descentralização; o seu faro de político arguto faz-lhe cheirar ao longe um odor a queimado; e como lhe parece que ministros e jornalistas começam a conspirar contra o *self-government*, reconhecendo o erro da sua aplicação à India, V. volta-se contra mim, iracundo e féro, e aponta-me as iras das multidões, clamando que a culpa do que sucede, a mim que cabe, e que eu, por inconfessáveis ambições pessoais, estou tentando estrangular as pequeninas liberdades concedidas a esta terra.

V. é levado dos diabos, meu caro Pereira Batalha! Mas nem assim me sinto zangado consigo; antes pelo contrário, a minha vaidade sente-se lisonjeada, e não cabe na pele de contente, perante o estrondoso reclamo que V. está fazendo à minha obscura individualidade, dando-lhe uma importância e um valor que eu nunca supuz que pudesse ter.

A propósito de um artigo de *Diário de Lisboa*, em que se afirma que a autonomia, longe de ter promovido a felicidade do povo da India, só produziu o descalabro económico e financeiro desta colónia, escreve V. :

> "A campanha que contra a autonomia se está fazendo nos balcões e, principalmente, num jornal que se diz órgão de um partido pro India, vinha produzindo os seus perniciosos efeitos. Já não é portas a dentro das nossas fronteiras que o regime autónomo sofre duros golpes. Estendem-se também à imprensa de Lisboa as críticas picantes à autonomia concedida a este Estado, e o escárnio ao que se passa nos nossos Conselhos".

E acrescenta:

> "A prosa dissolvente da *India Portuguesa* de Margao, espelhou-se num *Diário de Lisboa*, reflectiu-se noutros jornais, fez eco nos centros políticos onde as questões coloniais se agitam"

"Passa já em Lisboa como verdade axiomática que a autonomia só concorreu para o descalabro das finanças públicas".

Meu caro Pereira Batalha: - Se eu não tivesse a certeza (por o conhecer de perto e de tão longa lida) de que V. é um homem inteligente, ficaria a supor que V. era o maior parvo ou idiota que a Natureza colocou à face do planeta!

Que demónio! Eu sou uma criatura que, por mal dos meus pecados, lhe não faço bom cabelo. V. - polìticamente pelo menos - detesta-me, e todo o seu empenho (como de muitas outras pessoas que eu felizmente muito bem conheço) é o de me ver aniquilado e esfrangalhado.

Pois, então, é V. próprio quem vem apregoar que a "prosa dissolvente" do meu jornal "está fazendo eco nos centros políticos da Metrópole, onde as questões coloniais se agitam"?

Valha-o Santa Ugolina, que é protectora dos pobres de espírito, meu caro Pereira Batalha!

Diz V. que a campanha da *India Portuguesa* "se está reflectindo nos jornais da Metrópole", e que "passa já em Lisboa como verdade axiomática que a autonomia só concorreu para o descalabro das finanças públicas".

Mas, então, não me dirá V. que importância se liga na Metrópole à restante imprensa desta terra, que, muito ao contrário deste jornal, alardeia as excelências da autonomia e até demonstra com algarismos e factos concretos que o *self-government* só tem feito a felicidade da India?!

A autonomia, nesta terra tem a defendê-la a totalidade dos jornais - excepção feita do meu, tendo à sua testa a *Província*, que V. tão superiormente dirige. Pois todavia, é a "prosa dissolvente" da *India Portuguesa* que consegue sobrepôr-se e impôr-se no *Terreiro do Paço* ou nos "centros políticos onde as questões coloniais se agitam"?

Todos os jornais, sérios e cordatos, desta terra andam empenhados na gloriosa tarefa de cantar as belezas da autonomia. Todos eles querem o *self-government*, e todos garantem, juram e afirmam que a obra da autonomia tem sido benéfica para a India.

E no entanto - di-lo V. - só porque eu sozinho o afirmo, em oposição a tanta gente por junto, em Lisboa "passa já como verdade axiomática que a autonomia só concorreu para o descalabro das finanças públicas"!

A que conclusão pretende V. chegar com isto, meu caro Pereira Batalha? Quere V. dizer que não tem o menor peso nos centros políticos da Metrópole a opinião de todos os restantes jornais e que só a opinião da *India Portuguesa* o tem, a ponto de se ter *como verdades axiomáticas* o que se escreve nesta folha?!

É possível que V. - que não tem, como eu, *o crânio obtuso* - cuide que representa para mim uma grave ofensa, dizer que me cabe a responsabilidade da atmosfera que se tem criado em Lisboa, acerca da incapacidade política desta terra para o governo de autonomia. Eu penso exactamente o contrário; e *ex ore tuo* aceito, com muito prazer, a honra que V. me dá, atribuindo-me tamanha cotação nos centros políticos da Metrópole, que consideram lá *como verdades axiomáticas* o que se diz no meu jornal!

Com que, então, e a "prosa dissolvente" da *India Portuguesa* que se "está reflectindo nos jornais da Metrópole" e "fazendo eco nos centros políticos onde as questões coloniais se agitam"? Diga-o mais uma vez, meu caro Pereira Batalha, que eu gosto de o ouvir! Isto dá-me o direito de acreditar que toda a restante imprensa da India, que defende a autonomia, inclusive a *Província*, são vozes de burro ... que não chegam ao céu; e que só a voz da *India Portuguesa* é escutada nos "centros políticos onde as questões coloniais se agitam"–e escutada com tanta veneração, que, enquanto se riem com despreso do que dizem a *Província* e os outros jornais (que defendem a autonomia), consideram como *verdades axiomáticas* aquilo que eu digo, contra a opinião de tanta gente por junto!

Que maior glorificação queria V., meu caro Pereira Batalha, para a obra de um político moço e noviço, como eu?

V. pois, como está vendo, veio fazer-me um inconsciente reclamo, supondo, ingènuamente, que ia... liquidar-me. Não me liquidou: exaltou-me. Ergueu-me um pedestal, e tão alto me colocou, que, agora, quando espraio a vista e condescendo a olhar para a planície por onde palmilham, como rãs, os anões que tentam combater-me, os meus inimigos cada vez me parecem mais pequeninos, e, dentro todos, V., que nem por ser o mais anão de todos, é quem tem menos veneno que os outros, me parece, positivamente, uma formiga despresível e minúscula, que os gigantes, como eu, esborracham um dia, por desfastio, debaixo dos sapatos.

E, por hoje, vá roendo uma grande gargalhada que lhe envio o.

Seu *et nunc et semper*

J. I. de Loyola

3

THE LEGISLATIVE COUNCIL

A calm reflection upon the latest political events, namely, the conflict between the Governor-General and the elected members of the Legislative Council, indicates clearly that it is the government that has come out looking the worse in this struggle.

Dr. Jaime de Morais, a reputed politician, unfortunately has not maintained the dignity of his position in this case. Instead of remaining firm in his decisions, he has appeared indecisive and wavering. At first, though, he adopted an uncompromising attitude. What is in question is not whether such an attitude is right or wrong, so much as whether Dr. de Morais is as uncompromisingly firm as he appeared to be and not simply that having gone so far, he did not want to draw back. For his subsequent hesitations gave the public the impression that His Excellency regretted his initial high-handedness and that he wanted a retreat from the debate as soon as he could without losing face.

If the Governor-General attached any value or significance to the opinions of the Chamber of Commerce, he would have made the effort to listen to their views before submitting the new tax guidelines for the approval of the Council. Any modification that the Chamber of Commerce may have suggested to the guidelines, would have been included in the policy paper before presenting it to the Legislative Council. For once the guidelines are approved by the Council and converted into legislative diploma, by the respect owed to laws and the legislative body, they are not open to alteration.

Well, Dr. de Morais made no attempt to listen to the Chamber of Commerce at the time he should have. He did not even bother to listen to the elected members of the Legislative Council when they brought in the motion requesting the postponement of the debate. Instead, His Excellency showed callous indifference towards commerce, closed his ears to the moans of consumers, and above all, did not hear the protests of the people's representatives. At all costs, he wanted to go ahead with his tax proposals.

But now it seem he has suddenly remembered to submit his preferential tax guidelines to the Chamber when the guidelines have already been passed by the Legislative Council, although, when he had ample time to discuss the tax proposals with the Chamber of Commerce, he could not care less. It would appear from his behaviour that the Chamber of Commerce must be superior to the Legislative Council and further that whatever action the Council takes must depend upon the sanction given by the Chamber of Commerce!

What's the matter with you, Your Excellency?

If the Chamber of Commerce had no intrinsic value, and hence Your Excellency did not find it fit to consult them, why on earth did you approach them afterwards, when the tax guidelines had already been approved by the Council?

Clearly the Governor-General acted this way because, when the elected representatives boycotted the Council and did not show up for the session, he saw the gravity of the situation. Reflecting upon it he realized that it had been grossly imprudent to have approved the bill the way he did. In a skillful way, he engineered a way out to rectify the mess. For how would he explain his conflict within the Council to the Minister of Colonies? He therefore engineered a skilful way to rectify the mess. So now, if Lisbon were to ask him for an explanation of the conflict, he would be able to say that the tax guidelines were published according to an agreement reached with the Chamber of Commerce.

But, yes, here is the rub! If in the end, Dr. de Morais has had to make amends for having intervened in the business of the Chamber of Commerce, it would have been better certainly had he settled the disagreement first with the Legislative

Council. Among other things it would have shown that he does have some respect for the opinions of the people's representatives.

We are not interested in knowing whether all the Chamber's suggestions were attended to by Dr. de Morais, although from a moral point of view he ought to have, and not selected only some that appealed to his whims. What concerns us essentially in this case, is the Governor's earlier attitude, wanting to look for a reconciliation. Now, that is what he wanted and that is what he did.

The way Dr. de Morais handled the situation has pleased neither the Chamber of Commerce nor the Legislative Council nor has he resolved the conflict. Forcing the amendments of the Chamber of Commerce after the charter had been voted on and approved by the legislative body, he placed himself in a false position with the Legislative Council.

However, we want to be fair to Dr. de Morais and believe that he behaved thoughtlessly. He was merely drawn into the momentum of that moment without reflecting on the consequences of his behaviour. We would like to recognize that he would not consciously hurt the Legislative Council, which has always supported him loyally. At the same time, though, we lament that Dr. de Morais, who is astute and intelligent, did not show enough strength of mind to understand that he would be wrong if he took the step he was planning to take.

Resorting to political manipulation, he wanted to give a hearing to the Chamber of Commerce on the charter which had already been passed by the Legislative Council. In doing so, he provoked a great conflict, the first in his government.

The Governor-General left the Legislative Council in a shameful situation, it is necessary to tell him that. Far from achieving his objective, to remedy the harm done in the session of December 27, unfortunately, he created another aggravating state of affairs for the legislative members whose motion had been defeated. He showed that he was more willing to come to terms with the Chamber of Commerce than with the people's representatives.

(*India Portuguesa*, January 24, 1924)

O CONSELHO LEGISLATIVO

Examinando serenamente os factos políticos ùltimamente ocorridos, ou seja o conflito entre o sr. Governador Geral e os vogais eleitos do Conselho Legislativo, impõe-se reconhecer, à luz fria da razão, que, em última análise, quem ficou mal colocado em toda essa questão, foi o Govêrno.

O sr. Dr. Jaime de Morais, que todos aliás reputam pessoa muito versada em artes políticas, não soube estar, infelizmente,à altura do seu papel, neste incidente, porque, se é certo que, no primeiro momento, tomou uma atitude de intransigência orgulhosa, que, boa ou má, oportuna ou inoportuna, era todavia a atitude de um homem, que, tendo avançado demasiadamente longe, se não dispõe a retroceder, posteriormente o espectáculo das suas hesitações deu ao público a impressão de que s. exa., arrependido dos assomos de valentia com que entrara na contenda, procurava ansiosamente uma saída, não se importando de sacrificar neste jogo uma parcela da sua prosápia.

Que outra interpretação dar, efectivamente, digam os leitores, às negociações entaboladas com a Associação Comercial, já depois de terem sido votadas e aprovadas pelo Conselho Legislativo - na memorável sessão de 30 de Dezembro - as novas pautas aduaneiras?

Se o sr. Governador Geral tinha em algum apreço ou consideração a opinião da Associação Comercial, é manifesto que teria procurado ouví-la antes de submeter o projecto das novas pautas à aprovação do Conselho Legislativo. Quaisquer modificações, que a Associação Comercial pudesse sugerir, era no projecto que tinham de ser atendidas, antes da sua apresentação ao Conselho Legislativo, e não depois - pois que, uma vez aprovadas e convertidas em diploma legislativo, pelo respeito devido às leis e ao prestígio daquela alta corporação, as pautas tornavam-se intangíveis ou insusceptíveis de alteração.

Ora, o sr. Dr. Jaime de Morais não procurou ouvir a Associação Comercial em devidas alturas, quando era tempo de o fazer; nem quando os vogais eleitos do Conselho Legislativo apresentaram a sua moção de ordem, pedindo o adiamento da discussão do projecto. S. exa., indiferente ao sobressalto do comércio, indiferente ao sossobro dos consumidores, indiferente aos protestos dos vogais populares, quiz então ir para a frente, a todo o custo; e, não se tendo preocupado com a Associação Comercial, quando era ocasião de o fazer, lembrou-se de submeter as pautas à sua apreciação já depois de votadas e aprovadas pelo Conselho Legislativo: - como se a Associação Comercial fosse uma entidade superior ao Conselho Legislativo, e os actos deste estivessem dependentes da sanção daquela!

Porque o fez s. exa.? Se a Associação Comercial era um valor nulo, a tal ponto que s. exa. nem se dignava de a consultar quando foi elaborado o projecto das pautas, porque posteriormente quiz submetê-las à sua apreciação, já quando estavam aprovadas e votadas pelo Conselho Legislativo?

É, que, evidentemente, diante da atitude desassombrada e altiva dos vogais populares, que abandonaram o Conselho e deixaram de comparecer às sessões, o sr. Governador Geral, medindo a gravidade da situação, reflectiu e verificou que fora grossa imprudência fazer aprovar as pautas da forma como o fizera, e engendrou então uma maneira habilidosa de emendar a asneira, por modo a poder responder ao Ministro, se de Lisboa lhe pedissem informações sobre o conflito, que as pautas haviam sido publicadas, de acordo com a Associação Comercial.

Mas, que demónio! Se o sr. Dr. Jaime de Morais havia de transigir por fim, provocando a intervenção da Associação Comercial, melhor fora, certamente, que transigisse, de preferência, com o Conselho Legislativo, o que teria, sobre muitas outras, a vantagem de fazer supôr que professava, bem ou mal, um certo respeito pela opinião dos representantes populares.

Não se diga que nem todas as indicações da Associação Comercial foram atendidas. Porque, no caso, o que interessa essencialmente é o facto de o sr. Governador Geral, modificando a sua primitiva atitude, ter querido procurar uma conciliação; ora, desde que o quiz e o fez tanto valia, sob o ponto de vista moral, atender a todas as indicações como satisfazer apenas a umas poucas delas.

Pelo caminho que seguiu, porém, o sr. Dr. Jaime de Morais nem conseguiu contentar o comércio, nem conseguiu resolver o conflito com os vogais eleitos; mas colocou tão somente em falsa posição o Conselho Legislativo, sujeitando às emendas da Associação Comercial um diploma que, por aquele alto corpo, já fora votado e aprovado!

Fazemos ao sr. Dr. Jaime de Morais a justiça de acreditar que s. exa. não reflectiu nas consequências do seu procedimento, ditado certamente pela precipitação do momento, e de reconhecer que seria incapaz de ferir, conscientemente, no seu prestígio, o Conselho Legislativo, que sempre lhe deu um apoio leal.

No entanto, não podemos deixar de lamentar qe o sr. dr. Jaime de Morais, sendo aliás um homem perspicaz e inteligente, não tivesse tido a necessária serenidade de espirito, para perceber que era errado o passo que ia dar, recorrendo ao subterfúgio de ouvir a Associação Comercial, sobre um diploma já aprovado pelo Conselho Legislativo, e depois de ter conseguido a sua aprovação pela maneira como o fez, provocando um conflito grave, o primeiro da sua governação!

O sr. Governador Geral deixou o Conselho Legislativo em uma situação deprimente - é forçoso dizê-lo; e, longe de ter logrado o seu objectivo, qual o de remediar o mal feito na sessão de 27 de Dezembro, fez, sem querer porventura, um novo agravo aos vogais vencidos, mostrando que preferia transigir com a Associação Comercial, a transigir com os representantes populares.

(*India Portuguesa*, 24 de Janeiro de 1924)

4

THE ARMY

The army personnel, the sergeants of this native land, have been asking for years for a betterment of their salaries. But no one so far has paid any heed to their just demands. It is only right for the Minister of Colonies to look into this deplorable state of affairs.

In 1910, in the *Ordem a Força Armada* of this province, a decree (no. 5570) was published and it was put into effect on May 10 of the same year. According to this decree all army units from all the colonies were given better salary increments. But when this decree actually came into force, only European army personnel were given the benefits. The natives were ignored. This reveals nothing but hatred and injustice against the native army personnel.

The Commission that was responsible for the formulation of decree no. 5570 was composed of outstanding officials from the army. They were drawn from Portugal as well from the colonies and they knew the standard of living of this land. They had recommended that the benefits as set forth in the decree should be indiscriminately applied to both Europeans and Indians. However, it did not turn out to be that way. Their recommendations were pushed aside so that only European army personnel received the benefits, while the Indians were ignored.

This situation is completely out of line and most humiliating to our people. It should be stopped this very instant. The pay that the Indian army officers collect is not enough to meet even their basic needs. In the list below, we give you the pay-scale of the European sergeants and the corresponding one of the Indians. It will give you an idea of the discrimination between them.

Pay Scales in Force

Sergeants 1st Class (Europeans)	
In training	800
After commission	750
After probation	850
Emoluments	300
Colonial allowance	300
	3$ 000

Sergeants 1st Class (Indians)	
In training	450
after commission	300
emoluments	250
food allowance	196
	1$ 196

Sergeants 2nd Class (Europeans)	
In training	600
After commission	550
After probation	850
Emoluments	250
Colonial allowance	300
	2$ 550

Sergeants 2nd Class (Indians)	
In training	350
After commission	200
Emoluments	150
Food allowance	196
	$ 896

So, you will notice that the salary of the Indian sergeants of this colony is one-third that of their European counterparts and you will also notice the difference in emoluments and in residence allowances.

Though European and Indian personnel are subject to the same laws and to the same amount and quality of service, yet Indians do not earn the same privileges and salaries as their European colleagues. The salary discrepancy based on racial discrimination does not stop here. For example, a second class European corporal draws more in salary than a second class Indian sergeant. A European soldier without any rank, with his salary and emoluments, ends up drawing more than a second class Indian sergeant of this colony! No reasonable explanation can support this flagrant abuse of justice. Justice is unbiased. If its dignity is to be upheld then it is important that it should be put into practice in this situation as well as anywhere else.

If the living conditions of the Indian sergeants in service are bad enough, they are worse after their retirement. Their salary being one-third of that of Europeans, their retirement pension is also one-third of that of their European counterparts. For example, the pension of a second class sergeant of Indian origin is about 350 *réis* a day or Rs. 30 per month. This pension obviously is not enough to meet his own needs nor that of his family.

Experience has shown that it is well-nigh impossible for Indian sergeants to live on their pensions. The meagre amount heralds the bleak future that awaits them, and many, frightened of that future, have left the army prematurely to join the civil service.

To give an example, an Indian corporal, in the category of the first rank, knowing what was in store for him in the future, left the army and got a job as an ordinary servant in the health department.

For so many years the Indian sergeants have asked in a pitiable chorus that their deplorable and debasing pay-scales be improved. But up until today, no one has paid any attention to their complaints.

General Gomes da Costa, appointed to the highest military post to reorganize the army is at present here in our country. Given his incorruptible spirit, he should recognize the injustice committed against the Indian sergeants of this colony. Because of the injustice, the locals have neither enthusiasm nor willingness to make their careers in the army. The General, being a thoughtful man, should know better than any that soldiers should be treated with fairness, if they are to remain in the forces.

Of course, he has to look into the situation carefully and when he finds out for himself, as he certainly will, that the salaries of the unfortunate Indian sergeants are not enough to make both ends meet, he should put wheels into motion to improve their condition.

He should put into effect all the benefits that are stipulated in decree no. 5570 for the Indians as well. When that is done, their plight will be lessened. It is also a matter of urgency and importance that their salaries and pensions be based on the cost of living.

We hope that Gen. Gomes da Costa will address this shameful situation and put a stop to it. In so doing, he will save the honour of us all. Though the finances of this colony are in bad shape, it is unjust and immoral to balance the budget at the cost of minor army officials. It is wrong to deny rightful salaries and benefits for the Indian sergeants, while high officials who make more than enough, are given fabulous pay raises.

(*India Portuguesa*, November 8, 1923)

5

THE NEW CONQUESTS

The Press of this country, for years now, has been saying that the economic prosperity of Portuguese India depends upon exploiting the region of the New Conquests for profit. It has abundant natural resources, untouched until today. If explored methodically and intelligently, it would bring prosperity to this land.

In the vast and fertile region of the New Conquests there is a great opportunity to make the Portuguese culture felt. If the government was to apply itself seriously to the development of this region, the economic situation of this colony would be in a much better shape. The people who inhabit this region are not as advanced as the people in the Old Conquests; they are illiterate and backward. So many mistakes have been made, for so many years, with regard to the New Conquests. Both the government and the private sector have not taken any initiative to develop this region. This lack of initiative is detrimental to the public welfare and the economy. This region has been badly neglected. The newspapers do sometimes feature articles on this region (although only when there is nothing else to write about). Yet, nobody has taken any initiative to develop this region where natural resources are merely waiting to be tapped.

Portuguese India is a poor colony. There is very little employment in this colony. Even if one is employed, one finds it difficult to make both ends meet. The people of this colony emigrate to other countries for employment and the colony to a very large extent depends on the money remittances of the emigrants. Though the geography books say that the colony's economic mainstay is agriculture, it does not produce enough rice to feed its own people. The cereal imports that the colony needs are bought with the money remittances sent by hard-working emigrants to their families.

The lands of the New Conquests should be appraised and should be put to use. These uncultivated lands should be distributed to the tillers to be brought under the plough. And this should be done with a view to promote and enhance agricultural productivity to the extent of producing a surplus. The surplus would help to bring down the deficit. The first prudent step on the part of public administration should be to take advantage of all its sources of energy and use them intelligently. However, in this matter, the feeling of gloomy hopelessness is too deep within us for any changes to be brought about.

Once in a while, the Press will raise its voice requesting the government to put it's plans in motion in the New Conquests. Then the government seems to respond with enthusiasm, as it has done all the other times in the past when the Press raised the issue, and delivers positive speeches on the matter but, in the end, does nothing at all about it. The same old story is repeated as before. From our point of view, the faulty administrative system is the main cause of the backwardness of this region. The concentration of all power in the hands of the Governor and half a dozen high officials perpetuates the vices of the central administration, and thereby deprives the regional administration of sufficient autonomy to develop the region. This situation is very much similar to that of Panjim.

The New Conquests are kept in a state of uncertainty, in shameful stagnation and hence, they are not in a position to march forward at the same pace as that of the Old Conquests. Because of this handicap, they should be given special consideration, a measure that no one would contest. They should be administrated *in loco*, through an independent body, which has adequate administrative machinery. This administrative model should be like that of British India where some districts come under the collectorate. For instance, it would be a good move if military administration were to be established in the main districts of the New Conquests because these places are still inhabited by bush people, who are not yet civilised. However, this would mean that the civil authorities will have to relinquish their authority and pass it over to the military in order that this region may have an efficient administration.

With the proclamation of the *Carta Orgânica*, military administrations no longer exist. However, there is one still in force in Satari but this, because the government is afraid of the Ranes when it was established. There might not be any Ranes in Satari anymore but the military administration still exists. In a similar fashion, a military administration can be established in Valpoi, for it is indeed needed to steer development in that region. We are not saying that military administration is perfect. Far from it. We are aware of the abuses and the confusion that prevails in military administration. But we maintain that they should be rebuked and set right. Better statutes should be introduced in military administration and they never should be crossed out from the book–*tout court*. The administrative guidelines should be simple, like those of the *Carta Orgânica*.

It is our conviction that the districts of Canacona and Sanguem, if they are to develop at all, should be brought under a special status of administration similar to that of the collectors of British India.

(*India Portuguesa*, November 15, 1923)

AS NOVAS CONQUISTAS

A imprensa desta terra vem afirmando, desde há longos anos, que o futuro económico da India depende, em grande parte, da valorização das Novas Conquistas onde abundam recursos naturais até hoje inaproveitados, mas que, em sendo submetidos a uma exploração metódica e inteligente, podem assegurar a prosperidade do país.

É certo que, efectivamente, as vastas e férteis regiões das Novas Conquistas oferecem um largo campo de acção para a actividade portuguesa, e dúvida não há de que a situação económica desta colónia seria a estas horas mui diferente se os governos procurassem, mais a sério, promover o desenvolvimento daquelas terras, que, habitadas por uma população ignorante e inculta continuam a jazer em grande atraso, ao contrário do que sucede com os concelhos das Velhas Conquistas, que atingiram um notável grau de civilização e de progresso.

Longo seria enumerar os erros de muitos anos, mercê dos quais as Novas Conquistas, onde a iniciativa ou a actividade de governos ou de particulares não encontra, aliás, as mínimas dificuldades de penetração, têm continuado a permanecer, com grave prejuízo da economia pública e social, regiões fechadas e abandonadas à sua sorte, das quais só se se fala, de vez em quando, à falta de outro assunto melhor, nos artigos dos jornais, ninguém se abalançando, porém a pôr em prática qualquer pequenina medida de fomento, que possa valorizar os seus recursos naturais e elementos de riqueza.

A India Portuguesa é uma colónia pobre, que vive especialmente do expediente da emigração, não havendo, portas a dentro, emprego e ocupação para os seus habitantes, capaz de lhes dar o suficiente para as necessidades da existência. País essencialmente agrícola - como se lê nos compêndios de geografia - não produz sequer o arroz necessário para o consumo da sua população havendo que suprir o *deficit* cerealífero com as economias que os emigrantes, moirejando por terras estranhas, enviam às suas famílias.

Explorar e valorizar as Novas Conquistas, metendo a cultivo os seus extensos baldios, distribuindo pelos camponeses as suas terras, já para os prender ao solo, já para promover uma maior actividade agrícola, que pudesse debelar o *deficit* da produção, deveria ser, sem dúvida nenhuma, o primeiro passo de uma administração pública inteligente e sensata, que soubesse empregar as suas energias e esforço em uma obra reprodutiva e benéfica.

Infelizmente, porém, o que se tem passado e o que se está passando, é de jeito a semear o desalento e a desesperança. Umas vezes ou outras, a imprensa levanta a sua voz e pede que se olhe para as Novas Conquistas; os governantes dizem que sim e pronunciam grandes discursos; mas, no final, fica tudo como dantes, quartel general em Abrantes!

Ao nosso ver o atraso das Novas Conquistas tem tido como causa principal a organização defeituosa do nosso sistema administrativo, que, em vez de lhes ter dado condições de desenvolvimento, por meio de uma administração local dotada de amplas faculdades, tem querido sujeitá-las aos vícios de uma organização centralista, que congloba todos os poderes nas mãos do governador e de meia dúzia de altos funcionários e repartições superiores, com sede em Pangim.

As Novas Conquistas, enquanto não sairem da estagnação vergonhosa em que vivem atoladas, e se não tornarem capazes de marchar a par e passo com os concelhos das Velhas Conquistas, precisam de ser submetidas, ninguém o contestará, a um regime especial. Têm de ser administradas *in loco*, mediante uma entidade independente, apoiada em um maquinismo administrativo adequado, a exemplo do que sucede na India britânica, nos distritos submetidos ao regime de *collectorado*.

Neste sentido, a criação de comandos militares, nos principais concelhos das Novas Conquistas, obedecera certamente a um pensamento elevado, porque, em regiões como aquelas, habitadas por povos selváticos, que ainda se não integraram no convívio da civilização, as autoridades civis dificilmente conseguem dar à sua acção a eficiência que lhe podem garantir os militares.

A Carta Orgânica acabou, porém, com os comandos militares, à excepção de um único, o de Satari, que foi conservado, naturalmente, por medo aos ranes.

Mas não fora por medo dos ranes ou das revoltas, que haviam sido criados os comandos militares. Poderia não haver ranes em Satari; e, todavia, um comando militar em Valpoi seria de igual forma necessário, porque uma simples administração do concelho jamais lhe pode imprimir aquele forte impulso de desenvolvimento, de que Satari, como os demais concelhos das Velhas Conquistas, necessitam a olhos vistos.

Não pretendemos afirmar, com estas considerações, que os comandos militares eram isentos de defeitos. Não. Davam lugar - forçoso é reconhecê-lo - a muita casta de abusos, de desmandos e de tropelias. Mas os vícios que ocasionavam podiam ser corrigidos, aperfeiçoando a organização dos comandos, ou substituindo-os por outros organismos melhores; nunca, porém, deveriam ser suprimidos, *tout court*, e substituidos por simples administrações, como o fez a Carta Orgânica.

É nossa convicção que sobretudo os concelhos de Canácona e de Sanguém nunca poderão progredir, enquanto não forem submetidos a umas entidades, que, pela latitude das suas atribuições, correspondam, de algum modo, aos *collectors* da India Britânica.

(*India Portuguesa,* 15 de Novembro, 1923)

6

THE RURAL CREDIT BANK

The Rural Credit Bank which came into existence through the Legislative Diploma, is being discussed at great length in the Indian Press, and as such it has merited the attention of many, not only within Portuguese India, but outside of it. The Indo-Portuguese communities that reside in different parts of the British India have also shown their interest in it. For the past few years, the Legislative Diploma which instituted the Rural Credit Bank has been discussed to such an extent that *União Goana*, from Bombay, representing more than 100,000 emigrants sent a telegram asking for its suspension. Portuguese India is essentially an agricultural country. The public as such should have been happy to welcome such measures, measures that assist and protect agriculture. The Indian population which is often divided and split on many issues of collective interest, shows itself united for once, protesting against the Legislative Diploma which instituted the Rural Credit Bank, and that appears to be paradoxical. One does not often see Indians of one mind on any public or political issue. There are divisions among them. Their opinions are at the mercy of caste and religious differences. For example, if some are battling against a project, soon others, who belong to the same caste or religion and have the same political views, will encourage and approve the project without ever looking into it to see if it is beneficial or not to the country as a whole. Their understanding of the issues invariably is coloured by prejudice and caprice.

Well, in a country where political issues are evaluated on the basis of an erratic value system, it is indeed surprising to see the people united against the Legislative Diploma which gave them the Rural Credit Bank. In this one instance at least, forgetting the boundaries of caste, religion or political affiliation, they were in accord in launching their protest against the Rural Credit Bank. How does one explain this curious fact? No one will say that India does not deserve a Rural Credit Bank. Through the Press, public conferences and seminars, we have consistently clamoured for it because the people really needed a Rural Credit Bank. It is in fact a necessary institution to promote agriculture and the economic progress of the colony.

All this being so, one cannot understand the strong objections from all sides against the Legislative Diploma which instituted the Rural Credit Bank. We have shown our dissatisfaction against it by holding protest meetings. We have appealed against it to the Colonial Council itself and we have dispatched letters of protest and have sent representations explaining our discontent with it to the Minister of Colonies himself. Why? The people of India are not against the Rural Credit Bank. On the contrary, they have always wanted it; and they want it as much today as they wanted it yesterday. Their protests, their appeals and requests are not to annul or revoke the Legislative Diploma that gave them the Rural Credit Bank. But, what then? The people see that the Diploma as promulgated does not meet their desired objectives; and hence, they want it to be modified. It is this that they are demanding.

India is an agricultural country and most of her people depend on agricultural activities for their prosperity and for this very reason, they cannot afford to revolt against the Rural Credit Bank. But unfortunately the Bank that has been implemented in the colony is not an institution that is capable of dispensing the credit usefully or efficiently. This is not the type of institution that the people were demanding. This is something ridiculous, a perfect fiction that has been foisted upon the people. And hence the revolt and indignation of the public. The Legislative Diploma did not establish a Rural Credit Bank that genuinely met the needs of the agriculturists. Instead it brought into being a scandalous and swindling bureaucratic mechanism, which is in no way beneficial to the agriculture of this colony. This Bank is a sham, set up to put money into the pockets of some government allies and cronies. It is for this reason that the entire population of India, irrespective of caste, religion or political affiliation is against the Bank and demands that this institution be reconstructed to genuinely meet the aspirations of the people. Thus the public is not against rural credit banks in themselves, and their protests should not be wrongly interpreted. This is not a crusade dictated by the egoistic interests of the people, nor is it meant to as provocation for the sake of provocation. But if the authorities in the Metropolis were to look into these protests, they would discern the real truth behind them.

In principle, we accept making compulsory payments to agricultural associations and religious corporations and they in turn set aside a certain percentage of their gross or liquid income towards Rural Credit Bank. The simple system that had served so well has been made unnecessarily complicated. A bureaucracy has been established! Frankly, that is beyond understanding because they have established departments and offices that eat away the much wanted capital, depriving small agriculturists of possible loans. Such facilities for borrowing should have been entrusted to *comunidades* and *confrarias* of each village by creating a special fund for this purpose.

From this point of view, the educated and the independent opinion of India desires that the Legislative Diploma be modified.

(*India Portuguesa*, September 25, 1924)

7

POLITICS IN PORTUGAL

Those who care to read the parliamentary debates with attention will note with pain that they are futile, unproductive and spiritless. It is clear that no parliamentarian has taken the time to make a real study of the problems of the nation and no one so far has ,properly defined the course that the nation should take for the future. These debates without any decorum have a demoralizing effect upon the people. Parliament is like a boxing ring where the MPs, instead of exercising their brains to think about better legislation, behave like boxers, fighting each other brutally in the name of party politics. At each session there are tempestuous and rowdy scenes and that diminishes, not only the prestige of the legislators, but also the dignity of the institutions that they represent.

This kind of rowdiness may be due to the Latin temperament. Such parliamentary histrionics are not uncommon in the parliaments of Latin countries. Though this is true, there is a difference. In other Latin countries, such incidents of tumult and disorder in Parliament are only occasional events, not on everyday affair. In these countries, unlike in Portugal, the parliamentarians work hard and take the time to study the substance of the bill under discussion.

In Portugal, all rows are about daily bread matters. Their debates are the debates of threshing out party politics. It is a politics of factional interests. All their energies are channelled to achieve and to gratify either personal ambitions, their personal vanities, or those of the party that they represent. It is a politics of shame; it is a politics without dignity. In politics of this nature, the very interest of the nation is lost.

These episodes speak aloud of the bankruptcy of the parliamentary system in Portugal. Twenty-five years ago, Oliveira Martins, referring to the Parliament of his times, wrote the following words, which very much relate to the present time: *"Res, Non Verba"*.

One month of the parliamentary session is over; that is one third of the period for legislation. What have we achieved? The question is asked not to criticize anyone but as a sincere grievance, and it must be addressed. And the answer is, Nothing! It is depressing to watch this game of word play. Words wrapped in metaphors, words condensed with apostrophes and dashes. Words with hyperboles and analects and so the parliamentary rhetoric marches on into a desert of sterile ideas. The MPs may raise their hands so high as to reach the ceiling, raise their voices to electrifying depths and show faces that are inflamed with the heat of passionate concern for their country, but their words are no more than echoes resounding in an empty vessel. Their words are words without action.

We wish to see an assembly of intelligent, sensitive, articulate and knowledgeable parliamentarians who will put an end to these ineffective debates. Often, these trivial debates which last through all the sessions of Parliament, should be injected, if not with passion, at least with interest. If one were to read *O Diário das Câmaras* (Parliamentary Debates), it would be like journeying through a dry and scorching desert. Words, words, words!

What is the obvious explanation for this phenomenon? What adequate reason can be given for this situation, which we can in all truth call pathological?

First of all, according to our point of view, these incidents happen because of the following fact. The parliamentary opposition is not going the way it was meant to go. There is a conflict between the duties of the opposition and the way it exercises its duties. The opposition was supposed to be a moderating influence upon the government by ironing out partisan politics. But the truth is, all this eloquence of words obscures the dishonesty of the intent of the parliamentarians.

The other duty of the opposition is to look into the affairs of the ministries and whip them into shape, directing them at every stage in their responsibilities, commencing at the very beginning.

This explains why the individuals endowed with idealism and absorbed in their work are the first ones to confess the ridiculous situation that they are in. Any individual, however great he might be, if he is in a job that does not feel right to him, will always feel diminished. The ineffectiveness of Parliament is apparent to the nation, and this is detrimental to the reputation of the members of Parliament.

If one were to listen to the young debaters in Parliament fulminating against the crimes committed "against liberty", "against sovereignty" and other grandiose phrases that they use, one wonders where they get their zeal from. But they speak words without genuine commitment, creating an illusion. These young debaters are simply having a good laugh. They know better than anybody that, if they were in the government, they too would commit crimes against liberty and the collective sovereignty. They are not committed; they long to change places with the government MPs. This is the kind of politics by which we are governed.

The country needs a government that governs and not merely speaks. Words have quenched our thirst, but we are hungry for action. Words are sacred when they clarify a thought, but when they are used fraudulently they cause tragedy.

Our country should be respected and taken seriously by all of us. The first duty of the politicians should be to commit themselves to their task and learn to respect themselves. And to show that they have taken their task seriously, they could give up lying. They also have to forsake the foxiness that they indulge in to become members of Parliament and give up the skillfulness with which they grab power from the ministries into their own hands.

Portugal and other countries urgently need a parliamentary reform, separating the legislature from the executive.

(*India Portuguesa*, July 20, 1924)

POLÍTICA EM PORTUGAL

Quem acompanhe com atenção os relatos das sessões parlamentares, verifica, com mágoa, que a acção do actual Parlamento, sobre ser estéril e improdutiva, é profundamente desmoralizadora. Nem só ninguém estuda, com amor e consciência, os grandes e graves problemas que interessam ao futuro da Nação, mas a forma como decorrem os trabalhos parlamentares deseduca o povo.

O Parlamento, em consequência das lutas das facções, que se digladiam com encarniçamento feroz, assemelha-se a um ring. E os deputados, em vez de terem a linha grave da sua função de legisladores, parecem boxers. Em cada sessão, há zaragata, tumultos, cenas tempestuosas, que não concorrendo para o prestígio de quem os promove, só têm o merecimento de desprestigiar as instituições.

É certo que, para este resultado, muito concorre o temperamento exaltado da raça, e que espectáculo similar também o oferecem os parlamentos de quase todos os países latinos. Mas entre um e outros, há grande diferença, que não convem perder de vista: e é que, se nos parlamentos dos outros países latinos, pode haver ocasionalmente tumultos e desordens, são simples episódios de momento; mas não constituem a sua vida normal. Normalmente, naqueles países, trabalha-se e estuda-se. Em Portugal, não. Aqui os tumultos são o pão de cada dia; a discussão obedece sempre às conveniências de um partidarismo estreito e faccioso; votam-se a despreso os problemas de interesse nacional, para só se tratar dos interesses das quadrilhas; e malbaratam-se todas as energias e actividades nas pugnas inglórias de uma política sem elevação nem grandeza, que gira em volta das ambições ou vaidades de um homem ou de um bando.

De resto não é de hoje a falência do sistema parlamentar em Portugal. Há 25 anos, Oliveira Martins, referindo-se ao Parlamento do seu tempo, escrevia as seguintes palavras, que parecem escritas para a época presente: *Res, Non Verba.*

Está completo um mês de sessão parlamentar. Está decorrido um terço do período normal legislativo. Que há feito?

Esta pergunta não envolve censura para ninguém; mas exprime uma lástima sincera de que seja forçoso responder - nada!

É deplorável assistir ao espectáculo dos torneios estéreis de palavras, dos dilúvios cerrados de metáforas, dos nevoeiros densos de apóstrofes, e entimemas, de hipérboles e anancolutos, com que a retórica parlamentar avança em coluna no deserto de ideias, sonolenta e estéril, com o braço erguido para o tecto da sala, a voz tonitroante, a face inflamada e no espírito de todos a consciência do vazio em que se agitam, e da desproporção e dissonância entre os sentimentos e as frases.

Faz dó ver um congresso de inteligências superiores, de espíritos aguados, distintos, ou sabedores, disperdiçarem o tempo num palavreado estéril, e pôrem muitas vezes, senão paixão, pelo menos interesse, nas bagatelas que diàriamente ocupam o parlamento. Ler o *Diário das Câmaras* é o mesmo que jornadear num adusto e seco deserto.

Words, words, words!

Qual é a explicação óbvia deste fenómeno? Qual é a razão suficiente deste caso a que verdadeiramente podemos chamar patologico?

Ao nosso ver, a razão está, em primeiro lugar, no seguinte facto: o desiderato e a missão real de uma oposição parlamentar não é, como os teorizadores do sistema supuzeram, exercer o papel de crítico sobre os actos do governo e o de moderador sobre o espírito mais ou menos faccioso das maiorias. A verdade, que a retórica mascara mal, é outra: o dever das oposições é derrubar ministérios, quando estejam maduros, e moê-los, enquanto verdes, para que amadureçam.

Esta primeira razão explica o porquê de se encontrarem espíritos distintos ou superiores abarbados com tarefas que eles próprios são os primeiros a confessar mesquinhas, se não ridículas. Todo o homem, por grande que seja, colocado numa posição falsa, aparece diminuido. A esterilidade do parlamento não só é nefasta ao país: é deprimente para a reputação dos seus membros.

Ao ouvir os oradores da câmara fulminar os atentados cometidos contra a liberdade, as garantias da soberania despedaçadas, e outras frases mais rotundas, mas equivalentes, qualquer suporia que anima esses moços o mesmo entusiasmo (?) de há meio século. Ilusão! Esses moços riem de si próprios, sabem que todos, nas mesmas circunstâncias, cometeriam atentados contra a liberdade e despedaçariam as garantias da soberania popular. O único fim deles é substituir-se-lhe.

A isto se chama política, no feliz sistema parlamentar que nos rege.

O país quer governo, não quer discursos. De frases estamos saciados, de actos estamos sequiosos. A palavra só é um instrumento abençoado, quando esclarece. Quando chicaneia, é nefasta.

Para que o país nos possa tomar a sério e respeitar-nos, é mister que nós, políticos, nos tomemos primeiro a sério e nos respeitemos a nós mesmos.

E para que nós tomemos a sério é mister que abandonemos ficções; mas para as abandonar é também mister que as circunstâncias não ofereçam aos partidos esta tentação fatal de lhes proporcionar, com artifícios e ficções como todos aqueles que têm ocupado a câmara um mês e vão ocupá-la talvez outro mês ainda, o meio crónico de moer ministérios e trepar arteiramente aos bancos do poder.

O que em Portugal, como em toda a parte, urgentemente se reclama, é uma reforma do parlamentarismo; a separação de legislativo, e do executivo, e o fim deste sonolento reinado da frase tão rotunda como vazia.

PART II

8

TAXATION

1. According to reliable sources, the annual deficit of the colony, at this very moment, is about one million and five hundred thousand rupees. The public is seriously concerned. For a small country like ours, with limited resources, the deficit is enormous.

It is said that the local government, as a way of making a serious attempt to reduce the deficit, is planning to impose taxes on imported goods, including rice. But rice is a staple of this land, consumed by all of us.

A prominent member of the Legislative Council, concerned about the deficit, has formulated a proposal. In the last issue of this paper that proposal was published in its entirety. He recommends therein that the value of the rupee be raised to 450 *réis* instead to the present value of 350 *réis*. The present value of the rupee was fixed by a decree from Lisbon in 1911.

The value of the rupee which is now fixed at 350 *réis* fluctuates between 5 to 6 *escudos* in the daily exchange market. The plan to raise the value of the rupee was also put forward long ago by the Press of this country. It can be said, therefore, that the proposal that was introduced to raise the value of the rupee before the Legislative Council, is an old popular desire of the people.

In the meantime, however, thinking over all the consequences that would result if such a measure is to be taken, and not knowing whether it would be just and rational, we hesitate to give our unconditional approval to this proposal. We are also concerned about the way the proposal is formulated, for, if executed the way it is, the small functionaries, who are badly paid up to this day, would be the ones to suffer. Fixing the value of the rupee to 450 *réis* would have a disastrous effect on *Fazenda Pública,* curtailing its income. Though the State pays the civil service at the rate of 350 *réis* a rupee, it is equally true that the State collects most of its revenue by taxation, mostly seal (*selo*) tax, by regulating the rupee at the rate of 350 *réis* . Thus the State collects back most of what it pays its civil servants through taxes.

Therefore, if by tomorrow, the value of the rupee, *tout court,* is fixed at 450 *réis* what kind of economic parity would there be? Problems will arise when the State pays its public service and problems will arise when the State collects its revenue.

In the end, will the State benefit by introducing such a measure? We hope it will. Otherwise an idea of this nature would not have flowered in sane minds. Naturally, those who hold on to this idea with such tenacity must have computed the gains and losses, arriving at a conclusion that if such a measure is put into effect, the net profit would be huge and that there would be a tidy sum still left in the Treasury, even though there might be fewer returns in revenue.

To fix the value of the rupee at 450 *réis* summarily is not a good idea. The way we look at it is that the principle of the proposal is in the right direction but to put that principle into effect, a different path should be taken. Theory dictates that the annual deficit should first be reduced before raising the value of the rupee. So the first priority should be given to the annual deficit. Yes, there is another thing: to establish *modus faciendi*; to make this theory work without causing any chaos. But before we solve this problem, a pay-scale should be established. A minimum salary should be fixed and it should be based on the financial needs and the standard of living of the people.

Now, shifting our attention to the public service of this colony, there are three categories of public servants: (1) clerical staff of the secretariat, (2) heads and sub-heads of the departments, and (3) heads and sub-heads of the Public Service. Let us suppose, for example, that the minimum salary of the head of the Public Service is Rs. 500 in local currency, per month. Let us assume that his annual salary is 6 *contos.* Of this amount, let us assume that he is paid 2 *contos* and 100 *escudos* only, regulating the rupee at 350 *réis* and the rest of his salary is paid not only at the rate of 450 but even more, at 600 or 900 *réis* per rupee.

Anyway, this system, if adopted, would be like the one that is in vogue in the African colonies, where the functionaries are paid a small portion of their salaries, if we are not mistaken, in gold, and the rest in *escudos*. The benefits and salaries are adjusted according to the cost of living.

If this policy is put into effect here, we think it would help to reduce the deficit. In the end, we might even succeed in eliminating the deficit altogether. Then, a progressive taxation should be introduced and that taxation should be fair, just, and balanced and, above all, it should not destroy the small and the middle-income landlords, for they are the backbone of the economy of this land.

In India, the taxation system that is in force at present, is neither just nor fair. All the small landlords, who are small fry, using the picturesque phrase of the former Governor, are burdened with taxes beyond their paying capacity, while the privileged rich do not pay even one tenth in taxes, which by law, they ought to. One should put an end to this injustice immediately.

(*India Portuguesa*, September 2, 1923)

2. As we had predicted, this colony faces a deficit in its budget, and it is calculated now at Rs 1,500,000. This estimate looks dubious to us. Perhaps, there is an error in the calculation. Last time, the public, which was rightly worried about the government's expenditures, had clamoured loudly for its reduction and the local government, knowing the gravity of the situation, had published regulations in the *Boletim Official* to that effect. They too, being equally concerned at the mounting deficit, had asked the State to reduce administrative costs.

In this case, since both the people and the government were in accord, it was hoped that the State would not indulge once again in a disastrous spending spree. It was also hoped that the State, like the repentant Magdalene, would make a definite resolution and take the road towards austerity and reformation of character.

Moreover, a reformation was needed to usher in a financial and administrative autonomy. We also had an obligation to demonstrate practically that we were a wise people capable of exercising the rights of the majority.

Unfortunately, the views expressed by the Press coincide with the views expressed by the government in the paper. The government in turn, is determined to go to the very root of the problem in its attempt to reduce surplus expenditures. But often, it is true, the proposals that have been brought before the Legislative Council have been systematically rejected. Had they been approved, they would have brought respite to the Public Exchequer!

The Legislative Council so far has not approved a single proposal to help the economy. Thus, what recourse is left for reducing the deficit except imposing new taxes? But how can the government of this country demand new taxes? It is 13 years now that the Republic has been in effect but there has not been a single developmental project undertaken in this land, although lots of money has been spent on bringing in technical experts and creating new departments.

It is no use denying the reality of things. It would be prudent on our part to confess the truth. And the truth is that despite all that is being said about the high standard of education of the people of India, they do not have the necessary aptitude to lead an autonomous government to the best advantage of the country. Though they are intelligent and talented, they lack moral responsibility and intellectual integrity. And these two characteristics are prerequisites for the political development of any country.

Let me demonstrate by giving you an example. Let us look at the proposals that just a few days ago, were brought before the Council. The following briefs were placed before the Council: to eliminate some government departments in Daman and Diu; to eliminate the *Direcção Fiscal do Caminho de Ferro*, to eliminate the *Delegação Marítima de Mormugão*, and so on. Not one of them was approved by the Legislative Council, in spite of the fact that the elected members form a majority! They may aspire greatly but have no pragmatic sense.

Having lost hope of straightening out public finances by means of reducing expenditures, we are left with one solution only: increase taxes. What a solution!

Last week, an illustrious member of the Legislative Council brought in a proposal to raise the value of the rupee to 450 *réis*, instead of 350 *réis*, this value of the rupee was established in 1911. According to him, raising the value of the rupee would help reduce the public debt. We appreciate his view. But the colony is in dire need of a new taxation law. Small landlords pay more taxes than they can afford, while the rich landlords, who ought to pay more, pay less than their due. This tax system has to change. There should be equity in the system of taxation. The small landlords with minuscule incomes, who end up paying more, have hardly any money left to tend to their lands with the needed care. In the final analysis, taxes should be adjusted according to social wealth.

Every time new expenditures are brought in, they go beyond the financial capacity of the Public Exchequer, increasing the deficit. Then the government, with its obsession to raise revenues, imposes new taxes in order to balance the budget. But, unfortunately, this has been done without any thought or form. The very wealthy class has been given a preferential treatment. They hardly feel even the slightest pinch from taxation, while others are taxed mercilessly.

Considering the cumulative effects of the direct and indirect taxes that the people pay, it has been recognised categorically for many years that their capacity to pay more taxes has been exhausted. But does it mean the capacity of all categories of taxpayers is equally exhausted? *Hic latet anguis*! (Here is the agony!). This is because the government does not wish to analyse the naked truth of its taxation policy. It does not want to distinguish between those who ought to pay and those who ought not nor spare those who can hardly afford a shirt on their backs. The new tax measures, demanding sacrifices in the name of the country, are neither equitable nor just.

The fragmentation of agricultural land, mostly in the Old Conquests, has created many landlords. Excluding the labourer, almost everybody has a piece of land, a small homestead with coconut trees and a house. These small landlords are the backbone of the government's income from taxes and their income being almost minimal, any new taxes, however insignificant they might be, would have a devastating effect on the budget of the small landlords. They would be left without any money, unable to cultivate their small holdings. To demand new taxes from them is nothing but social injustice and misguided economics.

Besides these large numbers of landlords in rags who are taxed beyond their means, there exists another class, a very privileged minority, which is very well-off indeed, and its members hold prized real estate. Their annual profit at the end of the year is so huge that it almost equals the total annual income of all the small landlords. There are some such wealthy landlords in the Old Conquests and many in the New Conquests. After deducting all sorts of expenses, these wealthy landlords pocket two to ten thousand rupees a year. Surely, we cannot say that the capacity for more taxes of this class of people is exhausted.

Now an examination of the financial situation of the State, does indicate a need for more taxes to be levied upon the people. But the poverty of small landlords should establish that it is they who should be spared from being taxed anew and not the wealthy ones who make huge profits. They are in a much better position to make a few sacrifices for the good of the State without jeopardizing their own finances. It would be not only folly, but revolting barbarity to exact new taxes from poverty-stricken taxpayers!

From our point of view, before introducing any new taxes, the government should draw a boundary between those taxpayers who can afford new taxes and those who cannot. According to our understanding, in the present situation, the living expenses for a family is about Rs. 300 per month. This being so, the landlords whose yearly income is not more than Rs. 3,600 should be exempted from any new taxes. The government should introduce a scale of progressive taxation. That is, for those whose income is more than Rs. 3,600 annually, their first surplus of Rs. 1,000 or more should be taxed at 3%. However, those who make surpluses of

Rs. 2, 000, 3,000, 4,000 or 5,000 or more should be taxed at 3% for the first thousand rupees and at 4% for the others, *et ainsi de Suite.*

A taxation system of this nature would be fair and just. The wealthy and the small landlord would each pay his tax according to his means. Surely, those who have little should not be deprived of their livelihood, while the rich go scot-free.

(*India Portuguesa,* September 10, 1923)

3. The local government, a reflection of the Legislative Council, is a disgraceful institution that exploits the taxpayer. Under some pretext or other, it has increased every sort of tax on everything that it can lay its hands on, hurting many a poor man. But it has not touched those prosperous landlords from the districts of New Conquests who own vast and expensive estates, and they do not pay even one tenth of the amount of taxes which they ought to according to tax regulations.

The government claims that there is not enough money to meet its expenses. And so, in order to balance the yearly budget, it is demanding these new sacrifices from the people in the form of additional taxes. But this is just a game, for it is only the poor and the middle classes that are being taxed so ruthlessly.

Members of the privileged class who are rich indeed and who have higher revenues, should have been included in the new tax structure. But they are lovingly spared as if they belong to a class that should not be touched. This situation is revolting and scandalous, and public opinion finds it immoral.

If the government wants the right to levy new taxes on the people who are already burdened with taxes, it should ask itself beforehand whether it has the moral right to do so. Does the local government have such authority? No, it certainly does not.

It lacks this authority because the local government has failed to reduce public administrative costs to a minimum. They do not touch this issue, treating it as if it were something mysterious. Before the launching of new taxes, the new taxation policy should have been made impartial and equitable. But this was not done.

What right has the government then to impose new taxes upon the poor and the middle class?

To this day, the taxpayers of the Old Conquests complain that the district treasury offices have increased the land taxes without any auditing. But this is not the case in the New Conquests. There the taxes are ludicrously low, and this being so, the land taxation system is in need of urgent revision. Such a revision would enable the government to recover an enormous amount of embezzled tax money from the New Conquests, which by law, rightly belongs to the government. But the government is blind to this issue!

The finances are in bad shape and the government has no money to pay even a day's salary to its officials. One is at loss to understand why the government, which has been aware for many years that the wealthy landlords of the New Conquests pay less than their due, does not press them to pay their taxes. It appears that the government lacks the courage to force the wealthy to pay their taxes, but it can force new taxes on the poor.

The attitude of the government at this point is beyond anyone's guess. It invites severe criticism and lowers the prestige of established institutions.

The Press which is independent in this country has spoken sincerely and loudly, not once, but many times, reminding the government that it is advantageous and necessary to revise rigorously the land taxation policy in the New Conquests. But it has paid no attention. Why?

Is the government afraid of provoking a rebellion in the New Conquests? Or is the government favouring the rich landlords of that region? It is a known fact that the new developments which have sprung up in the government with the implementation of autonomy are dominated by certain persons who have important interests to safeguard in the New Conquests. If this is the reason why the wealthy in the New Conquests are being allowed to get away with cheating the government of taxes owed, then it is a grave situation indeed. It discredits the government, undermining its authority.

We will not discuss at this point why the government cannot balance the budget by lowering the administrative costs and hence is forced to increase the taxes in any manner it can. It is to be admitted that in order to decrease the deficit, it was but inevitable that the taxes should have been increased. But what we want to ask here is whether it is right to raise the customs duties which touch all the people of the colony, especially those less fortunate ones who are being suffocated by these new taxes? The land cultivation expenses are on the rise and the lands in the Old Conquests are bringing in lesser profits but the taxes continue to increase. Given these circumstances then, is it morally right for the wealthy landlords of the New Conquests to continue not paying their dues to the Treasury?

When requested either to approve an increase on revenues or an authorization to contract new loans, the Minister of Colonies ought to consult the local government on these matters. But before sanctioning such measures, he must make sure that the land taxation system is updated in New Conquests. Without such updating, no authorization should be given to launch new taxes or to contract new loans.

(*India Portuguesa*, August 31, 1924)

TAXAÇÃO (*Portuguese Version*)

1. O *deficit* orçamental desta colónia, que, segundo informações fidedignas, orça neste momento em cerca de um milhão e quinhentas mil rupias, está preocupando sèriamente a opinião pública, alarmada com a enormidade da cifra, que, efectivamente, parece grande demais para um país de recursos limitados, como é a India.

Diz-se que o governo local, não se afoitando a entrar, francamente, no caminho de uma rigorosa e inexporável compressão de despesas, como as circunstâncias exigem, pensa em lançar mão de novos impostos para fazer face à situação afirmando-se mesmo, com certos visos de verdade, que um dos seus planos é o de elevar os direitos aduaneiros sobre os artigos de importação, incluindo neste número o arroz, que é, aliás, um género de primeira necessidade nesta terra, pois que constitue a base da alimentação indígena.

Por seu turno, um ilustre vogal do Conselho Legislativo formulou uma proposta - que, no último número deste jornal, foi publicada na íntegra - alvitrando que seja fixado em 450 *réis* continentais o valor da rupia, que, por um decreto da Metrópole, promulgado em 1911, foi fixado, em 350 *réis*.

A alteração do valor oficial atribuido à rupia - e que continua a ser de 350 *réis*, quando, aliás, é sabido de todos que, ao câmbio do dia, a rupia oscila entre 5 a 6 *escudos* - é uma ideia que tem sido aventada, desde longa data, na imprensa desta terra, podendo dizer-se, por isso, que, de certa maneira, a proposta, que ao Conselho Legislativo foi submetida, traduz uma velha aspiração popular.

No entanto, ponderando todas as consequências que iriam resultar de uma semelhante medida - sem que ninguém possa contestar, no entanto, que seria justa ou lógica - hesitamos em lhe dar o nosso incondicional aplauso, não somente porque, tal como a proposta foi formulada, a sua execução pode originar um grave desequilíbrio na vida dos pequenos funcionários, ainda hoje mal retribuidos, mas ainda porque a fixação, pura e simples, do valor da rupia em 450 *réis,* teria um outro efeito deveras desastroso nas condições actuais, qual o de cercear os rendimentos da Fazenda Pública; pois, se é certo que o Estado paga o funcionalismo à razão de uma rupia por cada 350 *réis,* não menos certo é também que o Estado arrecada, da mesma forma, uma grande parte das suas receitas - que são as do imposto do selo - regulando a rupia, igualmente, a 350 *réis.*

Por conseguinte, se fosse amanhã definido, *tout court*, que a rupia passava a valor 450 *réis*, a par da economia que dali resultaria, pelo que de menos o Estado teria de dar para o pagamento dos functionários, uma desvantagem surgiria também paralelamente, pelo que de menos igualmente o Estado iria receber nos seus rendimentos.

Feito o rebatimento ou a compensação aritmética, entre a economia nos gastos e o cerceamento das receitas provenientes da medida proposta, ficaria o Estado a lucrar todavia, em resultado final? É possível, e cremos bem que assim suceda;

nem doutra maneira poderia a ideia ter medrado em cérebros sãos, que, se com tanta insistência a têm defendido, é porque, naturalmente, feitos os devidos cálculos, chegaram à conclusão de que as economias a haver seriam tamanhas, que, além de cobrir o que de menos resultasse nas receitas, ainda deixariam sobras apreciáveis.

Mas nem assim nos parece de bom aviso alterar sumàriamente a equivalência da rupia, fazendo que ela passe a valor, de um momento para o outro e para todos os efeitos, 450 *réis*. Para nós, se é admissível o *princípio* que à proposta presidiu, e que é certamente bom, a sua forma de aplicação tem de ser diferente; porque, assente, em tese, que não pode subsistir a fixação actual da rupia em 350 *réis*, tornando-se necessário alterá-la, como uma das maneiras de reduzir o *deficit* orçamental, não fica desde logo resolvido o assunto. Resta ainda por estabelecer o *modus faciendi*, de forma que a execução da ideia, aó passar dos domínios da teoria para o campo da prática, não vá causar perturbações e uma barafunda ainda maior.

Em nosso entender, como ponto de partida para a resolução desta questão, deveras emaranhada, a primeira coisa que se torna mister fazer é fixar, mediante um critério desapaixonado, o quantitativo do *mínimo* que devem ganhar nesta colónia - atentos os seus recursos financeiros e as necessidades locais da vida - os funcionários públicos, divididos, para esse fim, em três grandes categorias: empregados de secretarias, chefes e sub-chefes de repartições, e chefes e sub-chefes de serviços. Apurava-se, por exemplo, que o mínimo que devia ganhar um chefe de serviço, em moeda local, eram 500 rupias mensais. Pois bem. Se na tabela orçamental, vigente, o seu vencimento estava fixado - tomemos de hipótese - em 6 contos anuais, ser-lhe-iam pagos desta cifra sòmente 2 contos e 100, regulando a rupia a 350 *réis*; e o remanescente à razão não sòmente de 450, mas ainda de 600 ou 900 *réis* a rupia. De alguma maneira, seria, um sistema idêntico ao que vigora nas colónias da Africa, onde os funcionários, se não estamos em erro, recebem os seus vencimentos, uma parte menor em oiro - fixada conforme as exigências da vida - e a parte restante em escudos.

Parece-nos que desta sorte ficavam harmonizados todos os interesses, e teríamos dado um grande passo no caminho da redução do *deficit*, que, ao depois, seria debelado até a sua total extinção, lançando - se um *imposto progressivo* sobre as propriedades as fortunas em geral, fazendo pagar maiores contribuições aqueles que têm mais do que é necessário, e suavizando-se a condição doutros que, contràriamente, têm menos do que é estritamente indispensável. Porque não somente a incidência dos impostos tem de ser equitativa, justa e equilibrada, mas principalmente porque é de boa política não esmagar o proprietário pequeno e médio, cuja ruína é a que mais directamente influe sobre a economia e a prosperidade de um país.

Na India, mercê do regime tributário em vigor, a grande massa dos proprietários pequenos - que constituem o *peixe miúdo*, na frase pitoresca de um antigo governador - pagam mais do que devem; enquanto que com os grandes ricos - constituindo uma classe privilegiada - sucede o contrário: não pagam sequer a décima parte do que deveriam pagar. É uma injustiça, que não deve continuar.

No próximo número, voltaremos a tratar do assunto com maior desenvolvimento, afim de demonstrar até que ponto é imperioso reformar tal sistema, que, sobre ser arcaico e deficiente é absurdo, ilógico e anti-económico.

(*India Portuguesa*, Margao, 2 de Setembro de 1923)

2. Perante o deficit orçamental desta colónia, que, segundo dissemos, está computado em 1,500,000 rupias (salvo erro de cálculo, que, aliás, parece improvável), a opinião pública, justamente alarmada, tem pedido ùltimamente, em altos brados a compressão de despesas; e por seu turno, em vistosos projectos de diplomas legislativos, publicados no *Boletim Oficial*, o governo local descrevendo a gravidade da situação tem proclamado igualmente, alto e forte, a necessidade, imperiosa e inadiável de cercear os gastos da administração do Estado.

Em face desta perfeita concordância de vistas entre o povo e o governo, era lícito esperar que a India, afastando-se das veredas funestas da dissipação e da prodigalidade entrasse resolutamente- como Magdalena arrependida - no caminho de uma austera e severa regeneração, tanto mais que, tendo-nos sido concedida a autonomia financeira e administrativa, cabia-nos a obrigação de demonstrar, pràticamente, que estávamos aptos para exercer com proveito os direitos da maioridade.

Infelizmente, se é certo que por um lado, a imprensa - que exprime a voz do povo - berra noite e dia, reclamando a compressão de despesas, e se é certo, também, que, por outro lado, o próprio governo afirma, no papel, o seu propósito inabalável de cortar cerce todas as excrescências e gastos supérfluos, a verdade é que, todavia, no Conselho Legislativo, têm sido rejeitadas sistemàticamente todas as propostas de cuja aprovação poderia resultar um alívio sensível ao erário público!

Ora, se no Conselho Legislativo não consegue vingar uma só proposta que represente uma economia, que outro recurso existe, de que se possa lançar mão para debelar o *deficit* orçamental, que não seja a criação de novas receitas? E que novas receitas, que não sejam impostos, é capaz de criar o governo de uma terra, onde, durante 13 anos - desde a implantação da República até hoje - não tem sido empreendida uma única obra de fomento, apesar de se terem gasto rios de dinheiro com a criação de quantas repartições e entidades técnicas?

É inútil sofismar a realidade dos factos, antes é mais decente e honesto confessarmos com franqueza a verdade: - a India, apesar de tudo quanto se diz da ilustração dos seus habitantes, não possue ainda as condições necessárias para exercer convenientemente o *self-government* ou a autonomia; porque, se possue, em fartura, grandes talentos e inteligências, faltam-lhe outros elementos, de ordem moral, que junto com os de ordem intelectual, formam a preparação política de um país.

Será necessário apontar uma prova? Vejam-se as propostas que foram formuladas, ainda há pouco tempo, relativas à extinção dos governos de Damão e Diu, à extinção da Direcção Fiscal do Caminho de Ferro, à extinção da Delegação Marítima de Mormugão, etc. etc. *Pois, nem uma só foi aprovada*, apesar de que traduzem velhas aspirações populares e apesar de que no Conselho Legislativo, os membros eleitos estão em maioria numérica!

Perdidas, pois, as esperanças de endireitar as finanças públicas, mediante largos cortes no capítulo das despesas, a solução única que fica de pé é a de conseguir um aumento de receitas, por modo a fazer face ao *deficit* orçamental.

Mas qual o meio de o conseguir?

Apreciámos, na semana passada uma proposta, referente ao valor oficial atribuido à rupia, e que um ilustre vogal do Conselho Legislativo, no empenho de diminuir as despesas públicas, propoz que fosse fixado em 450 *réis*, visto não subsistirem actualmente os motivos que, em 1911, determinaram a sua fixação em 350 *réis*. E, por ocasião, preconisámos a necessidade de ser modificado o sistema tributário vigente nesta colónia, mercê do qual, enquanto os proprietários pequenos pagam mais do que podem, os grandes proprietários ficam pagando menos do que devem.

Efectivamente, a incidência das contribuições que vigoram nesta terra atinge por igual os ricos e os pobres, sem guardar entre uns e outros a devida proporção, dando em resultado que o proprietário pequeno, que tem rendimentos minguados, fique positivamente esborrachado, não podendo sequer granjear os seus campos com o necessário cuidado, o que, em última análise, redunda em detrimento da riqueza social.

Todas as vezes que, pela criação de novas despesas, incompatíveis com as forças do erário público, tem havido um desequilíbrio no orçamento do Estado, os governos, na obsessão de arranjarem receitas, para endireitar o fiel da balança, têm lançado mão de impostos novos; mas, infelizmente, com tão lamentável falta de ponderação e de critério, que, em vez de os fazerem incidir, de preferência, sobre as classes abastadas, os fizeram recair, indistintamente, sobre ricos e pobres, agravando descaradamente a condição destes, enquanto que aqueles não passaram de sofrer uma ligeira ... arranhadura.

Há já muitos anos que governantes e governados, considerando o avultado da soma dos tributos directos e indirectos que paga o povo desta terra, têm reconhecido e proclamado, categórica e solenemente, que *a capacidade contribuitiva do indo-português está esgotada*. Mas estará esgotada por igual a capacidade de todos os contribuintes, grandes e pequenos? *Hic latet anguis*; e é porque não se tem querido analisar detidamente os factos, fazendo uma escrupulosa destrinça entre os que não podem já pagar mais e os que ainda oferecem ... pano para mangas, que as tributações, novas, pedidas como sacrifícios, em nome da salvação da Pátria, não têm sido equitativas e justas.

Na India, a pulverização da propriedade agrícola, sobretudo nas Velhas Conquistas, dá lugar à existência de numerosos proprietários de chão, porque, exceptuado o proletariado braçal quase toda a gente possue um pedaço de várzea, algumas palmeiras e uma casa. Mas estes proprietários, que formam a grande legião dos contribuintes, têm rendimentos tão reduzidos, que qualquer imposto novo, por mais insignificante que seja, desequilibra o seu orçamento doméstico, impossibilitando-os de cultivar devidamente os pequeninos retalhos de terra que lhes pertencem. Pois, são estes os proprietários, cuja capacidade contribuitiva está esgotada, sendo um grave erro, social e económico, arrancar-lhes novos tributos.

Mas ... ao lado dessa legião esfarrapada dos pequenos proprietários que já não podem suportar o peso de mais impostos, floresce, rosada e nédia, uma minoria privilegiada de pessoas abastadas, que possuem riquezas importantes, e que, à roda do ano, chegam a fazer, *em sobras*, o que o geral daqueles outros não conseguem receber em total de rendimentos. Assim, há alguns proprietários nas Velhas Conquistas, e muitos nas Novas, que feitos os gastos da vida chegam a economizar, anualmente 2, 3, 4, 5 e até 10 mil rupias, ou mais: e em relação a esses, de certo se não pode dizer que a sua capacidade contribuitiva esteja esgotada.

Ora, perante a situação financeira do Estado, que exige a criação de novas receitas, verificada a inviabilidade da compressão de despesas, é nossa opinião que qualquer imposto novo, a ser criado, deve incidir tão somente sobre os grandes proprietários, que têm *sobras*, e que portanto, podem fazer ainda alguns sacrifícios, em benefício do Estado, sem que daí fiquem desequilibradas as suas finanças. Exigir novos impostos dos contribuintes pequenos, é que seria não somente um desatino, mas uma barbaridade revoltante!

Em nosso entender, deve o governo, antes de lançar qualquer imposto novo, marcar o limite ou a fronteira divisória entre os que já esgotaram a sua capacidade e os que ainda têm fôlego para pagar mais 300 rupias mensais, cremos que é presentemente, o mínimo com que pode viver uma família. Sendo assim os proprietários cujo rendimento anual não excedesse de 3,600 rupias, deveriam ficar definitivamente isentos de quaisquer impostos futuros; e os impostos novos, a serem criados, deveriam recair, em escala progressiva, tão somente sobre aqueles proprietàrios que tivessem mais de 3,600 rupias de rendimento anual. Pelas primeiras 1,000 rupias a mais, pagariam, por exemplo, uma contribuição adicional de 3 %. Tinham, porém, 2 ou 3 ou 4 ou 5 mil rupias a mais? Pagavam 3 % a mais sobre as primeiras mil, 4% sobre as mil seguintes, *et ainsi de suite.*

Teria este sistema a vantagem de manter uma proporção racional e justa entre as contribuições que pagam os grandes e pequenos proprietários, fazendo que pagassem mais os que possuem mais do que o necessário para a vida, e que, certamente por princípio nenhum, devem andar a par dos que têm menos do que o estritamente preciso.

(*India Portuguesa*, Margao, 10 de Setembro de 1923)

3. O governo local, que, à sombra do Conselho Legislativo, malfadado instrumento de espoliação do contribuinte, tem aumentado, a pretexto de tudo e de nada, toda a espécie de impostos, verifica-se que, no entanto, está fugindo, a olhos vistos, de ferir os interesses de uma minoria próspera e nédia de grandes proprietários, que possuindo vastas e valiosas terras nos concelhos das Novas Conquistas, não pagam ao Estado nem a décima parte do que devem. Diz-se que não há dinheiro; e, porque o não há, o governo, volta e meia, exige do povo da India novos ... sacrifícios. Mas, enquanto as classes populares e médias são tributadas sem dó nem compaixão, em nome do equilíbrio orçamental, (que, de resto, continua no mesmo pé), a classe privilegiada dos grandes ricos - daqueles sobre quem, por terem demasias de renda, deveriam incidir de preferência os novos

impostos - é precisamente a que o governo poupa carinhosamente, criando-lhe uma situação de previlegiada intangibilidade, que chega a ser revoltante e escandalosa e que, por isso mesmo, a opinião pública entende lesiva dos princípios da moralidade.

Um governo, para que tenha o direito de pedir ... sacrifícios ...às classes pobres, precisa de se revestir, antes de tudo, de autoridade moral para poder fazer aquela exigência. Tem-na o governo local? Não a tem, certamente; não e não! E não a tem, porque não somente as despesas da administração pública não têm sido reduzidas ao mínimo indispensável, como era mister que o fossem, em primeiro lugar, antes de se lançar mão de novos impostos, mas porque ainda o governo, no lançamento destes, não tem sido imparcial e equitativo.

Porque é que só aos pobres e aos remediados se hão de pedir ... sacrifícios!

Ainda agora, queixam-se os contribuintes das Velhas Conquistas de que as repartições de fazenda concelhias têm aumentado, sem audição dos lesados, as matrizes prediais. Mas não consta que se fizesse outro tanto nas Novas Conquistas, que é precisamente onde as matrizes são irrisórias e reclamam uma revisão urgente, afim de que o Estado desfalcado actualmente em enormes receitas, passe a cobrar o que de justiça lhe pertence.

Não faz sentido esta diversidade de pesos e medidas!

Se o estado das finanças públicas é precário, se a condição desesperada do Estado, que nem sequer pode pagar em dia os vencimentos do funcionalismo, exige do pobre povo da India novos ... sacrifícios, não se compreende como o governo, sabendo de há tanto tempo que os grandes proprietários das Novas Conquistas pagam menos do que devem, ainda não tenha querido ter a coragem de os obrigar ao pagamento do que rigorosamente lhe é devido.

A imprensa independente desta terra, que fala com altivez e sinceridade, não poucas vezes tem lembrado a conveniência e a necessidade de se ordenar uma rigorosa revisão das matrizes das Novas Conquistas. Porque é que o governo tem querido fazer ouvidos de mercador acerea deste assunto, fingindo que não ouve as indicações que lhe são feitas? Com o receio de provocar uma ... rebelião das Novas Conquistas? Ou pelo empenho de favorecer os afortunados proprietários daquelas regiões?

A atitude do governo, neste ponto, é inexplicável em todo o caso, e provoca comentários desprimorosos, que comprometem o prestígio das instituições. É sabido que, com a implantação da autonomia, nos organismos novos que o *self-government* criou, preponderam certos elementos que possuem nas Novas Conquistas importantes interesses. Toda a gente os conhece, e toda a gente sabe a influência de que dispõem nas regiões oficiais. Ora, esta circunstância é grave e autoriza interpretações que a uma governação, coisa dos seus créditos, impende o dever de conjurar.

Entende o governo que o equilíbrio orçamental não pode ser obtido mediante a compressão de despesas e que é forçoso aumentar de qualquer maneira as receitas públicas? Não discutiremos, neste momento, o seu ponto de vista quanto à possibilidade ou impossibilidade de reduzir os gastos da administração. Mas, admitindo como verdadeira a doutrina de que é inevitável aumentar as receitas, para fazer face ao excesso das despesas, perguntamos se será justo que, enquanto se elevam os direitos aduaneiros, que afectam toda a população da colónia tornando asfixiante a existência das classes desfavorecidas de fortuna, enquanto se aumentam, mediante processos sumários, as matrizes das Velhas Conquistas, onde as propriedades rendem cada vez menos porque as despesas de cultura aumentam cada vez mais, se será justo e se é moral que os grandes proprietários das Novas Conquistas, constituindo uma classe privilegiada, continuem a não pagar o que devem!

O sr. Ministro das Colónias, quando lhe pedirem em diante a aprovação de medidas conducentes ao aumento de receitas, quando lhe pedirem autorização para contrair novos empréstimos, que só Deus sabe como serão pagos, convem que simplesmente pergunte ao governo local - antes de sancionar semelhantes medidas - se as matrizes das Novas Conquistas já terão sido revistas ... E afirmar perentòriamente que enquanto o não sejam, nenhuma autorização poderá ser dada, quer para lançar impostos novos, quer para contrair novos empréstimos.

(*India Portuguesa*, Margao, 31 de Agosto de 1924)

9

CARTA POLITICA

Your Excellency,

I will comply with your order, once again. Your Excellency summoned me and ordered me to suspend the publication of the *Jornal da India* because of the security of the State and of public order and peace. This is not a valid reason. But I understand from the bottom of my heart and it pains me a great deal to know how all this came about. It happened because of a few irreverent articles that came from my obscure pen.

Yet on the other hand, some politicians and supporters, having taken into account those aspects of the newspaper that are perfectly reasonable (that is, not something that would disrupt public peace and order), demand that my journalistic career should not be interrupted. I am therefore determined to republish *Jornal da India*, before long.

To be quite honest, Your Excellency, I want to tell you in no uncertain terms that I intend to introduce another newspaper by the name of *Rebate*, and in this enterprise I wish to maintain an unbroken independence. I want you to know, Your Excellency, that I am counting on your support in this matter. For if a government governs as it ought to, then there should not be any problem regarding such things. However, your vigorous opposition shows that your government is unfit to govern.

Frankly speaking, even though it may not have been an intentionally ingenious move on your part, the suspension *of Jornal da India* in fact means a suspension of the Press, whose freedom is guaranteed by the Constitution itself. But since I am aware that my constitutional rights are still intact, I shall go ahead with my plans to launch *Rebate*, until I find the opportunity to restart publishing *Jornal da India*.

I hope that Your Excellency will have the goodness of heart to give me some warning ahead of time before you act this way again, not only because I would like be prepared for what you will do but also because I would like to discuss with you the action you have taken in this instance. For it might not be possible in the future since you might decide again that, the "security of the state, public order and peace" will be endangered. You see, I want to bring to your attention that I too respect and venerate the same three ideals that concern you. However, this may not be the right time for us to discuss your action since you are not at the moment in a receptive enough frame of mind in order for me to convey to you the right impression. Moreover, I am also not in a very enthusiastic mood at the moment.

By the way, here I am thinking deeply and prudently like a sixty year old man. It is rather a comic situation. Since words come to me easily, I want to choose the right ones and avoid disaster both for Your Excellency and for me.

Now, before I end this *Carta Politica*, I want to make a declaration, which viewed from all angles, is of great importance: "In case Your Excellency's intention is to erect a wall in the name of `security of the State' and of `public order and tranquillity', in order to stifle my voice in all the matters that offend your nature, as soon as I find out that *Rebate* does not have complete freedom to express its opinions, I will collect enough strength to open wide all the jaws and break them and also break all the handcuffs"!

As long as I can hear and see, you will hear me shouting heroically from the public park, standing or hiding. It is then, perhaps, that you will drag me and slam me into a gloomy prison cell.

But, I would like to tell you frankly that I prefer that Your Excellency do away with me with a gunshot. By the unlimited power that you have assumed, this act can be done.

I want to ask you another small favour. I would like Your Excellency to inscribe an epitaph on my tombstone, none can deny me this right, in good conscience.

Here lies he

Who in his austere life had characteristic frankness
Of one who speaks openly, never hiding his face,
Incapable as he was of infamy or vileness.
He died as he lived, just as he always dreamt to live
To love deeply his land.

(Published in 1913 when *Jornal da India* that Fanchu edited was suspended by the Governor F. M. Couçeiro da Costa)

10

AFONSO DE ALBUQUERQUE:

A Figure of Universal History

"*India will speak out for herself and for me*". These were the final words of the last letter of Afonso de Albuquerque to King D. Manuel. This was a farewell letter written in the ante-chamber of death on the morning of December 15, 1515.

The Hero, now old and enfeebled with no strength left in him, tired of wars, tired of fights and combats, worn out with sickness, was on his way to Goa in his warship, *Flor de la Rosa.* He was coming to this land, his home, the light of his eyes. He chose this land to be his last resting place. He had prepared a tomb, which he had left behind in this land, a tomb constructed with the most loving care and to grace it, he had saved six bronze lions which he had taken from the share of the booty in Malacca. But the *Flor de la Rosa* was shipwrecked in a storm and the lions went down to the bottom of the sea and Albuquerque, before he could disembark in the city, passed away at the dawn of December 16, in front of the gateway of Aguada.

Since then, India has spoken out and continues to speak constantly for herself and for Afonso de Albuquerque! Though she has spoken out, through an uninterrupted chain of events, she still goes on heralding her message and at this very hour of invocation and prayers, we have gathered here, the governed and the governing, to place our hopes and our appreciation before his statue. And before my dazzled eyes a shaft of light passes by, pouring out a lesson in history, exalting my soul. It is such a profound, suggestive, splendid and rare lesson, without any parallel in the history of the colonizing people. If no other titles could be bestowed, it would be only fair to legitimize the rights of the Portuguese nation by extending them to her overseas territories, which are spread throughout the five regions of the world.

This very pilgrimage which takes place year after year on the November 25, is a pilgrimage where the people come to fraternize. It is a pilgrimage of the exchange of patriotic sentiments. The hearts of Portuguese Indians and the hearts of the Portuguese in the Metropolis, throbbing together on the same wave length, come to pray "the prayer of the nation". Why would not India speak out for herself and for Albuquerque?

This unique man who had dreamt one of the greatest dreams which no other politician or statesman had dreamt, feeling the pangs of death, looked at the vastness of the ocean and then fixing his eyes on the blue dome of the sky, examined his conscience. He mentally reviewed his life and his actions. He squared the balance sheet of his work as a man and as a Portuguese, and he placed it at the threshold of eternity so that he could be accountable to God. He was so confident that he did his job well, that he felt very peaceful within himself. Yes, he was very sure that he did an excellent job. And then, he penned a letter with pride to his King who had been ungrateful to him. He wrote, "*India will speak out for herself and for me*".

Since then, and until now, a period of 400 years, on this day of the feast of St. Catherine, India has effectively spoken out for herself and for Albuquerque. Each time, the people of this land, their souls so stirred with emotion, as no other event has ever moved their souls before, come running to pay their homage of eternal gratitude and affection to him.

This experience of seeing the people of a conquered country come to glorify the memory of the conqueror through all these centuries, is uniquely extraordinary. To many of us, at first sight, this is a riddle, a paradox.

But, this marvel can be explained. Precisely because, for us, the people of Goa, though Albuquerque was a conqueror, he was a conqueror unlike other conquerors of this land or of any other land. He was not a sinister wolf that one sees defiling the pages of world history. When he took Goa away from the Muslims, he could have cleared the land and turned it into big plantations since this was the usual practice of the time. But he did not do that. Taking into consideration the values of our civilisation, and realising that the people of this land were not less intelligent than his own, and knowing that we were descendants of the Aryan race, just like his people, he planned the future of this land. By a deliberate attempt, he made this land an integral part of his country. He gave to the inhabitants of this land the same statutes as those of Portugal and in doing so, this land became part and parcel of Portugal, an extension of Portugal.

This concept of colonization was indeed an original one. This thought is profoundly intelligent, humane and Christian and because of that, the conquest can be justified and glorified. This was Albuquerque's magic wand, a wand which made it possible for faith and love to blossom in the hearts of the people of this land. And now, the descendants of the conquered people, shaking hands with the descendants of the conquerors, singing the same song of love together, with flowers in their hands, walk together to the statue of the conqueror to thank him. This is a miraculous spectacle that we are witnessing.

What pity I feel for this statue! For the sake of our honour, this statue should have been made of gold, standing with glory and triumph, watching out beyond the gateway of the Mandovi, with the rays of the sun prancing over its head in glory. The statue as it now stands, rough and unpolished, painted green like a pagan idol, is a humiliation to all of us. It is a humiliation to those who govern and to those who are governed. It is a humiliation to the Portuguese people of India and it is a humiliation to the Portuguese people of Portugal. The conqueror, who had never sheltered himself from the fire of cannons, is sheltered now by an ungainly dome, reminding me of a mushroom or an open umbrella protecting him from the vagaries of the Indian monsoons!

"*India will speak out for herself and for me,*" Albuquerque had said. He was proud of the land that he had conquered and above all, he was proud of her inhabitants. And I hope that India will speak out once again for herself and for Albuquerque. By taking into account the 420 years or so that have gone by after the conquest of Goa, we have to erect another statue of him so that we can continue to show our passion to his memory with more zeal than ever before!

And this passion continues to deepen. There is a reason for that. The wrongdoings of the leaders who came after him make our hearts yearn for the memory of the conqueror of Goa. He was very good and just to the people of this land! This second monument of Albuquerque that should be built to his memory, I am proud enough to tell him, would be a monument to represent our voice of protest against the iniquities that are rushing in like unceasing waves, subverting the very principles of fraternity and social justice, which the conqueror of Goa had embedded in India, when he had planted the banner of *Quinas* here. Sooner or later, the insanity, the blunders and the narrow-mindedness that are streaming in, will threaten to break up the spiritual alliance between the Metropolis and the colony, an alliance which Albuquerque had dreamt to be eternal and indissoluble!

"Matters of India create a great smoke of controversy," Afonso de Albuquerque used to say. And commenting on this, Oliveira Martins asks,

> "What sort of smoke was that? They were blunders made by all those narrow-minded people; they were blunders of vanity. The giant who had seen them like pygmies, busy like ants, feathering their own nests, was taken by surprise when he saw them later on. They were pot-bellied now, strutting in the courts like peacocks, bragging and testifying that they knew everything about the East."

Then as now, matters concerning India create a great cloud of controversy. The present day pygmies wearing statesmen's apparel parade and boast that they know all the concerns of India. By doing so, they are demolishing and destroying the little that is left of the past, by giving us an illusion that they are rebuilding it. These redeemers with their imperialistic and devastating attitudes can hardly measure up to the greatness of Albuquerque's thoughts. They are so puffed up with hot air and vanity that they admire themselves like that frog in the fable. Though things are quiet today, who knows what tomorrow will bring. In the future, because of these attitudes, the people will be hostile to Portuguese domination and will not hesitate to revolt and bring down the Portugal of the overseas. To save the little that is left of this great empire that Albuquerque founded, I think it is time for us to shout, "*Enough is Enough*!"

"*India will speak out for herself and for me,*" Albuquerque used to say proudly and prophetically and even at this very moment, India is speaking out for herself and for Albuquerque! She is voicing this statement before the statue of the conqueror, through my voice at this semi-religious ceremony.

The hour is calm and tranquil. Before this hallowed place let us pledge that we will be truthful to each other. Let us pledge to pursue new ideas, giving up on those that divide and split us, giving up on those that break us up and keep our mouths muzzled. Let us make a pledge not to give in to the ideas that would break the harmony in the Portuguese family. Let us make a pledge not to give in to repugnant ideas and let us make a pledge not to be spiteful to each other. These divisive ideas are like the welts of lashes given across the faces of some of us, and have taken away all our rights in favour of others. For such ideas, in the end, create two distinct classes of citizens: first class and second class, though we are all citizens of the same country. This bears no resemblance to the golden dream that Albuquerque had dreamt, nor is it anything like what the *Infante de Sagres* would have dreamed of nor is this a vision that navigators and warriors would hold or would have been held by those saints and heroes who have left their marks on the national epic history of greater Portugal.

Gentlemen!

I had to compose this speech, within 48 hours. This hardly gave me enough time to coordinate half a dozen ideas, my own personal ideas, which I wanted to voice on the conquest of Goa. Besides, more than half of those 48 hours were spent on affairs of my profession. These ideas may be good or bad, but I am going to express them anyway, so you may judge for yourselves.

Each time I think about the conquest of Goa, I believe more strongly than before that the conquest was neither the work of chance nor of circumstances. Oliveira Martins writes,

> "Piracy and looting were the two cornerstones of the Portuguese dominion: its nerves were cannons and its soul was spice."

If we analyze this brutal statement, it gives us a clue as to why Albuquerque conquered the city of Goa.

At the time, when Albuquerque was given the reins of the government of India, the Portuguese eastern empire was in reality a commercial empire. Though the Portuguese ruled over the seas of India and had factories and forts spread all over the settlements, they had nothing in the form of protection. Oliveira Martins, commenting on the consolidation of this developing empire, which did not have a defined boundary, writes,

> "The first need that arose here was to lay the foundation for a city, a capital city for this empire, which, so far, did not exist."

Commenting further, he writes,

> "Albuquerque chose Goa to be the capital city because she was situated in the centre of the western coast of the peninsula. She had a good port and all the favourable requirements to make her a capital city."

Once again, he adds this final comment on the same subject,

> "In February, 1510, Albuquerque took Goa by surprise; and, for the very first time, there came into existence a Portuguese state in the east. Since then, after the conquest, the territory became very important and the indigenous sovereignty was replaced by our own.
>
> Factories were established and forts were built with a view to protecting the commercial interests and to facilitating the collection of vassalage tributes and this was done according to the plan of the first Viceroy. In other words,

> Albuquerque was laying the foundation for a distinct order by launching an authentic Portuguese city. And with the coming of the new Governor, the ships from our dominion were unloading the goods on to firm land."

If this is a factual description of the reality of that time, the conquest of Goa was not an accident. It was well-planned, because Goa was essentially an important harbour for the defence of the commercial empire of the East, was it not?

Albuquerque was never the liberator of Goa. Never! He never conquered Goa to liberate Hindus from the oppression of the Muslim domination, as it is given to understand. Philanthropy never guided the steps of the conqueror of Goa. He was not a wandering knight of the Middle Ages, eager to plunge his violent sword into idealistic or romantic assignments. Goa was always on his mind as a city of conquest. If he conquered the city of Goa, he would have the *key to the whole of India* and that was imperative in his scheme of things. So, he wanted to conquer Goa, not because he wanted to free Hindus from Muslim exploitation, but because Goa's geographical situation fitted into his plans. In this game, it was Timoja who erred and was deceived himself.

Pinheiro Chagas writes:

> "Timoja thought in vain that he was going to conquer a sovereignty by accepting oppressive conditions. The conditions he agreed to were to be a vassal of Portugal and to permit the Portuguese to build a fort there. But in Albuquerque's mind, however, Goa had to be the future capital of our vast empire."

And further, he adds,

> "Timoja made repeated requests for Goa's sovereignty and promised that he would pay a huge tribute to the King of Portugal. He even spoke to the captains and requested them to take up his cause. The captains who

> were tired of Afonso de Albuquerque's unquenchable thirst for conquests and wanted to go back to Cochin, unanimously supported Timoja's request. Though Afonso de Albuquerque severely reprimanded them, he amply recompensed Timoja. Timoja was nominated Governor of the local people, riches were bestowed upon him, and for a hundred thousand *cruzados*, all lands of Goa were leased to him, with the exception of the island of Tiswadi. That was because Albuquerque never wanted to surrender completely the sovereignty of Goa."

He further writes:

> "Ormuz, Goa and Malacca, the three keys to the East, he [Albuquerque] leaves them as legacies to his successors ... and these were indeed astute choices, and even to this day, British politics acknowledge Albuquerque's policy as he had laid it down. When he [Albuquerque] attempted to establish himself in Aden, the English did not rest until they had established themselves there and when our great Governor settled himself at Ormuz, the English ships sailed there to occupy the island of Bandeira and this pattern was repeated in Malacca, Singapore, Goa and Bombay. The English, perceiving the advantage of all Albuquerque's plans, exploited them, as we have seen."

Your Excellency, the Governor-General. For us, as Indo-Portuguese, Albuquerque fascinates us. He excites our imagination, captivating our hearts. He wins our esteem and we pine for his memory not because he is the founder of the empire of the East not because he was a warrior who took Goa from the Muslims with his invincible sword, not even because he came as an ambassador of a Christian Europe to bring us the light of western civilisation and not because of the problematic superiority of a [western] civilisation over ours, ours, which is much more ancient.

He fascinates us, because he designed politics or the concept of colonization with revolutionary directives. The ideas that he introduced were unheard of before, nor were these liberal ideas conceived by any other man before him. As a statesman and politician, he was inspired to bestow the dignity of justice on the conquered people. The powerless people are not necessarily an inferior people. Albuquerque understood this truth better than anybody else. At one time, the people of India had a culture, a culture that would have been coveted by the people of Europe. And talking in ethnical terms, they had the same blood in their veins. They were the common descendants of the same Aryan family. Recognising this, he did not hesitate to give them equal rights of social standing with the conquerors.

The excellence of his genius lies in the nobility of this outpouring of liberal thought. His genius was ahead of his time. It was a big leap forward and it took centuries for the world to understand it. No doubt a hero to the people of the nation, he was also something more. He was a great statesman, administrator and politician, a personality in the history of the world.

Glory be to Albuquerque!

(*Diário da Noite*, November, 26, 28, & 29, 1932)

11

THE LACK OF SOLIDARITY

A society is like a living organism. The survival, growth and development of any living organism, whether plant or animal or human, depends upon the interaction of its cellular activity. Without the collaboration of its cells, a living organism cannot exist by itself.

In the same fashion, if there is not a cooperative effort among the various economic sectors of a society, that society becomes sluggish. And a stagnant society is a dead society. Death is not life. Death turns off the life-giving energy.

A society in which men are egoists, jealous of and inimical to each other, and whose members do their best to bring each other down, is like a man whose internal organs are on strike instead of reinforcing each other to do their task. The result is death.

No man is an island. But when the various activities of man join forces towards the achievement of the collective goal, that society is heading towards progress. The key to human progress lies in his social instinct and it is this social instinct in man which distinguishes him from other species.

There are no doubt some animals, like otters and beavers who live in communities of their own. Though this is true, they would not have been able to do so if nature were not there to provide for them. But man, because he is a developing being, cannot live by himself without associating with his fellow men.

So, man can only function as man in the society of men. The various human groupings which we call nations are nothing but reflections of the natural law which rules the human species. A society, in the end, means a solidarity of men.

But, in the society of this unfortunate land of ours, each one thinks of individual prosperity and that is contrary to the dictum of solidarity. For example, when the price of rice is fixed at a high level, paddy-farmers are content. However, if the coconut price is down, they are not worried about the plight of the coconut farmers. This kind of thinking is political heresy because when the economy of a country is in trouble the last thing that should happen is to ignore the prosperity of one sector in favour of the prosperity of another. This would be like neglecting to take care of one vital organ of the human body, for instance the liver, in order to keep another, the heart, beating.

A society thrives both economically and spiritually when there is a harmonious relationship among its various economic sectors. If one of the sectors is ailing, the whole economic system of the country will be affected. Interdependence between its various sectors is of paramount importance.

The various economic activities of the country cannot grow and develop in isolation. Nothing is gained by fighting among ourselves. No one profits when you are engaged in attempting to bring down your business associates. The key to success is to extend a hand to each other.

While the people in British India are marching ahead in various economic activities, we are going down the slope. For this, we have to blame ourselves. This happens because we hate each other and we are green with envy when our friends or neighbours prosper. Our rivalries and quarrels debase us. We do not possess a spirit of togetherness. We lack initiative. We cannot even establish an agricultural cooperative to export our agricultural products. We are not establishing one, it seems, because we do not wish others to profit from it, too!

Man's personal ambitions have no limits. But in our society, each one of us wants to achieve his personal prosperity without including others in the scheme of things. Those who have the means to start a business undertaking do not want to start one. They are afraid that others will also reap rewards from their initiative. Because we are trapped in this kind of mentality, we have not the foresight to see that establishing business undertakings produces saleable products and hence increases the land value. But we prefer to keep our economic situation as it is, stagnant.

We are a kind of people who do not trust others. We have no credence in honesty nor do we want to see good in others. If someone among us takes the initiative to start up a cooperative movement, others will insinuate that he is doing it for his own benefit or that he has some hidden motives behind it. They will denounce him as a crook, a man who cannot be trusted.

Because of our suspicious nature, we are skeptical of everyone and everything. We should not put down *bona fide* projects, when some of these projects are handled by men who have expertise in that field. Their contributing ideas to the project should not be rejected nor should their characters be maligned as a result of our cynicism. That is the worst thing that we can do to ourselves.

When we carry an unstrung mentality in matters of our economy, we have no right to blame the government for not generating economic activity and promoting prosperity within the country. Our misplaced egotism, our false values and other such traits stand in the way of our economic progress. Though we our proud to be Christians, our temperament is not Christian. We are phony. Kindness to our fellow human beings which is the corner stone of our faith is not in us. We do not want to see the welfare of others. On the contrary, we will do everything that we can to bring down our neighbour. That is how we are.

A country with a mentality like ours cannot march towards economic progress and, when we carry a mentality of this nature, we cannot point the finger at the government for not promoting economic prosperity within the country. We will not progress economically until we remedy our imperfections.

As politics comes, ours is the lowest. We plot against one another. We envy each other and we cannot see our neighbour with a shirt on his back. Our politics are cultist and caste-orientated. Our minds are filled with cobwebs and our hearts are filled to the brim with bitterness. Take this case for example: when the government established a subsidy for betelnut exporters, the others who do not export betelnuts started protesting loudly against these subsidies.

The owners of coconut groves, the owners of mango orchards, the paddy farmers all could not get a wink of sleep. They had an attack of colic, it seems, because the betelnut exporters were given subsidies. They too wanted the same kind of subsidies, not less, but equivalent to that of areca farmers, spelled out in a written agreement. Their demand had nothing to do with economics but was solely based on envy. What the areca farmers got, they wanted too. It is this kind of mentality that lies behind our economic downfall

Vasco Dias

(*Portugal e Colonias*, March 26, 1938)

12

THE ART OF GOVERNING

To govern is to look ahead into the future. In the field of social sciences one does not depend on the supernatural to foresee the occurrences that would unfold in the future. If we were to analyze the facts of today with our reasoning, we could predict the unfolding of the future events. By observing the course of nature, we know that the buds of today will blossom into flowers. In politics too, we see the same process. The thoughts and ideas that we sow today in the minds, will follow their due course, and we will reap the fruits accordingly. Man has no power over nature. But man can tame nature and put it to his use. Man can germinate seeds, grow plants and speed up the agricultural process by using fertilizers or other improved agricultural methods, or, he can also obstruct the progress of agriculture by using unwholesome agricultural practices. By the same token, in the field of social sciences, man by his actions can accelerate or retard human development. The speech of November 25, 1932, which I delivered in front of the statue of Afonso de Albuquerque was a claim for the equality of judicial rights for the people of India. The authorities were reminded that the people of India, like the Portuguese from the continent, had always been the heirs to these rights, and as such, these rights should be promptly reinstated. If not, they were warned, the Portuguese interests in this country would meet with ignominious end.

But those in the government, because of their narrow-mindedness, did not understand my speech in that way. Take for example the law of military recruitment. It is a law which legalizes discrimination. It debases the people of India, hurting their pride. The Portuguese conquest did not bring the people of India out of a state of barbarity or obscurantism to civilisation as it did in the case of the natives of Guinea or Timor. The people of India were not savages. They are heirs to a civilisation of millenniums. The very nature of this law has hurt the people of this country very deeply. This law is like a germ that has spread the disease of discontent among the people and now, the new laws that have followed, have deprived us of our civil liberties. It has further reinforced the resentment against such laws and what we are witnessing today is the manifestation of that resentment. We have to present this problem in very clear terms to the Governor-General. It is our moral obligation to do so, since we have to help him to arrive at a correct interpretation of the events which to some extent, have been caused by the demise of traditional laws. For instance, the only reason why it was possible for the government to hurriedly rush through the farcical election of November 18, was because old laws have been replaced by new ones. I have no desire to adorn myself with the feathers of a peacock and shy away from glories that are not mine. But I must speak my mind now, because during these last four or five weeks our country has gone through disturbances that demand the restoration of civic liberties. Though I am indifferent to this movement, I want to observe the facts and study its symptoms with the rigour of scientific analysis. And then, I want to present the study before those in charge in the government. I do not want to justify the symptoms, but rather to explain why they exist and then, ask the government for the symptoms to be removed before they cause irreparable damage. When human beings get sick, the doctor, by careful examination and study of the symptoms, arrives at a diagnosis and then prescribes a treatment. When the social organism gets sick, the same approach applies. The Governor-General is in a very precarious situation. And I would like to believe that he would like to be advised by a man of upright conscience who would tell him about the state of affairs, without circumventing the truth. That should help him to understand the significance of these happenings in all their aspects, so that he can plan with precision to resolve the problem that we are experiencing.

Unfortunately, one of my faults is to express my thoughts boldly. Santa Justa! Since I would find it unbearable if I were to be presented with a tangled web of incomprehensible statements, I do not wish to inflict the same on to another person and therefore attempt to express myself honestly and frankly, the way I understand them. The ideas I have put forward in this paper today, I would have voiced them in front of the highest powers of the nation, telling them that the election of November 18 was not an election but a mockery of one!

To fulfill the aspirations of the people of this country , I believe our country should be given a political status in accordance with the realities of its historical past rather than be treated as a colony, which she never has been, in the strictest sense of the term. We have never accepted and never will accept being placed in the same category as the people of Mozambique or Angola.

(*A Voz da India*, July 9, 1946)

13

A PUBLIC ASSEMBLY AT MARGAO

When the torrential downpour had abated for a while, Mr. José Inácio de Loyola braved the rain and climbed up on a table which had been placed on the platform. Taking charge of the assembly, he started the session. The umbrellas folded, and the assembly drenched in rain, listened to his speech as he read it out, applauding him now and then. Here is the presidential address:

Fellow citizens!

At this hour, as one of the greatest dramas in the history of the people is unfolding, it would be a sign of irresponsibility on our part, if we did not carefully reflect upon the words that we chose to say. It would be irresponsible to put forward proposals with the wrong choice of words or ambiguous words that may suggest more than one interpretation. It is for these obvious reasons that I have my speech on paper. All the speeches that will be delivered in this assembly will be read out from the paper.

Our ideas, because of the delicate problems that we have been called upon to face, have to be defined with perfect clarity, without any reservations or scruples on our part and in accordance with our aspirations. All our thoughts, all our intimate desires and all our anxieties have to be expressed with lucidity because it would be wrong on our part to present our protest in any other way and, we have to demonstrate our moral and intellectual capability to the media and assure them we are mature enough to wrest the political statute that we are proposing.

If the work of this assembly is denied its solemnity and the magnitude of the problems that we have come to discuss here is not taken seriously, if the effort that we have put in is not recognised, and the statute that we are seeking is not restored to us, it would be sentencing us to condemnation. If the statute that we want to reclaim, is denied to us because of imperialistic and arrogant selfish interests, and the additional political powers that we want in our hands is denied to us on the basis of immaturity, this too would be sentencing us to condemnation.

In my speech here, Mr. Vicente João Figueiredo, a good friend of mine, having taken the initiative to address this issue, has put together certain ideas. My intent is not to ask you to vote for our ideas nor am I attempting to solicit you into accepting our political point of view. These ideas have been public since my interview with *O Heraldo*. At the same time, they are not to be taken as mere suggestions and nothing more. They are my contribution to a larger effort put forward by the people as a whole. They are ideas for the common welfare of all classes of this land, for all levels of intellect to collaborate with each other, and all kinds of aspirations to come to fruition. Thus this assembly needs to fulfill many responsibilities that are of an exceptional nature.

I implore all of you, from this hour, to put aside all our quarrels, to forget our fights, our group rivalries and sectarian politics that have kept us apart in the past and weakened our moral unity and because of that, we hardly protested against injustice and never wrested our sacred rights into our own hands. But today let us give a new beginning to our politics. From today let us be brothers and forge together one fraternity, a fraternity without class distinction, without religious discrimination. From this moment let us forgive each other for past mistakes. Let us be a people united and strong and in this society, let the enemies of yesterday be the friends of today, let bygones be bygones. Let the slate be clean, wiping out caste differences. Let us be one people, brothers to each other. Let us build a society with our spiritual efforts, let our solidarity strive with all its components for the same ideal and then, let us bequeath this land of ours to our grandchildren so that they may be proud of us! By putting our past behind us, let us confront the future.

Inverting the words of a phrase which has been used often, I shall say to you. I am starting to see light where I could see ignorance before. I hope this is not an illusion. But I hear the distant rhythms of a song. It is a song of rejuvenation. It is coming closer to us to bring peace into our souls and joy into our hearts.

The statement made by the Minister of Colonies that India is not a colony but a state of Portugal, has a political significance to me. It is a message with an intent, which Portugal wants to convey to us. She wants to fulfill our legitimate aspirations. I do not believe that this statement was made thoughtlessly without taking into account the logical consequences that would follow. Dr. Marcelo Caetano, who is not unknown to us, is one of the eminent Portuguese jurists. The words that he chose so meticulously to express his ideas show the precision of his thoughts. Familiar with his juristic works, and also being conversant with his literary works on colonies and colonial problems, I do believe that his statement was made in all reasonableness and fairness before the people of this land. His writings fascinate the present generation of Portugal. He urges them to open their minds and with the strength of their soul, he says, they can enrich the empire beyond the seas. So, one can see that in his political thought, India does not occupy the position of a colony. This is because India is different from other colonized countries. Its social conditions do not offer the same incentives to be treated as a colony.

The ladies who form part of this assembly are making their contribution to solving the problem that confronts us. This is a good omen. Ladies, you are a source of inspiration to us all. Your support and participation in this assembly and the pledge that we made augurs a future of peace and happiness. It is a future where we renounce our wrongdoing of the past. Guided by your hands, I am sure our goal will be within our reach.

(The session began. Hindu, Christian and Muslim girls sang a song in Konkani to the accompaniment of the harmonium, especially composed for the occasion by Mr. Bhale, B.A.)

Ha amchem Gõy sobit kitlem!
Sogllea jogant vhodd nanv axil'lem
Amchi avoi bhy Gõy!

Fuddem pasun tachi vhoddvikai!
Amcho haves ani budvontkai!
Sogllea sonsarant Gõy gaztolem.

Avottan amchem Gõy zori lhan!
Bhurge tiche vhodd kortutvan!
Mogreachea fulavori vas tangelo!
Sogllea sonvsarant Gõy bhov mannkulem.

Aicho dis, atancho vell!
Onthokoronnant asum sodam kall!
Hindu, Kristanv, Moir soglle bhav!
Voir kaddat re Gõy amgelem.

Ha amchem Gõy sobit kitlem!
Sogllea jogant vhodd nanv axil'lem.

(How charming is our Goa
Esteemed the world over
Our motherland Goa!

From ancient times her greatness,
Our joy and our inspiration,
Renowned in all the world!

Though you are not big enough
Your hard-working sons,
Will shower your name,
The world over
The attar of the mogarim flower!

Today and this very moment,
May it remain forever in our hearts,
Hindus, Christians, Muslims all are brothers
Raise aloft our Goa.

How beautiful is our Goa
Much revered in all the world

After the singing was over, Mrs. Khrishnabai, the niece of Bairão Dempo and wife of a wealthy proprietor and capitalist, Mr. Datta Naik, spoke and then, Mr. Francisco Furtado read a speech, followed by Mr. Vicente João Figueiredo. The following motion was put before the people.

The text of the Motion

Taking into account that the declaration made by the Minister of Colonies that the *Estado da India* is not a colony but a State of the Portuguese nation; taking into account that this declaration has a special importance due to the way it was announced under certain conditions and opportunities; taking into account that this declaration will certainly be succeeded by a promulgation and statutes distinguishing the *Estado da India* from other Portuguese colonies; taking into account that the statutes that are brought in are fundamental and just, reflecting the aspirations and needs of this land and avoiding additional discontent, the Public Assembly which meets in the city of Margao resolves to ask the highest powers of the Metropolis:

1. that it should be promulgated that the *Estado da India* be granted a political statute guaranteeing the following rights, besides the ones that are defined in article 8 of the Portuguese political Constitution:

(a) that autonomy in administrative and financial matters be granted with a right to vote for a Legislative Assembly; exclusive powers be given to this State to develop its own annual budget, namely, revenues and expenditures, powers to generate and disburse its own taxes; powers be given to create departments of civil service of this State and powers to fix the salaries of civil servants;

(b) that powers be delegated to adjudicate and vote in the Legislative Assembly to enact salaries for the civil service that works within this State;

(c) that powers be delegated to adjudicate and vote in this State for the laws and public acts which are related to this State, and that the Central government issue a promulgation to this effect;

2. that the promulgation of this statute should include the document of article no. 10 of *Conselho de Governo*, of July 4, 1930;

3. that the promulgation of the statute should sincerely satisfy the claims of this land, and that it should be given top priority and put into effect from January 1, 1947.

The motion was approved and put to a vote.

Mr. Laxmikanta Bembro making various observations, demonstrated that the declarations made by the Minister of Colonies and by the Governor-General in their letter to Mahatma Gandhi, said that they would take into account the securing of the aspirations of the people of this land. Then he explained this in Konkani for the benefit of those who may not have understood Portuguese.

He made the following proposal, which said, "In order to make the message more effective, I propose a committee of the following:

Adv. Vicente João Figueiredo (president)
Adv. Polibio Mascarenhas
Mr. Manganlal M. Kanji
Adv. Panduronga Mulgaocar
Adv. Francisco de Paulo Ribeiro
Adv. Prisonio Furtado

Adv. António Xavier Gomes Pereira
Mr. Bascora Desai
Dr. José Paulo Teles
Adv. Álvaro Furtado
Adv. Francisco Pinto Menezes
Adv. Vinayaka Sinai Coissoro
Adv. Datta Phaldesai
Dr. Krishna Sansguiri

I, Laxmikanta V. P. Bembro.

The committee has the right to bring in more individuals representing all social classes and to replace the members who do not want to carry on the duties assigned.

The assembly approved the proposal unanimously.

About 3,000 men and women, boys and girls from all villages of Salcete and from other districts, from Bicholim to Canacona, and people from all walks of life, classes and religions, attended the assembly.

(*O Heraldo*, July 30, 1946)

14

THE COMING STRUGGLE

(Press Statement)

The anomalous situation prevailing in Portuguese India regards the freedom of thought, freedom of assembly and freedom of association, these three fundamental liberties are inseparable from human personality. It is my opinion whenever the people of a country, whoever they may be, are deprived of these essential liberties which are inherent to the development of human personality, it becomes the duty of all other people and especially of all lovers of democracy to rush to their aid and help them to regain their status. Dr. Lohia has unquestionably rendered a great service to the cause of democracy by bringing into the limelight the intolerable regime now prevailing in Goa. I feel deeply indebted to him for his valiant efforts to help the people of my country.

An attempt is being made in certain quarters to create among the Catholic section of the Goan population, the impression that Dr. Lohia's movement is directed against the Catholic religion. There is no truth whatsoever in this propaganda. This movement has nothing to do with any religion. It is a movement for all Goans, irrespective of caste and creed.

(*Free Press Journal*, September 26, 1946)

15

A LETTER TO HELIODORIO

My dear Heliodorio,

You are complaining very angrily about the shortage of servants and according to you, the problem is getting worse every day in the villages. In your letter, you say that the sons of *mundkars* after reaching the age of ten, and their daughters after reaching the age of twelve, emigrate to Bombay or Calcutta.

Because there is an excruciating shortage of servants, your wife, Senhora Dona Josefina, you say, is forced to grind curry-masala with her own hands. You also write that though *bhatkars* might have more than 10 *mundkar* households in their domains, yet you cannot get a single serf-boy to water the banana plants in your yard. And you are asking me if such a situation should be tolerated in a country where there is a government, laws and a judiciary. You are asking me also, whether the *mundkars* have the right to emigrate to foreign countries when *bhatkars* have no domestic help and, whether it is morally correct on their part to do so. Once again, you are asking me whether the Press should demand the enactment of a decree, which prohibits the emigration of *mundkars'* sons or daughters without the written permission of their *bhatkar*.

Put a lid on that grandeur of yours, my dear Heliodorio! I will not deny that you have legitimate reasons to be in a rage when you see your poor wife humiliated and forced to grind the curry-masala with her aristocratic hands. But you need to understand that social problems are not solved with threats and diatribes nor are they solved by yelling and shouting. Social problems, if they are to be tackled properly, demand that one should approach them with composure, with deep understanding and complete serenity of spirit.

Therefore, let us discuss the problem from a logical point of view, without getting excited about it. Let us discuss the problem step by step and reflect upon its various ramifications. After all, we are two individuals with gray hair, are we not? Bring in your cigarette of straw and I am going to light my pipe. Let us install ourselves in two rocking chairs and let us cough out our phlegm and arrogance and discuss this problem philosophically.

My dear Heliodorio, why do the sons and daughters of *mundkars* emigrate? Why do so many of them leave to go to unknown cities in British India to earn their daily bread?

Perhaps, you would say, the daughters of *mundkars* have given up on the values of their grandparents and so, you would answer, they are emigrating to Bombay and Calcutta to indulge themselves in profligate pleasure. Perhaps, you would say too, they are like prostitutes, attracted to the sensual and perverted seductions, dazzling vices, debauchery and voluptuousness of those big cities. You would respond too, perhaps, by saying, they emigrate to Bombay and Calcutta to trade their reputations and sell their virtue so that they can afford silk dresses, slippers with embroidered velvet tops or gold bangles or other such accoutrements.

My dear Heliodorio, let us assume that the daughters of *mundkars* emigrate to the cities of British India for illicit and sinful reasons. In some instances, let us suppose that they emigrate to give themselves cheaply as disguised prostitutes to the houses of Parsees and Khojas. But then, what is the reason for the sons of *mundkars* to emigrate? And why do the young boys of *mundkars* who are nine or ten years old, and who once passively looked after the *bhatkars*' goats and walked in the footsteps of their parents and grandparents, becoming tillers of the land, emigrate?

I can vouch, my dear Heliodorio, that those who work in the cities of British India as busy boys in the coffee houses of the Iranis, and in hotels or restaurants, work like beasts of burden.

They wake at 3.30 in the morning and report to duty by six. Without a break, they toil until ten o'clock at night, scrubbing floors, cleaning kitchen counters, polishing their bosses' shoes and they work on Sundays too. Late at night, they return to their *kudd* for a few hours' sleep and rest. If you were to see the drudgery of these people, who work without respite to earn a bitter crust of bread, you would see, not metaphorically, but literally, that the bread they earn is soaked with the sweat dripping from their brows.

The sons and daughters of *mundkars*, my dear Heliodorio, do not emigrate to Bombay and Calcutta, as you assume, to enjoy a loose life there. Their eyes have been opened to awaken their souls. They are now conscious of themselves as individuals, of being human. And that is how it ought to be. It is every person's right to feel socially emancipated.

Traditionally, the *mundkar* had offered himself humbly to look after his *bhatkar*'s goats, water his pepper plants, and so on. Along with this, the *mundkar* had also tolerated being his *bhatkar*'s slave. In return, the *bhatkar* was protector, brother and friend to his *mundkar*. The *bhatkar* could be seen, leaving early in the morning, dressed in his *cabai* of chintz gown, going out to supervise the farming of his land. A woman would follow behind, carrying a container of rice porridge on her head and behind them could be seen his *mundkars* in *langotim*, walking with their tools in their hands.

On arriving at the work site, the *mundkars* after spitting into the palms of their hands would begin ploughing the field. But the *bhatkar* would also work with his men. He would hitch up his gown and, taking the plough into his own hands, plough the field, directing, teaching and helping his *mundkars* in their work, thereby setting an example. And when the sun came overhead, they would break for lunch. Putting aside their working tools, they would all sit under the canopy of a cashew tree for shade, in a circle round the rice porridge pot, make the sign of the cross, and then partake of their meal, as if they were a family.

Those were the days, my dear Heliodorio. Those were candid times, patriarchal and rustic. In those times, the *bhatkar* would socialize with the *mundkar* and both had a passion for agriculture. In those bygone days, my dear Heliodorio, the *bhatkar* by his own movements set an example by demonstrating that agriculture was a noble occupation. The *mundkars*, from this practical lesson, understood that to toil on the land was fulfilling work.

But today, my dear Heliodorio, the *bhatkar* no longer wakes up early in the morning to go to his lands and there is no woman carrying a container of rice porridge on her head. The *bhatkar* no longer wears a *cabai* of chintz. Now, he dons himself in vestments made of cashmere. He is now a lawyer, a man of letters and handles other professions. He is not a farmer anymore.

The modern day *bhatkar* smokes cheroots brought in from Manila and his children now go to the universities to become physicians. He now feels degraded if he holds the plough in his hands and he thinks it is below his dignity to give advice on matters of farming. He wears shoes now and gives himself airs as if he were a white man, a *paklo*.

The *bhatkar* who owns the lands has no desire to look after his lands. He wants to be a public functionary and wants his son to become a physician and not a farmer. The *bhatkar* now despises the occupation of his forefathers. He dislikes the ways of simple ordinary people, the rustic life of his grandfathers, a life that in the past had brought happiness to their household.

My dear Heliodorio, what right have you to demand that the *mundkars* continue to be tillers of the land? What right have you to ask the sons of *mundkars* to look after the goats of the *bhatkars* and what right have you to ask the daughters of the *mundkars* to water the vegetable gardens of the *bhatkars* like their grandparents? When the *bhatkar* himself does not want to maintain the traditions of that occupation, how can you ask the *mundkar* to do so? Can you answer that?

The *bhatkar* has thrown away his *cabai* of chintz to dress himself in cashmere, so the *mundkar* has given up wearing *langotim*, and that is his right as a Christian. The *bhatkar* became a bureaucrat and the *mundkar* became a domestic. The *bhatkar*'s son went to the university to graduate as a physician and the *mundkar's* son went to Bombay or Calcutta to become a chauffeur.

Why should the *mundkar* stay in the village to toil in the fields of the *bhatkar*, when the *bhatkar* himself has given up agriculture?

My dear Heliodorio, let us be fair, up-to-date and candid in this matter! If you want the Press to support a decree, prohibiting the emigration of *mundkars'* sons and daughters without the written permission of the *bhatkar* then you must also let it be promulgated that the lands of the *bhatkars* be confiscated and given to the public.

I hope you agree with my proposal. Do let me know in your next letter.

Yours,
F. de Lemos
(*Portugal e Colonias*, April 2, 1938)

16

THE PROBLEM OF EMIGRATION

The current migration of Goans to foreign countries, mostly to British India and British Africa, has reached alarming proportions. Men, women, adults, boys and girls, people of all ages are migrating. It is like an epidemic that has spread among Goans.

Recently, the problem of emigration in all its aspects was debated at length in Margao, by our foremost intellectuals. Some among them defended emigration passionately, saying that it was good for the country. If it were not for emigration, they argued, the economic well-being of the country would not be stable. Others, on the other hand, strongly disagreed with that argument, attributing all sorts of social evils to emigration.

For two days we had the opportunity to be in the capital of Salcete. We took the liberty to meet with Mr. J. I. de Loyola and hear his point of view on the subject of emigration.

Luckily, Mr. Loyola was not busy when we visited him. He welcomed us in his usual amicable manner.

"What brings you here today, Sir? Is it the good wind that is blowing?"

Avoiding formalities, we broached the subject immediately.

"*O Heraldo* wants your opinion on the problem of emigration."

"What an extraordinary idea, that you people thought of asking me!", he exclaimed, touching his forehead lightly. And then for a few seconds, he was thoughtful, as if he were pondering, whether or not he should talk on the subject to us. In the end, he decided he would speak and the interview began with his views on the causes of emigration, followed by his views on its effects, on agriculture and finally, wages (Ed. *O Heraldo*).

Causes

Mr. Loyola: "The problem of emigration is nothing to worry about. The anxieties that are unfolding are not easy for me to understand. The way I see it is that Goan emigration is a natural phenomenon, nothing extraordinary. You certainly must have read Brouilhet. In a synthesis of admirable lucidity, he explains: "The repulsive factors that keep the people away from their own country, together with the attractive factors of the seducing countries of destination, may be interpreted as the causes for emigration." In *Estado da India*, perhaps, emigration is provoked by attractive causes rather than by the repulsive ones, and this is nothing to be surprised at. As Prof. Armindo Monteiro, who explains difficult contradictions such as these, says, people seek to go to far-off countries because there is not a high standard of living in their own country, or they think there is not. Well, looking at the facts, we have to recognize that the repulsive causes mainly affect the illiterate class, who are forced to look for jobs and salaries in neighbouring foreign countries. While the emigration of the middle class is dominated by a desire to seek better opportunities, in which they can utilise their talents, get secure jobs and better pay than they would have got in their own country and they believe that in the country of emigration they will have the opportunities to advance economically and socially".

O Heraldo: "Sir, are you in favour of emigration, then?"

Mr. Loyola: "My dear Sir, I'm simply stating the causes of our emigration. I'm looking at it objectively as a simple economic phenomenon. I'm neither for it nor against it. These are overwhelming facts governed by the laws of economics and hence, man has no control over them. You must be aware of Gresham's law: the inferior currency driving away the superior currency. If your newspaper were to ask me why the silver coins went out of circulation at a certain time, and why the market was flooded by paper currency, I would have answered, because of war, the paper currency did not inspire confidence, and besides, silver coins have intrinsic value. The currency that was considered inferior has expelled the superior one, which was considered to be a relatively good currency. From this explanation, would you think that I'm in favour of Gresham's law?"

O Heraldo: "But emigration does not fall into the Gresham law".
(Mr. Loyola received our impatience with a smile.)

Effects

Mr. Loyola: "Emigration should be looked at from two different angles. First, we must establish its causes, and then, secondly, we must study its effects. Although I do think of ways to remedy the causes of our emigration, for now let us look at its effects. You know that books on political economy classify emigration into two categories. One is called normal emigration and the other, pathological emigration. When the resources of the country are not developed on regular bases to absorb the surplus population into its economy, and when that population migrates, that emigration is normal. But when people migrate at the cost of population equilibrium, then it is pathological emigration. Or, according to the most recent definition, when there is a population increase within the country and the people migrate, that is normal emigration. It becomes pathological when people are forced to migrate due to miserable conditions. Normal emigration is beneficial and should be encouraged. The pathological one, when it is excessive, hurts the economy disastrously. Now, the emigration of Goans, is it normal or is it pathological? And, even if it is pathological, could it be excessive? You should have addressed the question in that fashion, my dear Sir".

(Mr. Loyola paused for a while, lit a cigarette and returned to the topic).

"Goan emigration, from my point of view, is absolutely normal. It has not only balanced the population, but it has raised the standard of living of the middle and the working classes. It is worthwhile to note here, in our case, it is the individual who migrates and not the family. In our case, our emigrants have continued to keep the bond with the native land, and also they have kept their blood and economic ties. It is true that the dislocation of men is always supposed to be dislocation of capital. You must be aware that some economists have developed a few procedures to find out mathematically the economic value of the emigrant. One of them is Engels. According to his calculations, the cost of raising a child before and after its birth, goes on increasing 10% every year, that is, over a period of 20 or 25 years. Then Pareto, for example, says that these costs should be added to the expenses incurred by the society for raising individuals born at the same time and those who died before they became adults. Another economist, Marshall, says that the economic value of emigrants should be determined according to the contributions that they would have made to the country, deducting the value of their future consumption.

I recall, some years ago, that Dr. Vitor Dias, if I am not mistaken, calculated Rs. 3,000 as the economic value of each inhabitant of the island of Jua. Whatever the case may be, the economic vacuum that the emigrants leave behind in their country, is compensated by the money remittances they send to the ones who depend on them in their villages and also the amount of money they bring with them on their return".

Agriculture

O Heraldo: "With so many young people going away, our fields lie fallow!"

Mr. Loyola: "If we had kept statistics on agriculture, but unfortunately we have not, I would have shown you, with figures to support me, that our agriculture has made progress in the last few years! Moreover, the *Direcção de Agricultura* has been in existence for more than 30 years. I have seen new lands cleared for paddy cultivation even at the foot of hills. The food crisis brought about by the war gave us an incentive, awakening our dormant energies, and we increased cereal production, growing it everywhere".

O Heraldo: "But, what about the coconut plantations?"

Mr. Loyola: "It might be true, speaking generally, that the coconut plantations are not looked after as they were before. But we have to realise that most of the *bhatkars* do not know that the standard of living has gone up. It has gone up not only for the middle class, but for the working class as well. If emigration is on the increase, it is because the living standards of the working class today are not the same as yesterday. The wages that they are paid in this land are hardly enough to keep them alive.

It is important, my dear Sir, to note that civilisation does not go backwards. The peasant today desires certain comforts that might have been a luxury to his grandparents, but to him it is a necessity, even though he is illiterate. But our *bhatkar*, imprisoned in the mentality of the past, refuses to see the reality of the facts, and appeals to the government to bring in legislation to freeze the wages of the working class".

Wages

O Heraldo: "Sir, are you of the opinion then that there should not be wage regulations?"

Mr. Loyola: "It is not possible in a country like ours to have a wage scale. We are not organised enough and no one gives any thought to organizing a system of medical services for the working class. Neither do they receive old age benefits nor financial assistance for the disabled worker nor any other social benefits.

These social benefits should have been made mandatory in the wage regulations for the workers. But do we have such a system? Our system forces the peasants to work for a few *tangas* a day. But what benefits are offered to him in return? Clearly, no one else knows either".

O Heraldo: "But the wage increase is a result, not only of the factors that you are alluding to, but also of emigration".

Mr. Loyola: "I agree. One cannot deny that emigration has an effect on wages. It should not have been so. But since there are not enough workers, the price of doing a job goes up. How can we stop emigration? I hope you are not thinking of resurrecting in this 20th century the law of Afonsinas, a law which prohibite the subjects to get out of the kingdom without royal permission? Since the proclamation of *Carta Constitucional*, we have had individual rights and we have the right to emigrate.

Well, I am aware that there is a school of thought which says that this right is not absolute and it might be possible to bring in restrictions to emigration by enacting laws to regulate it. In fact, a law of this nature is in force in Portugal. I do not consider it practical to introduce a similar law in this country. Most difficult of all is how we can define the term "emigrant"? Merely leaving the country does not make one an emigrant and his case cannot be investigated as such. The European countries have included regulations in their legislation that deal specifically with emigrant concerns in order to help them in the country of their destination. The regulations deal, for instance, with assisting emigrants in finding accommodation, orientating them in the lifestyles of the people of the country, finding ways of transportation, labour contracts, and so on. According to the Portuguese law of 1919, which is based on Italian law, the persons who are considered emigrants are those who arrive in the ports of foreign countries by travelling third class, those who travel in first or second classes but have intentions to reside in the foreign country, and lastly those who escape from their mother country by crossing the frontier and disembarking at the ports of foreign lands.

My dear Sir, I want to ask you if we can transplant the same legislation in *Estado da India.* Most of our emigration is to British India which falls within the same geographic area and we need no passport to go there. So to repress emigration here would not be practical. Even in Europe, most of the laws of emigration are indented to apply to trans-oceanic emigration, rather than to inter-continental emigration. And you certainly must be aware of the Indian Emigration Act of 1922 in our neighbouring country. According to this Act, only those who disembark on shore are considered emigrants. Reflect on the diversity of migration laws among other countries and on our own emigration laws. Due to our geographic contingency with British India, most of our emigration is in that direction. Think about it and give me your answer!

No, my dear Sir. We cannot solve the problem of emigration through legislation, even though our coconut groves are neglected and wages have gone up. In any case, the price of the coconuts have gone up too. In March coconuts fetched Rs. 150 to 180 per thousand. If the coconut production has suffered quantitatively because of lack of labour, the *bhatkars*, were amply compensated because of the high prices. But even otherwise, what right do we have to impede the right of those who want to emigrate to better their lives?"

O Heraldo: "But, Sir, do you distinguish between the emigration of educated classes and illiterate classes?"

Mr. Loyola: "I don't nor do I want to! On this topic,I frankly disagree with my friend Mr. Vicente João Figueiredo. In one of his articles to *A Voz da India* he makes a distinction between the emigration of educated classes and that of illiterate classes and, according to his viewpoint, the emigration of educated classes is beneficial while the emigration of illiterate classes is harmful. Most of the individuals of both the middle class and the upper class who emigrate to the neighbouring country are not really emigrants. Many of them do not go there for jobs. They go there to study at the universities, to take degrees in science, arts, politics and so on. And in the second place, do the individuals of the educated class need to get out in order to better themselves in their disciplines? In British India and Africa, Goans occupy positions in the bureaucracy, commerce, industry, and in other professions. These are the children of poor families who had emigrated as domestic servants. But their sons are doctors, engineers, officials. Because they emigrated, they were able to educate their children. And because of emigration, they were able to educate their children in the universities of Europe and America. If they had vegetated in their native villages, their children would not have fulfilled their aspirations. The children of Goan emigrants proclaim to the foreign lands the quality of our race".

O Heraldo: "But emigration is on the increase and that is frightening".

Mr. Loyola: "Frightening? Those who imagine dreadful things about emigration would do well, and their nerves would be calmer, if they carefully studied the demographic growth. According to the latest census, it appears that emigration is at a standstill. There are some in *Estado da India* who would agree that if emigration is at a standstill then it is of no consequence to worry about it".

O Heraldo: "Sir, in your opinion, we should not meddle with emigration?"

Mr. Loyola: "In my opinion, our emigration policy should follow the example of Italy. There they have orientation services for emigrants, the best in the world. They even have special classes for any future emigrants".

Comunidades

(The bell at the *Quartel de Policia*, a short distance away from Mr. Loyola's house struck twelve, announcing noon, and we stood up to leave. Since Mr. Loyola was in a good mood that morning, we ventured, innocently enthusiastic).

> "We have to return to your place, Sir, to inconvenience you once again. We want to talk to you about *comunidade* reforms. Since you were the former Inspector of *comunidades*, you will be in a position to throw light on the problems of the *comunidades* which are of a great interest to the economic and social well-being of our country."

(But our enthusiasm was greeted by Mr. Loyola with an indifferent shrug of his shoulders. With a tinge of irony in his smile, he replied),

> "The plans that I had the opportunity to formulate while I was the Inspector of *comunidades*, are only now beginning to be accepted. At the time there was a lot of opposition from our policy-makers, although of course I'm happy to know that some of the plans that were publicised a few years ago are being gradually put into practice. However, I am of the opinion that I no longer ought to use my sickles in the paddy field again. Allow me my peace, my dear Sir. Go and knock ón somebody else's door now".

(*O Heraldo*, June 2, 1946)

PART III

17

THE ECONOMIC AND MORAL DECADENCE OF THE PEOPLE

There was a time, my dear Luis Maria, in certain countries when the State sold public offices, just as we sell our community lands. In England, the sovereign sold the titles of nobility. The title of baron went for £ 10,000, the title of viscount for £ 15,000 and that of count for £ 20,000 (Taylor, *History of Taxation in England*).

Charles I made it compulsory for his subjects who had higher incomes to apply for the letter of nobility. Failing to do so, they would be heavily fined for contempt of the law. Not only were landlords made to obtain the letter of nobility but also merchants and businessmen were ordered to have the letter of nobility. "Charles did not restrict it to men of landed property, but included lessees, merchants and others." (Brodie, *History of the British Empire*).

In France, the sale of public offices was introduced during the reign of Louis XII, and it was the main source of State revenue. Louis raised money by the sale of offices, beginning that deplorable system which afterwards became so conspicuous an element in the finances of Francis I, an abuse which was paralleled only in the papal Curia. (G.W. Kitchin, *History of France*, 3rd ed., vol. 2, p. 148).

Though Louis XII established the trend of selling important public posts, Henry IV stretched this idea further. He sold public posts, making them hereditary. Francis A. Walker notes: "It was Louis XII who systematized the sale of offices, and Henry IV who first sold hereditary ones". (Francis A. Walker, *Political Economy*, 3rd ed., p. 479).

As financial difficulties continued to mount, said M. de Tocqueville, new jobs had to be created, with the sole purpose of bringing in revenue to the treasury. A number of these jobs were scandalous patronage plums. In 1664 Colbert set up a task force to find out how much money came into the treasury from the selling of public offices. It was found out that it brought in more than £ 500 million! According to one historian, though Richelieu abolished 100,000 jobs of this nature, more came into existence under new names.

These historic facts show us, my dear Luis Maria, that the State had other means of collecting revenues, besides taxing landlords. I want to believe, that in our country, the State could very well exempt those *bhatkars* who pay Rs. 25 or less from this tax. The State could have surplus revenue if public offices were put on sale, instead of having to compete for these positions. As you well know, the golden dream of everyone in our country is to secure a government job. Everyone, including those with primary education, or even without it, aspires to a government position. A physician is not interested in medicine. It does not bring him a steady income. But a job in the government is a sure thing, it gives him a secure income. In the same fashion, a lawyer hankers after an official position in the registry office; an engineer itches to be the head of the department, so that he can scribble reports and job applications; a bachelor of law aspires to be a teacher of a secondary school and a *bhatkar*'s son prefers to be an agriculturist. Since the public offices are so tempting, the big and the small, the literate and the illiterate go after them.

In my opinion, they should be auctioned. That would be an excellent idea. Those who offer higher prices, or those who would like to work for a minimum salary, these positions should be opened to them. This indeed would do away with resumes, letters of recommendation for influential politicians, favouritism, injustices and bribes. Each candidate could give his sealed tender, saying how much he would pay for the position and how much pay he expected for the same position. And then, the appointed committee could choose the candidates, in the same manner that the highest bid is selected for the contracts for a bridge or a road.

The disproportion between the salaries of civil servants and the incomes of those who pay taxes has caused a disaster not only in the economic sense but also morally. Once, we were people with dignity. As you are aware, our ancestors were very independent men with strong convictions who fought without any fear for their principles. They were men who would sacrifice their comfortable life and material well-being when their spirit and dignity were assailed. They were men who would not think twice to risk their very lives to defend their civic rights. But what do we see today, my dear Luis Maria?

Today, there is a society which is completely bankrupt. Today we see a race which is morally and intellectually decadent. Today we see a people who have fallen into abject servitude. How did it come to pass, my dear Luis Maria, that these people who once zealously safeguarded their dignity, fell into this degrading hopelessness? How did it come to pass, my dear Luis Maria, that this race which was once brave, fell into the abyss of moral stagnation? This is brought about by the disproportion between the salaries of the civil servants and the incomes of the taxpayers! This degradation of the people is caused because 99% of men in Portuguese India have their eyes on government posts. The high incomes of the civil servants is the cause of this economic disaster in Portuguese India. The civil servant having more money, has come to influence the habits and customs of the public of this land, the customs and habits which were modest, rural and simple.

The civil servant introduced new needs into this rural setting. These needs were beyond the reach of the taxpayer. The population of Portuguese India for the last fifty years was divided into two classes: *bhatkars* and *mundkars*. *Bhatkars*, who cultivated their lands with the help of *mundkars*, were people who took pride in their economic independence. In general, they were men without much education. But certainly, they had a passion for agriculture. They would economise, save year by year to increase their economic holdings, thus giving a boost to agricultural production. They were not misers, but provided all the needs of their families.

In the past, civil servants were poorly paid. The elementary teacher was paid Rs. 12, the secondary teacher was paid Rs. 40, a health official earned only Rs. 25, and the top official of the Treasury earned less than Rs. 30. But this was not the case with *bhatkars*. They had plenty and they were proud. They disdained civil servants. In those days, for a *bhatkar*'s son to seek a job in the government was a sign of humiliation. It was an indication to the public that his finances were in ruin. The government jobs were sought by the sons of those who did not have their independence. A rich *bhatkar* with an income of Rs. 1,000 or Rs. 1,500 lived like a king in his manor. In the morning, he was seen on his farm helping his farm-hands. In the evenings he was found discussing the various farming problems and debating the politics affecting his district with other farmers.

Those were the best times, my dear Luis Maria. A *bhatkar* was a very important man. He was the backbone of the economy. Being so, he disdained to work for the government. His principle was not to be servile to anybody. But soon things changed for him. The salaries of civil servants went up beyond one's expectations. The civil servant who was nothing in the eyes of the *bhatkar* was earning a better income, better than that of the *bhatkar*! Now the civil servants' salaries rose to five and twenty times more than before. His income now was five or six times more as compared to the top twenty rural farmers. He could now afford a flashy life, his wife who before could hardly afford a cotton dress, was now seen dressed in silk. Here his house, once lit with a small flickering lamp, was now lit with petromax. The *bhatkar*'s wife now wanted to attire herself in silk. She wanted to keep up with the civil servant's wife. The *bhatkar* to keep up his dignity in the village lit his house with petromax, and his children gradually adopted the lifestyles introduced by the civil servant in the village. The *bhatkar*'s household expenses increased to five and ten times more than before. What was the outcome of all this? The *bhatkar* became insolvent! A *bhatkar* who once closed his books with a surplus was faced with a deficit. His fortunes gone, he was a ruined man. He had to mortgage his lands.

The population which was once divided into two sectors, *bhatkars* and *mundkars*, now included a third category, the civil servants, who were at the top of the economic scale. *Bhatkars* fell to the lower rank, and *mundkars* remained where they were. The civil servant rose beyond imagination. He bought cars, the best real estate in the city, and became a money-lender. This is a new caste that came into existence in this country. The individuals of this new caste have become rich, while the former contributors to the country's economy are reduced to nothing. This new caste has been showered with honours, comforts and everything that life can offer. The *bhatkars*, who once were the pride of the nation, pillars of the society and the backbone of civic affairs, are now poverty-stricken people.

The *bhatkar* has been ambushed in a cage. When the incomes of the civil servants went up for the first time from Rs. 10 to Rs. 15 or from Rs. 25 to Rs. 30, the *bhatkars* could still keep pace with them without much economic hardships. Not wanting to be left behind, the *bhatkar* continued to imitate the lifestyles of the civil servant. Soon, the civil servants had another salary increment. From Rs. 15, it rose to Rs. 60 and from Rs. 30, it went up to Rs. 80. As their salaries went up, so did their standard of living and the *bhatkar*, wanting to keep up with the civil servant, was in a tight spot. His yearly budget was in a mess. He could hardly balance it. Meanwhile, the civil servants had another salary raise. From Rs. 60, it went up to Rs. 200, and for those who had earned Rs. 80, it went up to Rs. 400. Now it became impossible for the *bhatkar* to keep up with the civil servant. He was forced to pawn his silver cutlery, sell his wife's jewelry, and finally sell his community shares.

By increasing the salaries of the civil servants, the farmer, the backbone of the country's economy, were ruined, and brought economic disaster to our country.

You want to know whether the increased salary of the civil servants is a moral disaster. Yes, my dear Luis Maria, it is, indeed.

The *bhatkar*, seeing that his boat was sinking, and his lands were not bringing enough money even to pay his debtors, had to think hard. The only way he could put his finances in order was by entering his sons into the civil service. Thus, he made up his mind that one of his sons would be a farmer, and the other would enter the civil service. In this way, the son who was a civil servant would bring in his monthly pay and thus he would be able to meet the household expenses.

Once, these rustic farmers of our country were the living force of society. With integrity they defended the civic rights. But now, to balance their budgets, they encouraged their sons to enter the civil service. In doing so, the political courage, the high standard of morality, the integrity of the principles that they had, have eroded. Without being subservient, you cannot put your son into the civil service. You have to forget your principles. In order to get a civil service post for your son, you must learn to be servile to the influential politicians, you must learn to doff your *chapeau* to those rogues in high places, and you must learn to bend humbly before those dispensers of official favours. And then you have to dance to their tune. You have to go with the official view, even though you have a different opinion. That is how it works, once you have your son in the civil service. Now, you applaud the powerful, giving impetus to his power, and you act to safeguard the powerful.

This is how it is, my dear Luis Maria. Bringing up the salaries of the bureaucrats to five times more than that of the income of the *bhatkars*, has been the cause, not only of economic disaster, but of the moral decadence of the people. The people who once were aware of their political rights, are now without any dignity. All social problems are related to economics. How can we afford to have a patriotic soul, when we are bought with public offices? So in a country like ours, 99% of the inhabitants have their eyes on government posts. Thus our people have lost the moral courage, have no convictions of their own, nor sense of civic duties.

Do you know my dear Luis Maria, how many civil servants we have in Portuguese India? Whilst taking the census of the bureaucracy, we will exclude judiciary, the army, the health bureau, education, post and telegraph, forestry, and customs. The number of bureaucrats employed in all other administrative offices and community offices is 3,420 according to the Census. And do you know my dear Luis Maria, how many individuals know how to read and write Portuguese in Portuguese India? In 1931, the number of people who knew how to read and write Portuguese was: 28,567 males, and 15,458 females.

In the group of 28,567 literate males in Portuguese, we must take into account school boys and young men. In our country the minimum age to apply for a job in the government is 21. Now, let us see how many males of 21 years or older fall into this group of 28,567 literate males in Portuguese. According to the figures down below the total is 18,993, and they are distributed in this way:

Ilhas	3,801
Salcete	5,575
Bardez	3,878
Mormugao	2,165
Pernem	254
Sanquelim	557
Satari	130
Ponda	945
Sanguem	363
Quepem	474
Canacona	268
Daman	250
Nagar Haveli	172
Diu	161
Total	18,993

Now if we divide the number of civil servants, that is, 3,420 into 18,993 individuals who fall into the category of adults, we get 5.5 males who are 21 and more, who are literate in Portuguese!Further, the following table shows us the number of adult males in each district, who are literate in Portuguese and the number of civil servants in each district.

These figures, my dear Luis Maria, are an indication of our economic and political plight. These figures point out the tragedy of our public education. Public education does nothing to make us into better citizens, does nothing to elevate our minds to higher principles, does nothing at all to educate the masses. The only thing it does, is to produce civil servants! In other words, these figures demonstrate that the people of Portuguese India have no independent way of thinking. How many individuals in Portuguese India live on their own incomes? The number is 9,368 and the population of Portuguese India is 579,970 inhabitants. That means 2% live on their own incomes! While 9,369 individuals earn their own living, there are 3,240 bureaucrats and 1,368 men in the army. Thus the total number of individuals who depend on government jobs are 4,829 individuals.

Districts	*No. of adults literate in Portuguese*	*No. of Civil Servants*
Ilhas	3,801	939
Salcete	5,575	468
Bardez	3,878	695
Mormugao	2,165	192
Pernem	254	79
Sanquelim	557	156
Satari	130	59
Ponda	945	127
Sanguem	363	142
Quepem	474	91
Canacona	268	88
Daman	250	150
Nagar Haveli	172	138
Diu	161	96
Total	18,993	3,420

Now if we take into account the other civil servants in the justice department, health, post and telegraph, education, forest wardens and customs, the number of government servants goes up. Only 2% of the population earn their own incomes, while others live on government jobs or, we can say, government handouts. Then tell me, my dear Luis Maria, how can the people of this country have independent opinions of their own?

18

THE IMPORTS AND EXPORTS OF PORTUGUESE INDIA

Portuguese India is a country of paradoxes

My dear Luis Maria, you have already seen that the people in this country are poor, while the State is rich. You have seen too, that the public functionaries in this country move in cars while most of those who pay taxes go on foot. Now we look into another phenomenon which is more disorderly and unclear. Do you know by any chance how much our imports and exports come to? If you do not, let us look at the official statistics.

In 1901 the exports of Portuguese India amounted to Rs. 1,360,019 and imports in the same year came to Rs. 4,226,315. The trade deficit was around Rs. 3 million. In 1904, imports rose to Rs. 5,343,953 and exports remained almost stationary at Rs. 1,649,049. The deficit which was Rs. 3 million before, rose to Rs. 3,694,904. And in 1911 imports rose to Rs. 8,841,469 and exports rose to Rs. 2,622,311. Though exports increased slightly, the deficit came to Rs. 6,219,158.

Below is the balance of trade sheet, which I had the privilege of taking from the *Anuário do Estado da India*, 1932. These statistics do not include bars of gold and silver, gold and silver coins, or bonds.

Now what do we learn from these figures, my dear Luis Maria? These figures show that our exports have increased by Rs. 2 million but at the same time our imports since 1910 have continued to increase since then until now (1930). Our imports amount to

Rs. 11 million! The deficit which was Rs. 3,721,345 in 1910 went up in 1932 to Rs. 13,337,748. Think about it, my dear Luis Maria.

Year	*Imports in Rs.*	*Exports in Rs.*
1910	6,271,436	2,550,091
1911	8,557,746	2,622,311
1912	7,105,680	2,614,441
1913	7,562,005	2,915,435
1914	7,580,545	2,663,237
1915	7,844,848	2,971,141
1916	9,032,425	3,463,795
1917	8,339,380	3,059,495
1918	10,719,532	3,978,541
1919	13,992,834	4,444,221
1920	13,591,274	4,005,237
1921	15,067,113	4,004,820
1922	16,198,415	3,698,922
1923	16,332,990	3,933,676
1924	16,135,811	4,753,498
1925	15,253,378	3,949,247
1926	16,222,791	3,937,902
1927	16,756,129	4,047,150
1928	16,432,281	4,511,023
1929	16,727,423	5,186,396
1930	17,427,806	4,090,058

In the same year, we also exported unhusked cashew nuts to the tune of 23,601 measures valued at Rs. 97,736 and in the same year we also exported 10,536 measures of husked cashew nuts worth Rs. 295,745. But as you know my dear Luis Maria, the export of cashew nuts is not our real export. Most of the time we import cashew nuts from Portuguese colonies in East Africa, and we export them to the European and American markets. In 1932 the imports of cashew nuts with husk went up to 620,910 *ceiras*. And now, if we deduct these exports from our imports, we do not gain much, either.

The main exports of our country were the following in 1932:

Main Exports in 1932

	Quantity	Value (Rs.)
Coconuts (nos.)	30,549,417	905,885
Copra (*mãos*)	7,622	67,952
Betel nuts (*mãos*)	33,149	239,013
Mangoes (nos.)	5,993,052	198,743
Salt (*mãos*)	205,283	234,544
Solans brindão (*mãos*)	6,768	40,440
Bamboo (*mãos*)	218,320	19,633
Pineapples (nos)	106,095	10,783

Now let us look at our main imports in 1932.

Main Exports in 1932

	Quantity		*Value (Rs.)*
Rice (husked & unhusked)	288,509	*khandis*	3,247,919
Sugar	4,965,651	*ceiras*	581,160
Wines from Portugal	39,905	gallons	109,674
Foreign liquor	4,004	gallons	55,004
Beers	36,272	gallons	92,282
Tea	76,879	*ceiras*	101,187
Wheat flour	2,136,607	*ceiras*	289,305
Grain	17,353	*khandis*	227,092
Sugarcane jaggery	802,128	*ceiras*	145,053
Raw wood	11,064	tons	302,991
Indian butter	112,795	*ceiras*	158,641
Clay tiles	3,282,654	-	131,712
Tobacco roll	24,018	*ceiras*	12,977
Tobacco leaves	414,772	*ceiras*	265,996
Cotton cloth	548,792	-	1,776,702
Woollen cloth	47,350	-	114,404
Silk cloth	24,906	-	363,520
Wheat	16,420	*khandis*	216,581
Gas	409,664	gallons	438,896
Petrol	762,554	gallons	391,891

All these imports might show that we are people with a high standard of living, but unfortunately, the people of Portuguese India evidently cannot afford to attire themselves in silk, drink wine and beer, smoke, drink tea, have a car and a lot of other things. We do not produce these commodities and we have no means to produce them. But, my dear Luis Maria, we import many food items that we certainly have the ability to produce within our own country. At least, at this time, we will not discuss whether Portuguese India can produce enough rice to feed her population, We will keep our mouths shut on this sensitive issue. We will not discuss either, whether our country is in a position to produce enough tobacco for its own consumption. On this issue too, we will keep mum, since this too is a sensitive issue. Now let us look at some other figures of imports of 1932:

Bananas	1,020,135	(numbers)
Tamarind	115,509	*ceiras*
Saffron	50,494	*ceiras*
Ginger	25,535	*ceiras*
Mustard	19,711	*ceiras*
Potatoes	397,515	*ceiras*
Onions	218,950	*ceiras*
Long chillies	486,520	*ceiras*
Round chillies	3,090	*ceiras*

Value of imports of some of the items of 1932 in Rupees

	Rs.
Fresh fruits and vegetables	55,810
Potatoes and onions	64,344
Ginger	4,486
Long chillies	91,137

Imports of this nature to our country should put all of us to shame! These types of imports show that we should take a cane in our hands and put our economy in order. The people of Portuguese

India who boast that they are intelligent and hard-working should produce these items of food on their land. And the soil of Portuguese India is not less fertile than that of British India. Then why should we import all these food products from our neighbour? That is my question to you, my dear Luis Maria!

Hard-working and intelligent people, what a lie! Do you know how many people in this country claim to be farmers? They boast that their profession is farming. Their number is 140,710. And do you know how many people are unemployed in this country? The number of unemployed is 217,237! You might say that in this figure, I might have included children, invalids and old people. I might have. So, we will look at the statistics to find out how many children, invalids and old people there were in 1931. In Portuguese India, in 1931, there were 9,239 children less than one year old, 100,706 children between the ages of one and seven, 13,759 individuals between 64 and 70 years of age, and 7,755 individuals who were older. Total: 131,459. Now, if we deduct 131,459 as individuals who cannot be in the work force, we are left with 85,778 unemployed individuals. And because of these unemployed, my dear Luis Maria, Portuguese India has to import items of food such as: bananas, tamarind, ginger, mustard, round chillies and even green chillies!

How can one make these people work? That is what you are asking, is not it? I think it can be done very easily, my dear Luis Maria. It can be done by increasing by 500% customs duties on imports from British India, imports such as Indian butter, coconut and peanut oil, bananas, tamarind, ginger, green chillies and other food items. The idea behind it, is to make it almost impossible for these items to enter the country. With such legislation, a *ceira* of Indian butter would cost Rs. 10, a *ceira* of peanut oil Rs. 10 and a hand of green chillies would be Rs. 50 and so on. If this happens, soon you will see in the orchard of each house banana plants, milk cows, and soon you will also see that each house will extract coconut oil at home for its own consumption, just as our ancestors did.

A law should be enacted. When we import foreign goods, we should give preference to goods produced in Portuguese colonies, rather than import them from other countries. For instance, we should import sugar and beer from Portuguese colonies in Africa rather than from elsewhere. In this way, we could help to protect the industries in Portuguese Africa. To bring in such measures may not be entirely just. But this has to be done. We should give priority to essential foods and produce them in our country, instead of importing them. We should not tolerate the laziness of our people.

There are two ways to stimulate our economy. We can do it by persuasion or by force. The people of Portuguese India by nature are lazy. Passive persuasion would have no effect on them. The only way is to take a cane in one's hand and force them to work hard.

Our imports being Rs. 17 million and exports being Rs. 4 million, creates a doubtful problem. One wonders from where Portuguese India gets the money to bring in these imports. Our exports are worth Rs. 4 million. From where do we get Rs. 13 million? Imports depend upon the purchasing power of the people, and the purchasing power of the people depends on exports. The more the country exports, the more money comes into the country, increasing the purchasing power of the people. But in this case, we are at a loss to understand how we can import more than we export. How can we have money for imports, when our exports are much below our imports? My dear Luis Maria, how can this miracle happen when Portuguese India imports four times more than it exports?

You might indicate that remittances sent by the *émigrés* make up the difference. What you mean is that Portuguese India not only exports agricultural products, but it also exports men whose remittances give us the power to import more than we export. If you think, like other economists in our country, that these remittances cover the deficit, I beg to differ in this respect. Emigration itself does not cover our deficit. I do not think so. How many people are away from our country? According to the last Census, there were 40,852, given in this fashion:

Males 35,726 and females 15,126

As you are aware, we have Indo-Portuguese *émigrés* working in the British Empire, who come under these two categories:

(a) in the public service, liberal professions, medicine, commerce, industries, etc.

(b) servants, tailors, carpenters, craftsmen, etc.

The *émigrés* in the first category generally come from the *bhatkar* class and have their families with them, and hence they do not need to send any remittances back to the country. But some of them might have some members of the family in the village to look after their house and property. These do not need remittances, because they can afford to manage their finances from the income of their land.

The second category of *émigrés* falls under the *mundkar* class and these are the people who have families in the village. These are the real *émigrés* and these are the people who transfer their money to their country.

But there was a time once, when *émigrés* of all categories would transfer all their money from their toil to their native land. The emigrant doctor, or the emigrant engineer, or the emigrant public servant and other professional *émigrés* would come with a pile of money made in British India to his native village and build a cottage, or give a facelift to his ancestral home. He would buy paddy fields or some other properties, and invest his money in community bonds, or lend money with interest. But those times are no more. Today, the *émigré* who has some money prefers to make his domicile in British India. Once he does that, his wife and children join him there. Now he has no thought of coming back to his native village. He has no plan to build a house in his native village, nor repair the house that he inherited from his ancestors. Now he builds a bungalow in the suburbs of Bombay or buys land either in Calcutta or in Karachi. His money now is in British banks, his allegiance is now to the British, he becomes a naturalised British subject, he makes British India his adopted country. But there are some who come down to their native village once in three or five years. They come to visit their aging parents, their friends and to collect the community *jonos*, and sometimes, they might do light repairs on their rundown houses, which are rundown because they have been closed for years. Beyond this, they have no interest in the country of their birth. They are almost strangers. Their hearts and souls are where they live, in British India.

We will say that the number of *émigré* families that live in British India is 5,000, but I am of the opinion that it could be more than that. These families do not send monthly remittances to their native land. So we have to count these people out. These are not real emigrants. The real emigrants are those who make regular remittances to their families left behind in their native country. There are about 45,000 of these emigrants. They are employed in modest occupations and hence their remittances to their families back home cannot be that great.

Now we will consider how much money these *émigrés* can remit home. Out of 45,000 emigrants all are not males. Perhaps more than half of this total could be women and grownup girls who work as *ayahs* or servants and hence their yearly remittances could not amount to much. If let us say, each sends Rs. 100 a year, the total comes to Rs. 45 lakhs. This calculation is rather exaggerated because, there are about 25% among them who are unemployed. And all of them do not make fantastic salaries. The average salary could not be more than Rs. 15, and then, you have to deduct their personal expenses. The most one can save in these circumstances would be Rs. 60.

Studies made on Italian emigration by the economist Bodu, indicate that an Italian *émigré* remits 30 *escudos* (Rs. 75 according to the money exchange of 1914) per year to his country. (*Economia Política.* Lessons of Prof. Marnonoco e Sousa for a law course, from 1914-1915, compiled by José de Almeida Correia, p. 124). The Italian *émigré* is better prepared for emigration than the Indo-Portuguese *émigré*. The Indo-Portuguese *émigrés*, with the exception of a few, are mostly naive and illiterate. If the Italian *émigré* cannot remit more than 30 *escudos* to his country, I doubt, the Indo-Portuguese *émigré* can remit more than him.

The Italian *émigré* has better education than the Indo-Portuguese *émigré*. Italian emigration is unlike ours. There are special organisations in Italy that provide all kinds of assistance and orientation to the potential *émigrés*. They are given orientation at three stages: information of the place before departure, information about the mode of travelling, and information of what to expect at the place of destination. Armindo Monteiro states:

> "It is in Italy that such services have achieved perfection. Besides official bodies–*O Comissario Geral do Emigração, Os Comitati Mandamentali e Communali, Os Uffici Provinciali e Commnali de Lavoro*, there are many private organisations, *Italia Gens, A Sociedade Humanitaria, A Sociedade Bonomelli* provide useful information to potential *émigrés*, explaining in detail, and this is done through the Press, brochures or by any other means. Some of these bodies organize orientation classes for future *émigrés*" (Armindo Monteiro, *Ensaio de um Curso de Economia Politica* vol. I, p. 341).

The Indo-Portuguese *émigrés* do not have benefits like the Italian *émigrés*. And again, the working conditions of the Indo-Portuguese *émigrés* are different from those of Italian *émigrés*. Despite these observations, we will take for granted that our Indo-Portuguese *émigré* saves Rs. 100 per year, and remits them to his native country. Thus emigration brings us Rs. 45 lakhs or Rs. 4½ million annually. Now tell me, my dear Luis Maria, from where do we get Rs. 85 lakhs or Rs. 8½ million? Once again, we have to examine the budget, only then we might be able to solve this problem. The budget is the key to our economic and social problems.

The balance-sheet of Portuguese India for the economic year 1927, showed that the revenue was estimated at Rs. 9,939,053, and the expenditure for that year was estimated to be the same amount. If we deduct the salaries of public functionaries and

European military personnel, who most probably remit a part of their earnings to Portugal, the rest goes into the pockets of the local civil servants. With one exception, the small amount of money that is allocated for the promotion of public services and public administration, is the money that the State takes from the people and puts back into the economy of the country. Let us see, my dear Luis Maria, how many European functionaries there are in Portuguese India. Here is the chart:

Governor-General	1
Cabinet Chief	1
Aides (captains)	2
Chief of Protocol	1
President of Community Relations	1
Governor of the district of Daman (captain)	1
Governor of the district of Diu (captain)	1
Colonel (Police commander)	1
Lieutenant-Colonel (chief, pharmaceutical services) Majors	2
Captains (including military *intendente* of Satari)	1
Lieutenants	18
Judges	4
Delegates of the *Procurador da Republica*	5
Captain of the Ports	1
Maritime Delegate of New Goa	1
Director of Public Works	1
Director of Civil Administration	1
Chief of Customs	1
Inspector, Post and Telegraph Services	1
Head of Department, Post and Telegraph Service	1
Fiscal Director of the Railway	1
Teachers at the Central High School	3
Normal School teachers	2
Administrator of Nagar Haveli	1
Patrão-mor	1
Sergeants	36
Corporals & soldiers	27
Total	125

How much do you think these 125 European functionaries make, including their bonuses, colonial allowances and other privileges? The amount is not more than Rs. 9 lakhs. Let us be generous and say that these European functionaries make about Rs. 15 lakhs. Deducting Rs. 15 lakhs from the expenditures for the administration of the colony (9,939,053-1,500,000), we are left with Rs. 8½ million. From these 8½ million the local functionaries are paid and the rest of it goes for the promotion of public services.

I do not have the time nor the patience at this moment to give you the exact sum that is absorbed by the Public Service nor do I have the patience to find out the amount of money used for the promotion of the Public Service. I do not think I would be far from the truth, if I were to say that Rs. 6 million pays the salaries of the public functionaries and the remaining Rs. 2½ million are used for the promotion of the Public Service. Now these Rs. 6 million, the salaries of the public functionaries, remain in the country, and to this capital we should add the money in circulation within the country. So the wealth of our country is made up not only from exports, not only from the emigrants' remittances, but also from the salaries of local public functionaries.

The public functionary, my dear Luis Maria, who is more than handsomely paid and lives fabulously, is the cause of the trade deficit. Our imports kept on increasing year by year. In 1910 the imports were valued to Rs. 6,271,436 and in 1930 they came to Rs. 17,427,806, and this because, as the salary of the public functionary increased year by year, his appetite for imported goods also increased.

To these Rs. 6 million, we have to add the money that comes into the country through the sale of lotteries from British India. More lottery tickets are sold in British India than in Portuguese India. I would say, that about Rs. 30 lakhs come into the country annually from British India through the sale of lottery tickets. Besides Rs. 4 million that come into the country through exports, we have three other sources that bring money into the economy. They are,

(a) Rs. 4½ million from the emigrant remittances

(b) Rs. 6 million from local public functionaries

(c) Rs. 3 million from lottery ticket sales in British India.

These figures indicate that emigration does not bring that much money into the country to generate the economy, as heralded by many journalists. The local public functionaries contribute two-thirds to the economy, and one-third comes from lottery ticket sales in British India. Though we have talked a lot against the public functionary, he, in a way, helps to keep an equilibrium in public finances! The public functionary, earning a kingly salary, consumes more imported goods than the *bhatkar*. It is the public functionary who has four and five times more income as compared to the top twenty landlords of each district. He has more purchasing power than the others in the country. The key to our economic problems lies in this phenomenon: Portuguese India imports four times more than it exports. That is the problem.

19

THE MARKET VALUE OF COCONUTS

The Press of our country is urging us to put flags in the windows to celebrate the glorious and historic date of the discovery of the island of Angediv. The public is busy brushing off their Sunday clothes in order to don them for this festive and commemorative service. But you and I who live away from the city are not fortunate enough to take part in these recollective solemnities. You, because of your rheumatism, and I, as I have no overcoat to wear. Therefore, my dear Luis Maria, we will try to exchange our ideas on less poetic topics. We will touch on the gloomy realities of our everyday lives. We will not discover new islands, but we will look into the market price of our coconuts. The coconut price in foreign markets has gradually decreased. Today the coconut sells for Rs. 10 to 12 per thousand, whereas before, it sold for 25 to 40 per thousand. So, my dear Luis Maria, let us exchange ideas on this problem and investigate, not the actions of our ancestors, but rather the ideas of what is needed to secure a future for our grandchildren.

At the moment, it is true that neither you nor I hold any responsible political position in our country. You are not a member of the government council, and I am not even a member of the village administration. You are just an ordinary citizen with rheumatism living on the 9% interest from your securities. And I, a humble lawyer without land or capital.

So, you might say that you and I have nothing to do with the problem that the coconut business is facing today. The *bhatkars* who met in the Town Hall of Salcete appointed a commission to look after their interests and did not even invite us to that meeting. Why should we bother? But the crisis that the coconut business is facing also affects us, even though you might live on the interest of your securities and I on my profession. If you look into it, you will understand. Since your capital is tied to real estate, and you earn interest from it, what will happen to it now? The coconut price being Rs. 10 to 12 per thousand, how do you expect the debtors to pay the interest on time? This crisis has brought land prices down, and your capital is tied to the value of the land. In this case you might bring debtors to court, or you might take away their land against your debt, or you might auction their land. But with the price of the coconut being what it is at the present time, who is going to buy that land? The result would be that the market economy would come to a standstill, and the income of the mortgaged land would go to the trustees. You would be left with nothing.

And what about me, dear Luis Maria? I do not have any coconut plantations or agricultural land. My sole income comes from my law practice. The coconut price being Rs. 10 to 12 per thousand, the planters have no money to indulge in lawsuits. The poverty of the *bhatkars* results in empty stomachs for lawyers like me. Is this what is going to happen to me?

My dear Luis Maria, you and I are victims of this economic crisis. Because of this, we should put our heads together and try to come up with a solution that will fetch better prices for our agricultural produce on the market. I am afraid that if we do not try to find a reasonable solution, both of us will be on the verge of financial ruin, you, because your capital is tied to the land and I, because my income depends on the prosperity of the *bhatkar* .

We will be magnanimous, and will not be upset because the *bhatkars* had not the decency to invite us to their meeting at the Town Hall of Salcete. Neither will we lose any sleep because we were not made members of the Commission that was authorized to talk with the nation about this economic crisis. But you and I, who are knowledgeable in economics, will do something for the good of the public by giving them our free advice to help find a solution to this economic problem.

This economic crisis that the *bhatkars* are debating reminds me of water, which is composed of two elements: oxygen and hydrogen. In this case, the two important factors are the fall of coconut prices in the foreign market and the decline of its production at home. It is not enough, dear Luis Maria, to investigate why coconuts from Portuguese India are not fetching the price they did before. We must research another factor as well. That other factor is the fact that we must once again recapture the foreign markets. That being taken care of, we must search for ways to increase coconut production to the level of past years. We cannot solve these problems in isolation with a fitting solution for both.

To solve these problems we need to do as medical doctors do. Just as they first check the temperature of the patient, we must establish mathematically the loss of income of the *bhatkars*. With the help of export statistics from the years 1931 to 1934, let us begin analyzing this problem.

	Export of Coconuts		
1931	**1932**	**1933**	**1934**
31,334,405	30,594,417	24,087,424	23,453,053
	Value in Rupees		
924,669	905,885	669,526	596,978

My dear Luis Maria, when we look at this chart of coconut exportation, we notice that there has been a progressive decline each year. From 1932 onwards, the productivity of coconuts has fallen by one-fifth of the production. The coconut value shown in the chart is calculated at Rs. 25 per thousand, but in fact, the coconut fetched much more in 1931 as compared to 1934. But let us concentrate, not on that, but on the statistics so that we can have a clear view of the matter. When we take into account the number of coconuts sold from 1931 to 1934, at the rate of Rs. 25 per thousand, we can understand the economic pinch the country was feeling during those years.

Unfortunately, I do not have statistics for 1935 to 1937. But we can at least theorize about what may have happened during those years. Let us assume that for the years 1935, 1936 and 1937 the agricultural production and the coconut exportation of the country were the same as in 1934. That being assumed, my dear Luis Maria, we can understand the economic suffering of the *bhatkars*. This is simple mathematics. Quantitatively, let us allow the coconut exports to be the same as those of 1934 but we will lower the coconut price. Let us assume that the price of the export coconuts is Rs. 15 per thousand in 1936 and Rs. 12 per thousand in 1937. This gives us approximately Rs. 350,000 in 1936 and Rs. 250,000 in 1937. The income loss of the *bhatkars* then becomes the following: in 1936 there are Rs. 245,000 less than in 1934, Rs. 320,000 less than in 1933, Rs. 555,000 less than in 1932 and Rs. 575,000 less than in 1931. And in 1937 they lost Rs. 345,000 as compared to 1934, Rs. 420,000 as compared to 1933, Rs. 655,000 as compared to 1932 and Rs. 675,000 as compared to 1931.

The total loss of income for the *bhatkars* for 1936 and 1937, when compared to 1931 is Rs. 12,500,000. These figures, my dear Luis Maria, would send shivers down anybody's spine! They are an indication that the low production and low prices of coconuts put big holes in the pockets of the *bhatkars*. Imagine, that for those years they lost Rs. 12½ lakhs! From these figures we can calculate that in 1931, my dear Luis Maria, the income of the *bhatkars* from coconuts totalled Rs. 924,669. Out of this income the *bhatkars* paid for all their expenses, which included clothes, food, their children's education, costs and taxes paid to the government. But in 1936 their incomes amounted to Rs. 575,000 or less, and in 1937 their incomes amounted to Rs. 675,000 or less, so they had less money to meet their annual budgets. These figures show that the *bhatkars*' incomes have been reduced to one-fourth what they were in 1932, and that is the most frightening thing of all!

During those years, the market price for the coconuts was Rs. 35 per thousand. Now, the coconut production has fallen to one-fifth of that earlier production. A *bhatkar* who harvested 5,000 coconuts in 1932, harvested 4,000 in 1936 and 1937. In 1932 with his coconut harvest being 5,000 and the market price of the coconut being Rs. 35 per thousand, his yearly income amounted to Rs. 175. But his income in 1936 and 1937 came to Rs. 45. This is the case because the production of coconuts fell to 4,000 during those two years and the price per thousand was between Rs. 10 and 12. Though we see that the economic situation of the *bhatkars* was already bad to begin with, it got worse during 1936 and 1937. What can we do to make a difference, dear Luis Maria? How can we help turn the economy around?

The solution to this problem is to increase coconut productivity. This solution would not be easy considering that the soil has been exhausted. To solve this problem, you might suggest that coconut palms should be well looked after by being fertilized by fish and salt, the same way our grandfathers did it. Instead of taking that route, our *bhatkars* are conducting meetings to bring their plight to the attention of the nation. Though the nation might oblige and say that it would help and protect the farmers, it will not do their work for them. This being the case, how can the *bhatkars*, who are reduced to the state of penury, take care of their palm groves? And after they get less productive returns from their land, how are they supposed to be able to pay the land tax?

You and I, my dear Luis Maria, who both understand economics, can condemn this land tax the *bhatkars* pay to the State because it is an unjust tax. It looks as if *bhatkars* go through all these sacrifices and deprivations for the sole benefit of the State. Their incomes are reduced to almost nothing, and the little money that they are left with is taken by the State in other direct and indirect taxes. And the worst of it is that these taxes are not based on reality. According to past law, it is obligatory for landlords to pay one-tenth of their incomes to the State. This deduction is taken from their profits, without first deducting their necessary expenditures. This is unfair, because as the situations stands today, the coconut planters make no profit at all. Since the plight of the *bhatkar* is less productivity and price depreciation, how can a *bhatkar* pay one-tenth of his profit to the government, a profit that does not even exist?

In theory, the portion of the taxes that goes into the government coffers is based on the surplus income of the entire population or the country. For this golden rule to be put into practice, there is a condition that the citizens of the country as an aggregate have surplus incomes. This is because the nation's poor are not taxable. In addition, there are properties which are valued as unprofitable, and hence they are exempted from land tax. This being the principle of taxation in Portuguese India, we know that there are two classes of landlords: those with higher incomes and those with no incomes, those who pay the tax and those who are tax-exempt. As the economic condition of the *bhatkars* stands today, should they be included in the category of those who can afford to pay taxes? That is a vitally important question.

We have seen already that the present income of the *bhatkars* has been reduced to one-fourth, that of 1932. Formerly, they used to harvest 5,000 coconuts and sell them at Rs. 35 per thousand, making Rs. 175. Presently, they harvest 4,000 coconuts and sell them at Rs. 10 and 12 per thousand, hardly making Rs. 45. The logical conclusion is that coconut farming is not a profitable business. The only thing that a *bhatkar* is then left with is the public status that goes with land ownership and that in itself does not contribute much to his financial status. With Rs. 45 in hand, a *bhatkar* has to maintain the coconut plantation, pay the wages of the labourers and the coconut harvesters, pay the transportation costs, and a host of other costs. This puts the *bhatkar* in debt, a bad place to be. This being the case, my dear Luis Maria, why should he have to pay the land tax? In fact, the government should compensate the *bhatkar* for his losses not tax him. The National Assembly should also pass legislation that would honour the coconut farmers of Portuguese India with the Order of Good Merit for producing coconuts at a loss! But, all kidding aside, my dear Luis Maria, this is indeed a serious matter, an important subject that concerns our political economy.

The truth of the matter is, the small *bhatkar*, who used to collect 5,000 coconuts, now only collects 4,000 and thus, if he maximizes his efforts on his small coconut plantation, he still ends up with a loss. After all his expenditures, this small *bhatkar* is left without any money to pay land tax to the government. And another thing: not all *bhatkars* are the same, in that not all *bhatkars* end up with a loss. There is another kind of *bhatkar*, a big *bhatkar*, who collects about 50,000 coconuts and makes Rs. 2,000 and pays one-tenth of this sum as land tax to the government, i.e. Rs. 200. These *bhatkars* should not be put into the same category as that of a small *bhatkar*. Even if he now only collects 40,000 coconuts instead of 50,000, he still makes a profit. This profit is, and should be, taxable. The large *bhatkars*, unlike the small ones, have a profit margin, though smaller than before, that puts them into a taxable bracket.

So, my dear Luis Maria, we have to make a distinction between two groups of *bhatkars*: the big and the small *bhatkars*. The small should be defined as those who cannot make a profit by selling the produce of the land. The big ones are those who have enough land to make a comfortable profit on the selling of the produce of that land. The boundaries thus being set between these two, the law should be that the smaller ones be exempted from the land tax, while the land tax paid by the larger ones should be adjusted according to the incomes they make from their lands. This task is difficult to accomplish, in that it is difficult to settle on a demarcation between these two groups. We have set into motion the principle that only those *bhatkars* who make a profit should be considered for taxation. This should be understood to mean that "profit" refers to the liquid cash that a *bhatkar* holds in his hands, after making the proper deductions for his farming costs.

Taking this definition of profit into consideration, it is not difficult to follow through with the process of demarcation. To help make this matter clearer, suppose that a landlord pays Rs. 25 as land tax. This tax paid is the one-tenth of his income after deducting his expenditures. After the deductions, his income would be Rs. 250. This example would have to represent past income, since at present his income has been reduced to , of that amount, since coconut productivity is declining, and the market price for agricultural produce is low. If this is indeed the case, his present income would be Rs. 82. One-tenth of that would be paid to the government as land tax. After paying that tax, he has Rs. 4 and 8 *tangas* for his monthly expenses. What a life!

In the past, it was not so bad when a coconut plantation would bring in Rs. 250. Even if a *bhatkar* paid one-tenth as land tax to the State, he was still left with Rs. 225. That means he had about Rs. 20 a month. Though this is not a large amount of money, this sum at least guaranteed him his daily two meals of rice and curry. But now his income is reduced to Rs. 82, and he is not in a position to meet the average expenses on the coconut plantation. He is now a man in debt. I ask you, how can a man who makes no profit from his land be asked to pay land tax to the government? To further emphasize this point, I offer a quote from an economist of our times, Charles S. Devas:

> "Five percent taken from an income of 5,000 involves immensely less sacrifice than five percent taken from an income of 50, and considerable less sacrifice than five percent taken from an income of 150". (Charles S. Devas, *Political Economy*, 3rd ed., p. 597).

In any case, my dear Luis Maria, the tax should not be thrown to the public irrationally. The State might establish that a citizen is the owner of a piece of property and thus falls into the taxable bracket, but that is not a good reason to tax a citizen. The tax department should not tax a citizen when doing so for it deprives him of his personal necessities. In other words, the taxes should be just, reasonable and above all, fair. In no way, should they take away the funds needed to support the basic needs of daily life. In this case, I want to remind you of the wisdom of the old maxim: *prima vivere, deinde tributum persolvere.* Justice demands that citizens who can hardly pay for their daily necessities should be exempt from taxation.

According to some economists, not only should the expenses of the daily needs of the citizen and his family be excluded from taxation but the government should also take into consideration the lifestyle of the citizen, the lifestyle that he is accustomed to. In Florence, for example, my dear Luis Maria, the citizens are allowed to make many tax deductions. They are allowed not only to deduct family expenses, but can also make deductions in order to maintain their lifestyle status. They also have other privileges, depending on the social position of the taxpayer. Only after all these deductions are made, are the residents of Florence taxed on their remaining income. This kind of taxation may not be a realistic option for us, but *bhatkars* in Portuguese India still need to demand that taxes be better regulated, taking into account the expenses incurred by raising a family, and other costs. After deductions are made for everyday expenses, this leaves the average *bhatkar* about 8 *tangas* a day, compensation for supervising and assisting the labourer on the farm. This amount may not be much, but at least it is something.

My dear Luis Maria, now that we have clarified why small *bhatkars* should be exempt from the land-tax, you may ask under what criteria should coconuts from Portuguese India be priced? You may also ask how coconut farms can be more productive, and how can it be arranged that coconuts fetch a better price in the foreign market? I know you are eager to learn the answers to these questions, and I will answer them as best I can. You and I may not be the owners of coconut plantations, but we still have an undeniable and reasonable interest in these questions and their answers. You have the right to be interested because you have loaned money to *bhatkars* from the mortgage of your village lands, and you want them to pay the interest on the money on a timely basis. As for me, a *bhatkar* who is free from debt will have money to employ my services to pursue lawsuits. Which class of *bhatkar*, the large or the small, takes up a mortgage? Indeed it is the small one. And which class of *bhatkar* files lawsuits, the big or the small? It is the small one, in general. When exempted for land tax, *bhatkars* will pay their interest, and seek my services to file lawsuits. Because of these reasons, it is in our definite interests that coconuts should have a better market price, and that the production of coconuts should be increased rather than decreased.

And in regards to the national economic interest, a commission was appointed to look into these affairs at the meeting of the *bhatkars* in the Town Hall of Salcete, Thank God, neither of us was part of that commission.

Are we in accord?

20

THE STATE'S BENEFITS FROM COCONUT PLANTATIONS

As you might know, my dear Luis Maria, in France the fiscal accountants understood that among all the rich sources for revenue, only land rendered profit above the cost of production. Therefore, they concluded that all the State income should come from land taxes (Clamageran, *L'Histoire de l'impôt en France*) writes,

> *"Ils tablissent d'abord que la terre seule donne un revenu net, cest-à-dire, un revenu qui excéde les dépenses nécessaires pour l'entretien des cultures et cultivateurs; ils établissent ensuite que ce revenu net est la source qui alimente tous les autres revenus; ils en concluent qu'il est inutile de poursuivre les revenus mobiliers à travers des mille canaux où ils circulent: qu'il est plus commode et plus juste de les atteindre à leur source, et ils s'obstinent à la théorie de l'impôt unique sur le revenu foncier".*

So the fiscal school supported only the principle of land taxation, and opposed taxation on moveable property. In practice, this theory had a great advantage. It made tax collection easy and simple. "The distinguishing feature of the best tax," said J. R. McCuloch, "is not that it is nearly proportioned to the means of the individuals, but that it is easily assessed and collected, and is, at the same time, conducive to public interest."

These are experimental economic ideas, my dear Luis Maria, and they sound right. In the name of progress, economic science has thrown away, like old shoes, the services of the public welfare. Public welfare should be the most important notion at work today, and the collection of taxes should be based upon a system that upholds that principle. In order to maintain the collective welfare of all, every citizen has to make a contribution to the State according to his income. Not only should those who make a living from the land be taxed, but also those who earn their income from other professions and services should be taxed.

But in our country, as we have seen my dear Luis Maria, only *bhatkars* pay more taxes than anybody else. The professionals, merchants, government officials and others whose income is much more than the *bhatkars'* do not pay any tax. For example, industries, insurance companies, physicians, lawyers, public notaries and others do not pay any tax to the State. All insurance companies that are doing business in our country are outsiders. No one in the government so far has remembered to subject these insurance companies to taxation laws.

You might be aware, my dear Luis Maria, that life insurance premiums keep going up. Do you know how much policy holders pay these insurance companies yearly? Let us say, about Rs. 15 lakhs. And do you know, my dear Luis Maria, how much the insurance companies pay annually to the families of the deceased or to their heirs? It is not more than Rs. 25,000. In other words, these foreign insurance companies take away Rs. 15,000,000 and only Rs. 25,000 comes back to the country. And these insurance companies who do business in our country do not pay a single paisa as tax to the State. They scorn our taxation laws.

More than three hundred years ago, De Lugo, a theologian preached that while raising taxes (*in tribute impositions*), all sectors of the society should contribute equally to the expenses of maintaining the public welfare system. That meant that taxes should be raised according to a geometric progression. In other words, those who earn more or make more money should pay more, and those who earn less should pay less (*ut ii majores viras habent, plus sovant, et qui minores, minus*). To put it differently,

> "the distributions of public positions may look as if based on unconventional equality, but it is based on wealth, and hence it would be the most unjust" (*De Justitia et Jure, Disput.*, p. xxxvi).

The geometric progression which De Lugo talks about in mathematical terms may not be easily understood. But it makes a solid statement in moral sense. Well, my dear Luis Maria, if we were to apply this principle to our country, what do you think would be the results? We have already seen that in Portuguese India taxes do not go up in a proportional manner. The citizens contribute to the State expenditure not in geometrical progression, but inversely. The rich pay less and the poor pay more.

The *bhatkars* who pay Rs. 10, 15, and 25 as land tax are economically bankrupt. And besides this, they are obliged to pay 10% to the State from the income of a sale. But this income does not exist at all. It is a pure fantasy. On the other hand, commerce, industry, public servants, physicians, lawyers, contractors and all those prosperous people who earn sumptuous incomes, have the privilege of paying nothing at all to the State. Even to this day, my dear Luis Maria, we are hooked to fiscal theories that the land alone should shoulder the responsibility of funding public expenditures.

Besides, we demanded from the justice system that the civil servant should have a remunerative salary because of the trappings of his office. It is also demanded from the justice system that his comfort and well-being be secure and that his income should be such that it guarantees him and his family security for life. The one who contributes to his opulent lifestyle, has a life full of worries. So there is no correlation between the State expenditure and the wealth of the nation. The nation is poor, the State is rich. There is no correlation between the income of the taxpayers and the salaries of the civil servants. The latter move in cars. The taxpayers go on foot.

This absurdity, my dear Luis Maria, goes still further. The official statistics (*Anuário Estatistico - 1932*, p. 301) states that the total production of coconuts in Portuguese India was about

100 million coconuts. This figure is based upon the registered coconut palms from five districts: Ilhas, Sanquelim, Ponda, Daman and Diu. What about the other districts? In a way, let us presume that the production of coconuts is about 100 million. But a few years ago, the coconut production should have been about 80 million. We have gone through this before, and since 1932, coconut production has gone down by one-fifth.

This being the case, we will look into the economic returns that coconut palms bring into the coffers of Portuguese India. Then, we will compare the profit that *bhatkars* make from the land to the profit that goes into the coffers of the State.

Now, 80 million coconuts at Rs. 10 to 12 per thousand, would make roughly Rs. 900,000. First, from this amount we have to deduct the plantation expenditures, such as, the upkeep or the plantation, labour and other related expenses. It would not be an exaggeration to say that the operating costs could amount to Rs. 300,000. So the economic returns from the coconut plantations of Portuguese India would be Rs. 600,000 after deducting the operating costs.

The following are land taxes collected by the State for the five years:

1930-1931	Rs. 516,788
1931-1932	Rs. 511,982
1932-1933	Rs. 526,647
1933-1934	Rs. 516,916
1934-1935	Rs. 516,927

The above figures are the aggregate land taxes, including not only the land under coconut plantation, but also paddy cultivation.

Let us suppose, my dear Luis Maria, that the land taxes that came into the State Treasury were from the one-third of land that is under paddy cultivation. The other land taxes that came into the Treasury are from coconut plantations, and should roughly amount to Rs. 344,000. To this, we must add the other monies that came into the Treasury from coconut palms allocated for sap, from which alcohol is distilled. In Goa alone this activity in 1932 brought the Treasury Rs. 535,102.

To these returns, we must add the taxes that come to the State Treasury from the coconut palms allocated for jaggery. This amounts to Rs. 11,673. And also the taxes that come from the coconut palm sap allocated to the preparation of bread come to Rs. 1,977. To avoid confusion, we will stick only to the figure that the State collects from coconut palms allocated to the distillation of spirits.

The chart below shows the various districts of Goa that brought in the tax from sap distillation:.

Ilhas	Rs.	57,307
Bardez	Rs.	68,138
Pernem	Rs.	81,086
Sanquelim & Satari	Rs.	8,738
Salcete	Rs.	132,715
Quepem	Rs.	34,865
Canacona	Rs.	26,575
Mormugao	Rs.	57,248
Ponda	Rs.	52,685
Sanguem	Rs.	15,745
Total	Rs.	535,102

Now we will add Rs. 535,102 which the State collects from the coconut palms that are allocated for the distillation of spirits to the land tax from coconut planters which amounts to Rs. 344,000. Thus altogether the State pockets Rs. 879,102 from coconut plantations.

Below are the economic returns of the *bhatkars* and the State from the coconut palms:

Bhatkars	Rs.	600,000
State	Rs.	879,102

I know what you are going to say. You are indicating that I have not included the income that comes to *bhatkars* from coconut palms allocated for sap extraction. But the official statistics that give 100 million coconuts as the yearly production in the country, is not specific about this. The official statistics give credence that the coconut palms that are allocated for sap extraction are also included. But let us look into this matter. The coconut palms registered, during various periods for sap extraction in 1932 was 119,996. (*Anuário Estatistico*, p. 280). The average coconut production of these palms, i.e., palms rented for sap extraction would be 20 to 30 coconuts per palm. Taking as a round figure 120,000 coconut palms for sap extraction, their coconut production would be roughly 3,000,000. Though according to official estimates the coconut production is 100,000,000, we have shown that it is not so. According to our estimates the coconut production is about 80 million. To this we add 3 million and this makes the annual production move up to 83 million. In the same fashion, the value of coconut production in rupees goes up from Rs. 600,000 to Rs. 635,000.

The economic returns now for the *bhatkars* and the State are as follows:

Bhatkars	Rs.	635,000
State	Rs.	879,102

Again you might express your disapproval of my calculations. You might say that the coconut palms rented for sap extraction should be calculated in rupees and not in coconut production. Now let us talk about this. Each coconut palm rented for sap extraction brings in on the average Rs. 3 to the *bhatkar*. You must remember too that a coconut palm rented for sap extraction for a year should be kept idle for two years. So the real income that a *bhatkar* gets from the coconut palms rented for sap extraction is about one-third of the exact number of coconut palms rented for sap extraction. This being stated, 120,000 coconut palms that are rented for sap extraction would seem to bring to *bhatkars* an income of Rs. 480,000. But that is not so. The actual income that *bhatkars* pocket is Rs. 160,000. Now we will add Rs. 160,000 to Rs. 600,000 (this being the original income from the coconut palms rented for sap extraction). From the new calculations, we will compare the economic returns of *bhatkars* and the State.

Here they are,

Bhatkars (600,000 + 160,000)	Rs.	760,000
State	Rs.	879,102

Every way you look at it, my dear Luis Maria, it is the State that gets the best economic returns from coconut plantations in Portuguese India.

In this situation, who needs to be a *bhatkar*?

21

INCREASING COCONUT PRODUCTION

The economic measure that I have discussed in my previous letter, neither solves your problem nor mine, dear Luis Maria. Let us suppose the small *bhatkars* who pay Rs. 25 or less as land tax are exempted by law. Even if this tenet becomes law, you are of the opinion that a *bhatkar* would not be in a position to pay punctually the 9% interest on borrowed capital to the creditors. Nor would he be in a position to litigate his complaints. A relief of Rs. 25 a year does not make a difference. It is like a drop in the ocean. That is your opinion. You earn your living by lending money to *bhatkars* and I am a lawyer. We are in the same boat. Your capital is at risk as before. This measure is not of much help.

My dear Luis Maria, let us find out ways to evaluate the rural lands in our country. Let us push ourselves, my dear Luis Maria, to find better prices for our agricultural produce, and also my dear Luis Maria, let us be in earnest to introduce coconut palms that produce more coconuts! I know this problem is a vicious circle. That is what you are saying, is it not? Or, you are going to argue that there is not any point in increasing coconut production when the prices are down. In fact, to fetch better prices the coconut production should be brought down. This is how the law of supply and demand works. That is your argument. But my dear Luis Maria, these are just economic theories and you are taken in by them. Let me remind you that in the domain of social events, there are no laws, but tendencies. In the domain of social events, my dear Luis Maria, all assumptions are hypothetical.

Do you remember what happened in England in 1846 with the repeal of the corn laws? According to the dictates of economic principles, wheat prices which were supposed to come down immediately with a bang, did not come down at all. Wheat prices remained constant. This happened because of the poor potato harvests, the Crimean War, and specially the depreciation in the price of gold. Who in his right mind can predict that with the increase of coconut production and more coconuts in the market, the prices will go down?

The effects of supply and demand, my dear Luis Maria, do not always come into play. The laws of supply and demand come into effect when there is an increase in production but demand remains stationary or when there is an increase in demand but the production remains stationary. But where there is an equal increase in supply and demand at the same time, the laws of supply and demand are not effective. To quote Keynes,

> "An intensification, for instance, in the demand for a commodity may take place concurrently with an increase in supply and hence the absolute effect of the change in demand may not be apparent in any actual change in price". (John Nevelle Keynes, *The Scope and Method of Political Economy*, 3rd ed., p. 220).

Who can predict what tomorrow will bring, and who can foresee in this complex world of today, what the influence of new industries in the near future will be upon agriculture? But it is a fact, at the present moment, that the market in British India, the only export market that we have, is saturated with coconuts. And I would not deny, at the moment that coconut supply in the external market exceeds demand. But it is also true, day by day, that coconut products are being used in large quantities. The new industries that are springing up use coconuts daily to bring out a variety of products. So, the point is we cannot anticipate that the increase in coconut production will bring its price down. To do so would be unwise. We should not be intimidated, nor be afraid of hypothetical events. Let us be men of courage, optimism and faith. Defeatism and pessimism belong to mediocres. Let us face the future with equanimity. The two of us know the heritage of our ancestors, those brave forefathers of ours who discovered the island of Angediv 450 years ago!

According to official estimates, the country's coconut production is 100 million. This figure I find is inflated. In 1862, the coconut production in the country was an estimated 23,108,457 (F. Luis Gomes, *A Liberdade da Terra e a Economia Rural da India Portuguesa*, p. 40). At that time the population of Portuguese Indian was 347,000. Coconut then, as now, was our source of agricultural wealth.

At this time, we will not discuss if we have quintupled our coconut plantation in 75 years to give us five times more coconuts today. In 1931 and 1932 the coconut exports of our country did not exceed 30 and 31 million, respectively. And they were good years for coconut production. Even at the present, we have estimated that coconut production is about 80 million, which is less than one-fifth that of 1932. This being the case, my dear Luis Maria, why do not our coconut exports go beyond 23 or 24 million? What happens to 56 or 57 million coconuts? Do we consume them within the country? If we do, how? If we look at the official statistics (*Anuário Estatistico*, 1932, p. 213), we see a very different picture. We import at present the following kinds of cooking oils:

Cooking oil imports

Peanut oil	3,051	gallons
Coconut oil	1,216	gallons
Gergelim oil	13,180	gallons

The imports of these cooking oils in large quantities indicate the state of economic affairs in the country. We even import coconut oil which was once produced in our homes. How do we then use 56 or 57 million coconuts that are not exported? You mean to say, we use 56 or 57 million coconuts only for curry? That is too much for curry, is it not?

I know we export not only coconuts, but also copra. And

if you are suggesting that I have not taken into account the copra exports, you are right, very right. Our copra exports in 1931 were 7,082 *mãos;* in 1932 they were 7,622 *mãos*; in 1933 they were 3,943 *mãos* and in 1934, they were 25,961 *mãos.* I do not know how they arrived at this figure of copra exports in 1934. But let us take the average copra exports to be 7,000 *mãos.* How many coconuts are involved to produce this much copra? Let us be generous and say 3,000,000 coconuts.

We will add these 3 million coconuts to the 23 and 24 million coconuts we export. Taking this into account, the coconut exports for 1936 and 1937 will go up to 26 and 27 million. The coconut production being, in our estimate, 80 million, now deducting the copra exports from that we are still left with 54 or 53 million coconuts. What do we do with them, my dear Luis Maria? In British India, the population of 352,837,*778 (Census of 1931)*, consumes yearly 400 million coconuts, according to official estimates. (*Handbook of Commercial Information for India*, 3rd ed., p. 237). This population is distributed in the following manner (round figures):

British India

(Area: 1,096,171 sq. miles) 272,000,000 inhabitants

Native States

(Area: 7,122,508 sq. miles) 81,000,000 inhabitants

In British India there are extremely poor people, and these people do not use any coconut in their diets. These people fall into the regions of native states and hence we will exclude them. But we will take into account the states which are directly ruled by England and the population there, as we have seen is 272,000,000. We will assume the yearly consumption of 400 million coconuts in British India is by these people. So, each individual in British India consumes less than two coconuts per year.

According to the *Census of 1931* the population of Portuguese India was 579,969. Let us be very liberal and assume that the population in Portuguese India is better fed than in British India. This being the case, we will also assume that the people in Portuguese India consume five times more coconuts than in British India. This would give us 10 coconuts per individual for a year in Portuguese India. Thus the internal consumption in Portuguese India would be 5 million and 800,000 coconuts: Are you indicating that these estimates are wrong? Are you saying too that my comparison of eating habits between the two populations is not on the right track? Well then, let us look at it from a different angle.

My dear Luis Maria, we will take for granted that in Portuguese India each individual, including the newborn, consumes 50 coconuts per year! This would give us yearly consumption of 19 million. Even with this amount of consumption, we are left with 24 or 25 million coconuts. We know that we export 26 or 27 million coconuts yearly, and we have hypothetically shown, and this in exaggeration, that we internally consume 29 million coconuts per year. What do we do with the 24 or 25 million coconuts that are left? In you wildest dreams, do you imagine that these are consumed by the people of the country? The point is, my dear Luis Maria, the official estimates of 100 million coconuts in Portuguese India is not accurate. It is a figment of the imagination. The coconut production in Portuguese India, therefore, fluctuates between 50 and 60 million and not beyond.

My dear Luis Maria, you might say that it is unwise to increase coconut production and that it does not make economic sense. It is like taking a chance, playing a lottery. You also might say that day by day the factories and new industries that are springing up in British India consume a lot of coconuts. That is right. But it is also true, that Ceylon which once exported its coconuts to Europe and America, is no longer exporting coconuts to these markets. The coconut prices in those markets have fallen. Now Ceylon floods the markets in British India with its coconuts. You have observed also that in British India itself there is a trend to increase coconut production. Given these factors, you are of the opinion that we are not in a position to compete with Ceylon and British India in the coconut market.

I want to pose a question. Why do we not process our coconuts, and start an industry of that nature? Let us not dream big dreams. Big dreams mean big factories, large capital, high technology, expert directors and a skilled working force. Given our modest means, my dear Luis Maria, we cannot afford to lay the foundation for big undertakings. But we can establish small-scale industries, and set them up in our villages. They do not require machinery, nor graduate technicians, nor capital that runs into five figures.

The great mistake in our thinking is that when we talk of a coconut processing industry, we think of the processing of coconut kernel. We think of industries that refine coconut oil, coconut butter, sap and other related industries. We never think of coconut husk. A coconut husk processing industry would bring in good profits to coconut planters and at the same time, it would provide employment to lots of people of both sexes. This would bring economic well-being into many households.

The coconut husk industry in British India is well-established in the state of Travancore, and there are signs that it is doing well in Mysore and Orissa. In certain districts of Bombay too, there are signs that it is doing well. The number of workers in these industries in 1931 was 224,788. Of this total 154,312 were women. Before the Great War the main export to Europe and America was coconut oil. But today coconut husk products have taken its place. The charts below will give us a comparative idea of these products:

Export of Coconut Oil 1934-1935

	Quantity	*Value (in £)*
	32,742 gallons	3,124

Export of Coconut Husks

	Quantity	*Value (in £)*
Fibre	31,319 tons	598,241
Cords and ropes	2,649 tons	55,200
Total		653,441

To this we must add the figures for the export of doormats and carpets of coconut coir which in 1934-1935 amounted to 63,222 cwts and the value was £ 142,224.

My dear Luis Maria, this export of the products of coconut coir to the tune of £ 653,441 in 1934-1935 is not a random happening. The market for coconut coir products in Europe has been very regular. You will have a better understanding when I put the figures of exports for five years before you.

Exports
Fibre of Coconut Coir

Year	*Tons*	*Value in £*
1931-32	6,390	565,036
1932-33	26,904	451,284
1933-34	31,102	577,104
1934-35	31,319	598,241
1935-36	34,223	656,192

Exports
Coconut Coir Cords

Year	*Tons*	*Value in £*
1931-32	2,228	64,014
1932-33	2,295	57,949
1933-34	2,115	49,149
1934-35	2,649	55,200
1935-36	2,408	51,393

These figures show, my dear Luis Maria, that your objections hold no water. These figures indicate that it is not risky to increase the coconut production in Portuguese India. It is not playing a lottery. It shows that we should not necessarily depend on the markets in British India. It is in our hands to take the maximum advantage of coconuts. So we have to think differently. Instead of thinking of processing coconut kernel which requires a large amount of capital and experts, we would do better extracting the fibre of coconut husk. This would give us a valuable export. You must also remember that the extraction of coconut fibre takes time. First the green coconut husks must be kept for at least eight months in open pits. These pits would be at the river banks, so that the tide that comes in will soak them. After eight months they can be prepared for fibre extraction. About five husks give clean fibre, weighing about a pound. The coconut production being about 60,000,000 according to my calculations we could produce £10,000,000 of coconut fibre.

I have to bring to your attention, my dear Luis Maria, certain aspects of coconut fibre. Raw coconut fibre has less commercial value. For example, the export of raw coconut fibre during 1934-35 in British India did not exceed 54 tons and brought in £ 730. In order to get better export prices, it needs to be spun. Once spun, it should be carefully cleaned and bad threads should be removed. Then it is made into yarns by hand. The fibre of 3,000 coconuts gives one cwt. of fine thread. The fibre of 60 million coconut husks would give 20,000 cwts. of fine thread, which comes to 1,000 tons and its commercial value is about £ 20,000. This is not as worthless as mud.

During the last two years of the Great War, British India supplied 150,000 sq. yards of mats of coconut coir every month to France. You might be aware of it. These mats were used as curtains or as screens in military operations, a method of camouflage. Who knows in the next war what the war strategists will do? Perhaps they might use the coconut coir mats on a greater scale. How do you know that new ways may not be found to use the various coconut products in the future? The thing is, we have to have confidence in the future. I hope now you are convinced that the increase in the coconut production does not necessarily mean depreciation in coconut prices. By increasing coconut production, we are not pushing the national economy down the hill.

The question is, how do we increase coconut production? That is what you want to know, is it not? You want me to come up with a practical method, a sure method that would make our coconut palms yield more. In my opinion, this can be achieved by passing an act of legislation, declaring that the coconut is a national product as we did with rice and then fixing a remunerative official price for coconuts, the same way we did for rice.

My dear Luis Maria, you want to know how coconuts can have a fixed price when their production is increased. You must be thinking that I am joking. But I never joke about serious matters. Truly, my dear Luis Maria, legislation has magic powers to render fields and farms fecund and yielding in abundance. Christ's miracle, the multiplication of loaves pales before what legislation has done in our country for agriculture. You still do not believe me. In that case I ask you to read the act of *Conselho do Governo* (session of August 5, 1937), where the highest colonial power has shown it with figures, my dear Luis Maria! The supernatural powers of the legislative act, the act that was brought in to protect the national production of the paddies, has indeed increased the rice production. This miracle, my dear Luis Maria, was performed without any fertilizer, without better work tools, without new technical innovations and the least distribution of the paddies. And this increased paddy production to 150,000 *khandis*!

It is a proof, my dear friend, that legislation works wonders. When the legislation fixed a compensative price for local rice, rice production in the country went up and rice imports fell to 150,000 *khandis*. Any other reason why the rice imports came down is of no consequence. The only conclusion that one can deduce is that the right type of legislation can make agricultural lands bloom. Since you doubt me still, my dear Luis Maria, I give you statistics from the colonial authority, and the statistics do not lie. Take hold of your glasses and go through these figures very carefully. I know that there are many like you. You can show this legislative miracle to them.

Conclusion

In 1936 the rice imports that came through our Customs amounted to less than half, as compared to 1932 rice imports.

From these we deduce,

(a) A few lakhs of rupees remained in the country.

(b) Rice production increased progressively.

(*Acta da sessão do C. do G,* August 25, 1937)

Here are the rice imports for 5 years

Year	*Quantities (khandis)*	*Value* (Rs.)
1932	226,294	3,247,919
1933	274,198	3,162,512
1934	124,750	2,337,939
1935	192,476	1,901,191
1936	137,493	1,593,221

Now, my dear Luis Maria, you must be convinced of what the passing of a legislative act can achieve. By fixing a remunerative rice price to local production, the rice production more than doubled in the country. If a rice farmer in Paroda was given bone fertilizer, if the rain water was trapped to irrigate the paddies in Ponchvali or Sancoale, or if some paddies had been converted to produce two harvests, or if rice farmers were ordered to clear land for more paddy acreage in Cabo da Rama, then these figures could have been interpreted differently. We could have said that the rice production increased because of the trapping of rain water. We could have said that the rice production increased because some paddies were converted to produce two harvests, or we could have said the rice production increased because more land was cleared for paddy acreage. We could have said all these things, but the fact is the rice farmers were not given such incentives. The acreage of rice paddies under cultivation remained the same as before, the irrigation system remained without any improvement and yet, the rice production increased to 150,000 *khandis*! This, my dear Luis Maria, we can only attribute to the absolute power of the legislative act!

This being the case, my dear Luis Maria, we request our government to pass legislation in favour of protecting a remunerative price for coconuts. A guaranteed better price for coconuts, would indeed increase the coconut production in the country. The *bhatkars*, disheartened because their coconut production had gone down by one-third, would now fill their barns with plenty of coconuts. The coconut plantation, their value now down, would go up in price. This would make the farmers happy. This would make both of us happy and there would be no more sleepless nights for us. If this comes to pass, you will collect your interest on your capital punctually. And with plenty of coconuts, my legal profession will blossom, lawsuits, contracts and lots of other legal work.

22

THE LIQUOR INDUSTRY IN PORTUGUESE INDIA

Truth should always come before everything else, my dear Luis Maria. In my last letter, I said that there were not any industries in Portuguese India. I was wrong! I apologize. I hasten to rectify this error.

In Portuguese India there is a booming industry, a very prosperous industry. This industry annually brings Rs. 8 lakhs into the State coffers. This is the industry that produces local alcohol. There are three kinds of alcohols produced in Portuguese India: one is from coconut palms, the second from cashews and the third is from *cajuri* in Daman. We also produce alcohol in small amounts from sugarcane, about 26 gallons. We will not take this into account.

In Goa in 1932 there were 2,430 licensed depots for coconut palm alcohol and 1,216 licensed depots for *caju* alcohol. All this distilling activity took place within an area of 3,806 sq. kms. This is something to be proud of. This industrial activity makes the people of Portuguese India not lazy at all, but speaks eloquently about their industriousness! To have 3,646 distilling depots in 3,806 sq. kms, means that there is one depot to one sq. km. One has to doff one's hat to such an achievement!

Unfortunately, the government has not revealed statistics about coconut palm alcohol production. Cashew alcohol production in 1932 was 147,293 gallons.

The statistics say nothing about the quantity of alcohol production in the districts of Daman and Diu. However, the receipts of *abcari* seized by the State show the following about alcohol production in those districts:

Daman	1931-32	Rs.	147,331
Diu	1931-32	Rs.	50,789

The above figures show, my dear Luis Maria, that not only Goa, but also Daman and Diu have a booming native alcohol industry!

In 1862 when the population of Goa was 347,000, 62,000 coconut palms were leased for toddy tapping (F. Luis de Gomes, *A Economia Rural da India Portuguesa*, p. 44). Today the Census in Goa is 501,281 inhabitants and coconut palms leased for toddy tapping were 119,996, all these were licensed for spirits. Though from then to now the population has increased a little more than one-third, coconut palms licensed for spirit production have doubled. The toddy production in 1862 was 28,924 barrels. These divided among 347,000 inhabitants, allows a barrel for 11 individuals. But the actual production of toddy could be calculated at 57,000 barrels and divided among the present-day population of 501,281 inhabitants. In this case, 9 individuals get a barrel! Do you know, my dear Luis Maria, how many taverns there are that sell native liquor in Portuguese India? In 1932 there were 417 taverns in Goa alone. They were distributed in this fashion.

Ilhas	104
Bardez	61
Pernem	6
Salcete	152
Quepem	5
Canacona	3
Mormugao	51
Sanquelim	6
Satari	2
Ponda	20
Sanguem	7
Total	417

The population of Goa, as we have already seen is 505,281, according to the last *Census*. This population is divided according to sex, in this fashion:

Males	263,345
Females	241,936

The population can be further subdivided according to religion in the following manner:

Catholics	247,570
Hindus	250,443
Muslims	6,981
Parsees	22
Protestants	98
Others	125

Hindus and Muslims, as you know, my dear Luis Maria, do not consume alcoholic beverages. In the cities, there might be a few Hindus who might partake of an alcoholic drink. Those who drink the local spirits are mainly Catholics or other Christians. It is the Catholic or Christian males that you see frequenting the taverns.

The *Census* data in Goa with regard to sex and age is:

Age	*Males*	*Females*
0 to 15	96,690	92,158
16 to 49	112,529	130,559
Over 49	32,596	40,511

The Hindu and Catholic population in Goa is half and half. Therefore, the total number of Catholic males who are over 16 and permitted by law to drink alcoholic beverages, is about 77,000. Now dividing 77,000 consumers of alcohol by the 471 taverns that exist in Goa, we have a ratio of 185 males per tavern! You are aware, my dear Luis Maria, that a considerable number of women also go to taverns to quench their thirst. Let us say that 10% of the female population over 16 goes to the tavern. This 10% of the female Catholic population over 16 who drinks, should be roughly 9,000. Adding these 9,000 females to 77,000 males, we have a total of 86,000 consumers of alcoholic beverages. And dividing these alcoholic consumers by the 417 taverns, we have 200 consumers of alcohol to a tavern!

These numbers, my dear Luis Maria, indicate that in Portuguese India we have a very sound and booming industry of taverns! These numbers also demonstrate that the population of Portuguese India has not yet learned how to produce sugar, has not yet learned how to make sugarcane jaggery, nor have they learned to establish a cement factory, but they have mastered the art of producing spirits from coconut palms! This industry, producing spirits from coconut palm sap has indeed made tremendous progress in our country.

I have been unappreciative of our government in accusing it of not introducing any industry into our country. In fact, in my last letter to you, my dear Luis Maria, I wrote that Portuguese India is a country without industries, an industrially backward country. Sorry, I sinned! Here is an industry that has made gigantic progress in our country. We are champions in this industry, among all the peoples of this planet!

23

AN ECONOMIC AND SOCIAL VIEW OF PORTUGUESE INDIA

"Man's value is in the few things he creates and not in the many possessions he amasses."

Kahil Gibran

Dedication

Your Excellency, I would like to have the honour to dedicate this book to Your Excellency. But I would not dare put your Excellency's name on the page, without your consent. If I did that, it would be presumptuous on my part. I am pleased to inform you that this book is my dedication to Your Excellency. That is all. I will not put my name on the cover, since everybody knows who the author is.

Often a writer of my level dedicates the fruits of his intellectual labour to another writer who has made a name for himself in the society. Or he dedicates the book to a prominent politician in the country. In this fashion, he obtains the preface to his work from the distinguished writer or politician. An endorsement of this nature enhances the value of his book which otherwise would have been neglected by the public. This is a strategy a writer uses, knowing that individuals in high places can help him to climb the ladder of his ambition in the distant or near future. But these are not my intentions, Your Excellency. Being the grandson of farmers, my only wish is to cultivate some banana plants in my orchard. And since in our small society everyone knows everybody,

I do not need letters of recommendation. My credentials are enough to present this book to the public.

Why do I dedicate this book to Your Excellency then? Because I find Your Excellency is the only competent entity to take into account what I am going to expose in this book. It is like when one has a toothache, one goes to a dentist, or when one has a headache, one goes to a pharmacy. At this very moment, Your Excellency, I am suffering acutely from intellectual torments because of a certain law. So I come knocking at Your Excellency's door, not for any other reason, but because Your Excellency is the one who promulgated such a law. I cannot go anywhere else. You are the only one who can help to alleviate my intellectual pain. In this sense, Your Excellency is my doctor.

The law which I am talking about, Your Excellency, is the Law of the Press. That is the law which has made my very existence unbearable. Your Excellency might argue that this law is neither oppressive nor tyrannical, but it is. With the benevolence of your heart, Your Excellency could have abolished this law. But instead, Your Excellency went to the lengths of meticulously explaining the duties and obligations of the Press. Obviously, Your Excellency kept silent about the rights of the Press. That may be because at that moment Your Excellency's mind might have been distracted by something more pressing than the rights of the Press. This syndrome of distraction is not uncommon. Even the great Homer would slip into a trance now and then.

Admitting that it was an oversight, Your Excellency should come out now and define the rights of the Press with the same zeal and clarity. This is the reason why I humbly dedicate this book to your Excellency.

To cite article no. 21 of *A Constituição Politica*, which says, "the Press exercises the character of a public function." By token of this article, which incidentally I support passionately, there is a decree no. 13,841 which stipulates that:

> "In case of a lack of higher qualifications or special training, the candidate for the chief editorship of a Press should be interviewed and judged fit for the said discipline".

Whereas, part 2 of article no. 4 says,

> "the purpose of this is to investigate whether the candidate has the moral ability and technical know-how to be the chief editor".

In order to consolidate the position of the periodical press better as an institution of public character, decree no. 23,228 was introduced. It establishes high standards for new periodicals that are published in the colonies. According to this decree, the publishing of the periodicals demanded a prior deposit, and stated that,

> "it should not be less than 50,000 *escudos* or equivalent with regard to a newspaper that is published four times a week or it should be less than 25,000 *escudos* or the equivalent with regard to others".

Later, this legislation was improved by passing decree no. 26,589, and article no. 20 of this decree says,

> "any publication, periodical or otherwise, provided it is subjected to the regime of the existing censor, can be established provided it recognizes the intellectual and moral ability of those responsible for the publication. Further, there should be sufficient proof that these individuals have the financial means to run the said enterprise. It is understood that if they do not submit the deposit and a financial guarantee from the bank, showing sufficient salary and wages for the correspondents, as well as funds for the expenses of collaboration, composition revision and printing within the period of six months, they will not have the possession of the firm".

In justifying the innovation of this ruling, a magistrate referring to the preamble of decree no. 126,589 said,

> "In truth we should be zealous in the elevation of our publication of periodicals because we have not authorised them to be familiar with the whims of public opinion, which is no doubt, of low calibre and responsible for the degeneration in society. Our publications should be free from doctrines and diverse ideologies".

These series of laws therefore kept careful vigilance on the social function of the Press. In doing so, they carefully laid solid foundations in the institution of its public character. They were incorporated in such a way into the body of the nation, that decree no. 23,228 made it obligatory to publish the official bulletins of the colonial Governor which ran in not more than two columns. Failing to publish them, the penalty was not less than 5,000 *escudos* or the equivalent of that amount.

The Press thus happens to have the honour of your original collaboration, being the Governor of the colony. In the Metropolis, the newspapers are sub-agents of *Diário do Governo.* In the colonies, they are the sub-agents of *Boletim Oficial.* These publications are at the service of the nation, semi-official organs for the interest of the State.

There is more to come. The Press, now assigned to be the semi-official voice of the State, was legally forced to condemn vociferously grave acts against the security of the State. The directorial general services of the Press censor in its circular of August 28, 1931 for the censor committees in Portugal, says, (and says it quite well):

> "One should not however, tolerate newspapers (except those that serve the nation) that exert a harmful influence on the leading papers of the nation and upon public opinion by applauding even indirectly or covertly violence and disorder, false ideology, or wanting to support the very criminal and absurd acts which the nation repudiates, the consequences of which can only be assessed by tears".

No man of sound mind and moral standard could measure up to this excellent orientation. At one time, the Press was regarded as an organ of public function, an organ to orient society in the right direction. But now, it is seen as a voice that creates panic with a tendency to corrupt the national conscience.

No doubt, all these impositions, both intellectual and moral are just, if we do not enter into a debate. But what I want to ask Your Excellency is where are the rights and privileges, and where are the material and moral benefits in these laws granted to the periodical Press in return? If the Press fulfils a public function, where are the sources of this function Your Excellency?

According to article no. 186 of *Reforma Administrativa Ultramarina*, no lawsuit, either civil or criminal, can be brought against public servants without the authorization of the government. This being so, I ask Your Excellency, how is it that the law permits the arrest of the chief editor of a newspaper while exercising his rights in the course of his duty, just like a public servant? Once again, let me quote to Your Excellency, article no. 21 of *A Constituição Política* which says that the Press has, "the function of a public character."

The public servant, Your Excellency, receives remuneration for his services rendered to the nation. But the journalist, who is also a public servant, renders his services gratuitously to the nation. Moreover, the journalist cannot exercise the function of a public character because of the various impediments put in his way. So, for making all these sacrifices for the good of the nation, why should not he have the right to certain privileges?

Besides, the Press has been consecrated as having the character of a public function. And the chief editor publishes his newspapers with money from his own pocket, and he is subjected to publishing literary works. They are the official bulletins from the colonial Governor, which do not exceed more than two columns of the newspaper. And let me remind your Excellency that the public servant (who often writes ungrammatically) does not use his own stationery for his briefs and notes as the journalists do. If the newspapers exercise the character of a public function, the logical deduction is that they should be exempted from postage as official publications are.

The decree no. 12,008 in article no. 8 establishes that in continental Portugal, all publications which are non-periodicals would send a sample copy to the libraries in Lisbon, Porto, Braga and the University of Coimbra. Decree no. 12,869 orders that colonial publications send a sample copy to *Arquivo Histórico Colonial*. In this regard, I ask Your Excellency why it should not be made obligatory that the editors of all publications also send a sample copy to the publications of the newspapers which have a social function to guide the moral and intellectual standards of the society.

This should be done with the collaboration of the departments of public administration. In my opinion, sample copies of all the books that are published in various fields and in constituencies should be sent to the Press for critical reviewing.

I could have given Your Excellency examples *ad infinitum* of this nature, but the two that I gave are sufficient. You are aware of many more that are in existence which were brought in with urgent necessity to impose on publications of periodicals as various duties of the Press.

Your circular dated August 28, 1931 in article no. 186 to *A Direcção Geral de Censura Imprensa* states: "a prudently guided newspaper can be a helpful tool for the services of the police."

But in practice when a journalist asks for information from the Public Service, he is not given any. When a journalist criticizes the wrongdoings of a government servant, no one bothers to take action about it. When the editor of a newspaper needs any information for publication, he is treated like an ordinary citizen, as if he were seeking that information for his own personal use, and hence he is asked to make a request on legal paper *(papel selado*). If the journalist has anything to say against the government servant, the government law is that the journalist must present his case through legal channels, signing it before a notary. Well then, Your Excellency, where is that "character of public function" that the laws attribute to the Press?

One of my compatriots, named Francisco Luis Gomes, while taking part in the parliamentary debate of January 17, 1866 in the *Camara dos Deputados* made this point. There is an opinion among some that the Press ought to have a special jurisdiction and they insist that the journalist should not exercise his rights as an individual. This is because his is the highest social mission. His is a political function. The voice that he raises is done not in his name, but he does it in the name of a party or the society. Thus the dialogue that he establishes is a dialogue of ideas with ideas. So a journalist has some power, some attributes to exert, to carry out some function, about his job description.

At that time, when Francisco Luis Gomes was talking about the Press, *Constituição Politica* did not recognise that the Press was an organ of public institution. In the name of rationalising the law of the Press, he was stating that because journalists are subjected to common rights, they are denied a special status as representatives of the society before the courts. I, in the same fashion, in the name of rationalising the law, come today to demand the privileges and rights of the periodical Press. These are inherent rights of the Press which enable it to exercise its public function. Once again, according to the new laws that Your Excellency has promulgated, the Press even now has "a function of public character." I do not understand as a chief editor of a periodical Press, how the Press could be subjected to the jurisdiction of common rights when the law explicitly says that the Press has "a function of public character". On the one hand, the periodical Press has been given the attribute of having a public character, but on the other hand the law refuses the guarantees, privileges and rights that are usually accorded to an organ of public function.

I would like to take the liberty to suggest to Your Excellency that article no. 186, which I have referred to, and also the privileges of articles nos. 190 and 197 *of Reforma Administrativa Ultramarina* be applied to the editors of newspapers. Taking into account that the Press exercises the "function of public character" judiciary assistance should be guaranteed for the Press, or the Press be exempted from expenses and postage. Either passively or actively, the ministry of Public Affairs should treat the Press with reason.

I could have given you more indications of this nature. From the little that I have said your Excellency's perceptiveness will uncover the rest.

I hope this plea meets with your approval.

I beg to remain,

Your humble servant,
J. L. de Loyola

(*Portugal e Colonias*, Bombay, 1938)

24

LARGE AND SMALL-SCALE INDUSTRIES IN PORTUGUESE INDIA

Besides the exports of coir fibre, which other industries can stand a chance of succeeding when introduced into Portuguese India? That is what you are wondering, my dear Luis Maria, is it not? You are naughty! You are afraid because your capital which is tied to the rural land properties, and which earns you interest, might go to pot if industries are introduced into our country. But aside from that, you are also mentally preparing to collect all your credits and declare bankruptcy. However, you are anxious to know beforehand how best you can invest your capital in such business schemes. You are anxious to know if you can get a return of 9% on the investment of your capital without any risks. I understand. You have a right to know these things. You are a prudent and careful man!

The industries which have a chance of succeeding in Portuguese India depend upon the accumulation of our own capital, my dear Luis Maria. We can divide them into two categories:

(a) Industries that operate on steam or electricity and need technical directors and skilled workers.

(b) Industries with simple machinery, and which do not require technical directors nor skilled workers.

In the first category, I would put two industries, a sugar factory and a cement factory. In my opinion they have a chance of succeeding in this country. For example, Portuguese India consumes

5 million *ceiras* of sugar (excluding sugar imported in the district of Daman for the production of alcohol) and imports 3 to 4 million *ceiras* of cement every year. This imported sugar is worth Rs. 6 lakhs and the cement Rs. 1½ lakhs. Sugar has reached its capacity of consumption in our country, and cement too is used more and more in construction and as the years go by, there will be more demand for cement in the country.

Since Portuguese India consumes 3 million *ceiras* of sugar, I think we can afford to have one or two sugar factories in our country. In British India there are about 130 sugar factories and they are modern. They produce about 600,000 tons of sugar, sometimes more and sometimes less.

The great problem in our case is that we do not have sugarcane fields. Our agricultural land is all allocated to paddy cultivation. Now, would it be possible to convert some of our land to sugarcane plantations in order to feed one or two sugar factories? Here is the rub. As you might be aware, sugarcane cultivation requires a lot of water, not less than one cubic foot of water per acre, ten times more than paddies take for the same area. The existing reservoirs that capture rainwater can hardly irrigate our paddy fields. So the existing reservoirs would be inadequate to irrigate sugarcane fields.

Nowadays a lot of progress has been made in hydraulic agriculture. In my opinion, we can solve the water irrigation problem by installing artesian wells, which are becoming common in British India. When France was colonising Algeria, the lack of water was their main concern. Jules Duval pioneered the idea of constructing artesian wells there. By 1909 there were 40 artesian wells between Chott Melghir and the city of Tongourt, a distance of 120 kilometres, thus giving three wells per kilometre. The English did the same in Australia. Australia had vast arid plains, without any vegetation. But they solved the problem, and with happy results, by introducing artesian wells.

Such results encouraged engineer Armando Xavier da Fonseca to approve enthusiastically the introduction of artesian wells in the archipelago of Cape Verde. He writes:

> "The hydraulics would help us not only to use artesian wells, but also on the islands of S. Tiago and Santo Antão where there is always water even during the worst of the dry season, we could use hydraulic pumps at diverse points of the streams, pumping water to altitudes, where flood hardly reaches" (*Portugal em Africa, Suplemento Colonial*, 16, no. 199).

From then to now, a lot has happened!

In British India hydraulics has made astonishing progress. The Ganges Plain, which has subsoil springs, has made great progress in hydraulic irrigation. In the United Provinces by 1929, they had 400 artesian wells, 200 were big ones and the other 200 were small. The big ones use electric pumps for irrigation, and the smaller ones draw water by using Persian wheels pulled by oxen. The study made of 71 artesian wells, built in 1928-29, gives us an idea of irrigation expenses. Irrigation expenses per acre would shift between 12 *annas* and Rs. 2½, including 15% interest on capital and depreciation on machinery. The expenses to install these wells were not too much either. They came to Rs. 36 to Rs. 884 for each well.

In 1932, 223 more artesian wells were installed in the United Provinces, 35 of these wells had a diameter of 5 to 10 inches, and the remaining 188 had a diameter of three and three-eight inches. In 1933 studies with estimates were made to install 327 more artesian wells, 47 of these wells would have a diameter of 5 to 10 inches and the rest of them would have lesser diameters.

In Punjab, between 1928 and 1929, they built 519 artesian wells with various dimensions of diameter and in 1932 they built another 276 artesian wells and still 173 more artesian wells were built in 1933.

The department of Agriculture created permanent bodies in each province to study and survey the land in order to facilitate the construction of artesian wells. In the United Provinces in 1932 they had 1,499 surveys and in 1933 they had 1,714 surveys of this nature. 71% of these surveys yielded satisfactory results. The

Province of Punjab too had surveys of this nature. In 1932 they had 2,404 surveys and in 1935 they had 3,565 surveys. In this last case, 72% were with successful results.

The hydroelectric section of the department of Irrigation Services in the United Provinces, has a big project on its hands which it is going to complete in the current year of 1938. According to this project, the State is going to build 1,353 artesian wells, irrigating 350,000 acres of wheat fields and 150,000 acres of sugarcane fields. The estimate for this project is about Rs. 105 lakhs.

The artesian wells have brought astonishing results in agriculture in British India, and I believe, my dear Luis Maria, that we too in Portuguese India can introduce sugarcane on a large scale. The paddies are no longer remunerative. I am of the opinion that the introduction of sugarcane in the country would be economically advantageous, and hence, a part of our community lands should be allocated for sugarcane cultivation. You might be aware, in Bengal, jute cultivation is slowly being replaced by sugarcane. It is calculated that in 125,000 acres of this area during the last few years, have been used for sugar plantation, in this province.

As we stand today, to establish a sugar industry in our country, without sugarcane plantations, would be something big to accomplish. It would require lakhs of rupees, a capital which you do not have. Hence, in this case, we have to raise this capital by creating a limited company with stocks. The same process can be applied to raise the capital for a cement factory.

In your case, my dear Luis Maria, I understand that you are not interested in a limited company with stock and the complications that go with it. I know what you are interested in. You want a small industry, financed by your own capital rather than by raising capital through shares. If that is so, how much capital do you intend to put into an industry of this nature? Maybe Rs. 20,000? Or maybe Rs. 30,000? In order to be on the safe side, let us open the statistics on imports. That should give us an idea which industry would be suitable for your range of capital, which would give you a secure investment and bring in 9% profit or more. The statistics on imports show us, my dear Luis Maria, that we import yearly a lot of umbrellas. In 1933 we imported the following kinds of umbrellas:

	Numbers	*Value in Rs.*
Silk umbrellas	1,015	1,000
Cotton umbrellas	31,659	46,750
Waterproof umbrellas	214	304

We will not take into account silk umbrellas, nor waterproof umbrellas. But the statistics show that we import 31,659 cotton umbrellas, valued at Rs. 46,750.

Besides these imports of umbrellas, many more umbrellas come into the country through Customs, brought into the country by the people coming from British India. You might have observed, my dear, Luis Maria, that any individual from our country going to British India, on his return, brings at least two or three umbrellas, one for his wife, one for his children and one for his neighbour. These umbrellas escape Customs duty, because the one who brings them into the country passes one each to his travelling acquaintances, collecting them after crossing the border. Let us suppose, 15 umbrellas per day come into the country in this way. But actually, it should be more than 15, because we have two kinds of entry points, sea and land. So in the course of a year about 5,500 umbrellas come into the country. Now we will add these 5,500 umbrellas to the yearly import of umbrellas brought in by the merchants. So the actual import comes to 36,500 cotton umbrellas.

Now my dear, Luis Maria, if you make up your mind to establish an umbrella factory to produce 36,500 umbrellas, umbrellas the country imports from British India, you would end up making a yearly profit of at least Rs. 12,000. And to establish this business venture, let us suppose you have invested Rs. 20,000. This brings you a 55% return on your investment! This kind of return you do not get by lending money on interest, you know that, because you make your living by lending your money at 9%. Do you think that

I am joking with you? Not at all. Let me assure you that this is not mere fanciful thinking. I am going to demonstrate it to you.

These expenses to produce 3,000 umbrellas of inferior quality are overrated. To produce 3,000 umbrellas, according to me, could not cost more than Rs. 1,500. In that case, to produce one umbrella would cost 8 *annas*. But let us stick to our original estimate, it is always good to be liberal.

Selling one umbrella for a rupee, you would make Rs. 3,000, and after subtracting the production expenses (Rs. 2,000), the profit would be Rs. 1,000 per month.

The production of 3,000 umbrellas would cost per month:

(a)	cotton material	Rs. 450
(b)	rods and iron gear	Rs. 300
(c)	bamboo, wood, handles etc.	Rs. 500
(d)	two carpenters' salaries	Rs. 60
(e)	two blacksmiths' salaries	Rs. 60
(f)	two tailors' salaries	Rs. 50
(g)	two painters, salaries (to varnish)	Rs. 50
(h)	paints and varnish	Rs. 50
(i)	packing material	Rs. 30
(j)	one manager's salary	Rs. 90
(k)	administration expenses	Rs. 150
(l)	rent for the building	Rs. 60
(m)	other expenses	Rs. 150
	Total	Rs. 2,000

Your mouth is watering now, is it not?

This venture sounds very successful, a sure thing. You invest Rs. 20,000 and you are sure to make a profit of Rs. 12,000. If that is so, you are asking me now, why did not anyone so far start an umbrella factory?

They are afraid of the competition. Do you not know what happened when machines for unhusking rice came into the country?

The first man who imported rice husking machines into our country was doing good business. Seeing that he was doing well, others imported rice husking machines, and soon there were too many of these machines in this country, one in each ward. This was unhealthy competition!

An umbrella factory in our country might meet the same fate. Like rice husking machines, you might see umbrella factories mushrooming in Portuguese India. Such a competition is disastrous and makes no economic sense. Portuguese India has room only for one or two umbrella factories, and not more. But our greed is blind. Our spirit of competition is unreasonable. No one wants to make a study of the statistics of imports, no one cares to see what imports we consume. But when you put up an industry, and they see you are prosperous, everyone wants to go into the same business. Without legislative protection in this country, it is not easy to establish an industry, however small.

In order to install industries in our country, the industry owners should be given a monopoly over their manufactured goods for 5, 10 or 15 years.

In the meantime, the legislators should study the consumption habits of the people, and only then should another industry of the same type be allowed to come into existence, and only if it has a chance to succeed. Without such procedures, to start an industry in Portuguese India is suicidal. This is the reason why many are reluctant to start any industrial venture. Because of this, my dear Luis Maria, we are dependent on our neighbouring country. Our capital, for this reason, is shy and non-participant. Our capital runs away from all initiatives and is suspicious of all undertakings.

Besides an umbrella factory, one can invest in many other small-scale industries, requiring capital within the range of Rs. 20,000 or Rs. 30,000. But for these industries to come into existence it would require protective legislation, giving one a monopoly for 5, 10 or 15 years. This period of years would give them a chance to become established and make profit. However, if a rival industry were to be established before this period ended, it would be fatal to the economy. Allowing many hunters to hunt on the same hunting ground when game is scarce, makes no sense. So it would be better, my dear Luis Maria to keep your capital engaged where it is. A cure in this case, is worse than the disease.

Customs statistics indicate that Portuguese India imports the following articles, some from British India and some from other countries, either Europe or Japan.

Here, then, are some of the small-scale industries in which you can invest your capital. If you were to invest in any one of these industries, I am sure it would bring you 25% profit on your investment. But our legislators, my dear Luis Maria, though thoughtful in protecting industries in the Portuguese colonies of Africa, have not given any thought even now to bringing in incentives to industrialise the primary resources of this colony.

Imports in 1932

	Quantity		*Value (Rs.)*
Gambolins and vales	88,132	*ceiras*	42,161
Soap	415,262	*ceiras*	23,411
Toilet soap	21,015	*ceiras*	32,849
Fine and thick mats	77,232	*ceiras*	34,071
Quality shoes	2,302	pairs	11,270
Non-quality shoes	67,772	pairs	52,645
Cotton caps (big & small sizes)	7,419	numbers	1,662
Woollen caps	4,909	numbers	1,226
Caps with wool & cotton	2,220	numbers	950
Silk caps	2,196	numbers	1,347
Matches	120,594	gross	88,330

The economic neglect in Portuguese India is responsible for killing any initiative in an entrepreneur. On the other hand, our exports are taxed. Coconut exports are taxed, mango exports are taxed, salt exports are taxed, betel nut exports are taxed and so on. This does not make economic sense. S. Evelyn Thomas in *Elements of Economics* (4th ed., p. 613) says,

> "Export duties are imposed chiefly for revenue, but only in very special cases can they succeed in exacting a contribution from the foreigner. This may occur when the exporting country possesses an almost complete monopoly of the supply of the commodity taxed, when its producers are in effective combination to maintain export prices, and when there is a strong demand in the importing country. In the absence of these conditions, the duty will tend to be paid by the home exporter. The foreigner is not likely to pay the tax if he can obtain supplies elsewhere in the world market, if he can use substitutes, or if he can reduce his demand. Trade will therefore cease or seriously diminish".

In no way, would I want to diminish the importance of tax imposed by Customs upon our exports. But this Customs tax in our country goes against the very principles of economics. It does not make economic sense. How can industries flourish in a country which does not understand the elementary principles of economics?

It is a fact that England imposed an export tax on coal in 1901 to meet South African War expenses. It is also true that British India imposed a tax on the export of opium to China. But in the case of England, the export tax on coal made economic sense, because England had a monopoly on coal. This is not so in the case of Portuguese India, even with regard to our exports of salt and betel nuts. We do not have the luxury of being the only producers of these commodities. In the case of opium export in British India, they are in a better position to impose tax on this commodity, than we are to impose an export tax on coconuts. Our situation is totally different from theirs. We are not exclusive exporters of these products. There are other countries who export these products. In the buying market there is fierce competition, and our products have to compete with those of other countries.

The tax on exports could be justified in the following two hypothetical situations:

(a) when the exporter country has a monopoly over the merchandise in which case, the tax will fall on the importing country; and

(b) when the exporting merchandise is no longer beneficial to the national economy, i.e., the State has to push this merchandise out of the country for export. This is based on the economic system called mercantilism.

S. Shield Nicholson in *Elements of Political Economy* (2nd edition, p. 479) writes:

> "The mercantilists imposed special heavy duties on certain exports, e.g. on the raw material of manufacture and on the instrument of production. These duties, however, were intended to check exportations rather than to yield revenue and in the extreme case, which was very common, they were intentionally prohibitive".

Portuguese India, as we have observed, does not have a monopoly on its exports. So the export tax in this case does not fall on the importing country but on the national producers of the products and this diminishes production profits. These taxes are not constructive, and legislation of this nature puts constraints on exports. Then, tell me, my dear Luis Maria, what kind of criteria does our fiscal policy follow? What are the grounds for these taxes? It is obvious, my dear Luis Maria, that we do not have any national economic policy at all! This indicates that the only preoccupation of our State is to generate revenue, anywhere possible and in any way possible. It does not care if it destroys agriculture. It does not care if it destroys industries and it does not care if it destroys the populace.

It is my opinion that in this country, we can establish some industries and produce our requirements, instead of importing them. We have already looked into some of these industries which have a potential to succeed in this country.

Let us consider a soap industry, for example. We import soap to the value of Rs. 123,000. This is not right. Our country has all the necessary raw materials to produce soap, and that too in abundance. In British India the soap industry is now well-established. They not only have big soap industries but also cottage industries. There are families who make soap at home. In this way, earning a little extra, these families supplement their income. To establish a soap cottage industry does not require a huge amount of capital. With Rs. 200, one can set up a small soap industry at home. And it is not difficult to learn soap making.

Or take another industry, like the manufacture of matches. It stands a chance of succeeding in our country. We annually consume matches in this country worth up to Rs. 88,000. Why can we not establish a match-making factory in our country? Why do we have to import matches from Sweden? British India no longer depends on other countries for matches. They make matches in their country for their own consumption. If they can do it, we can too, and I see no reason for us not to succeed.

Portuguese India has excellent craftsmen. Our shoes are the best. The Indo-Portuguese shoemaker is very skilful, much better than the Chinese shoemaker who dominates the shoe industry in British India. And in the meantime, we buy non-quality shoes from other countries to the tune of Rs.½ lakh! Why do we import shoes, my dear Luis Maria? Why? Because in our country there is no legislation to protect our national industries. In this case, the imports on raw materials, which should have been excluded from taxation are taxed 14%. This sort of legislation puts a damper on the shoe industry at home. And the exporters of shoes to our country also buy 20% *ad valorem* rights. A pair of shoes in this case, including both quality and non-quality, should have been taxed at least Re. 1 or Rs. 2. Non-quality shoes, 67,772 pairs, imported into Portuguese India in 1932, were of wool with crepe rubber soles, made in Japan. I ask you, my dear Luis Maria, why on earth should we give preferential treatment to Japanese imports, when our shoemakers are vegetating in idleness?

We should declare war against Japanese imports into our country, exactly because their products are cheap! The flooding of cheap goods of inferior quality into the markets is a threat to all people, mostly to our people. This is one of the reasons we are industrially backward. Our handmade products cannot compete with their machine-made products, because they produce them in large quantities.

My dear Luis Maria, I can see you laughing at my ideas on the sly. You are thinking that my economic ideas are outmoded. You think that I want to return to the times of Colbert. Or you might think that I want to go back to the times of the Marquis of Pombal, when he ordered the farmers to pull out vines planted at Tejo, Vouga and Mondego and grow cereals instead.

Colbertism, my dear Luis Maria, is an economic system. It advocates that each nation should be a self-sufficient economic entity, evaluating its resources and regulating its own commerce and industry. I understand very well that Portuguese India does not have all the requirements necessary for economic entity. What I am proposing is that certain small-scale industries that have an opportunity to succeed in our country, should be given a chance to get established.

This can be achieved by bringing in legislation to protect these industries. We should stop importing products from outside, when we have them in the country. The outside goods that come into our country are sold cheaper than our native goods. Such an attitude does not give an impetus to our industries. In fact, such imports kill our native industries. This, then, exerts a disastrous influence on our country, a country which depends solely on agriculture! You, Luis Maria, above all, who understand various aspects of economics, simply cannot dismiss this economic aspect. Frederic List in *Systeme National d'Economie Politique*, as you know, talked about a mixed economy, agriculture and industry being complementary to each other. In Portugal, Duarte Ribeiro de Macedo, also had the same idea, when he said,

> "these two means of subsistence, agriculture and industry, help each other reciprocally. You cannot have many farmers in a country, where there is no trade and where trade flourishes, there are plenty." (*Discurso sobre a introdução das Artes' em Portugal*, 1675).

In the same vein, José Acurio das Neves says:

> "A country which has only an agricultural economy will never reach its peak, without the help of trade and manufacturing. On the other hand, a country which has established its factories, will see increased production in its agriculture. This kind of experience, you will see all over in Azeitão, Cascáis, Alcobaça, Covilhã, and above all Marinha Grande. This truth is very evident" (*Variedades*, vol. 1, p. 11)

Cauwes once expounded the theory that in order to make profits, there must be either plenty of capital and cheap labour, or the land revenues and the price of the products should be raised. Sometimes, given both these factors and a dense population, an essential element, the industries tend to flock close to the site of agricultural production. In this way, capital and fertilizers would be plentiful, creating a strong demand for agricultural products, and the price of the first would pay the cost of the other, thus making a profit (*Precis de l'Economie Politique*, vol. 1, ch. 1, 1878).

Dr. José Frederico Laranjo, a Portuguese economist following Cauwes' thoughts, wrote:

> "This is the reason why nations which have no industries have little agriculture, Portugal for example" (*Princípios de Economia Política*, p. 47).

Here they are, my dear Luis Maria, the reasons why I want legislative intervention. It is because I want to promote the growth of industries in our country. This can be done by exempting taxes on imported raw materials, by abolishing taxes on exports, by enacting high taxes on foreign products, products which we can easily produce in our country.

As you are aware, the population of Portuguese India is increasing. According to the *Census of February 1931*, our population was 579,969 and distributed in this order:

District of Goa	505,281
District of Daman	58,001
District of Diu	16,687

This shows an increase of 48,038 as compared to the *Census of March 1921*. The population in Portuguese India has a yearly average increase of 4,804. This phenomenon should not surprise anyone. In countries where many people emigrate, the population has a tendency to increase. The opinion among various economists, even those belonging to different schools, is that the emigration takes place in order to increase the population of the country. So, Leroy-Beaulieu is of the opinion that as the emigration increases, so does the population (Marnoco e Souza, *Sciencia Social*, p. 739).

This increase in population, is it good or is it bad?

An increase in population has been considered throughout time as a fountain of progress in societies. Herbert Spencer writes:

> "From the beginning this pressure of population has been the proximate cause of progress. It produced the original diffusion of the race. It compelled men to abandon predatory habits and take to agriculture. It led to the clearing of the earth surface. It forced men into the social state ... and developed the social sentiments. It has stimulated progressive improvement in production and has increased skill and intelligence." (*Principles of Biology*, vol. 2, New York, 1910, p. 536)

The increase of population in Portuguese India has not given us the best agricultural culture, as it should have, nor has it given us any industrial development. But in the near or distant future we will realize that the laws of economics are not fiction.

A country with a vision for the future will not wait for the economic laws to fall into place. A country with a vision will not tarry to bring in the necessary measures to give impetus to a certain number of industries within the country. The growth of population and the growth of industries should go hand in hand, like parallel lines. To hope that industrial growth will follow the pressure of economic laws, to hope that industrial growth will come by itself with the automatic growth of the population, is to abdicate the responsibilities of governance.

25

THE FICTITIOUS PROSPERITY OF PORTUGUESE INDIA

Ramsay Macdonald, a keen and shrewd observer of social phenomena, wrote, referring to the rural population of British India:

> "Better clothes are being worn, cigarettes are being consumed, shoes are more general, umbrellas are becoming more common. The people's wants, too many of them debased, are becoming more costly to meet. As evidence of increased prosperity, I place little reliance upon such facts. These things no more show prosperity than expensive weddings or extravagant funerals." (Ramsay Macdonald, *The Awakening of India*, pp. 177-178).

One could say that Macdonald was referring to the people of Portuguese India, mostly when he alludes to expensive weddings and extravagant funerals.

Portuguese India is showing off a fictitious prosperity. The people dress well, live in better comfort, consume more products, mostly imported ones. The Customs Department makes more money, and the government coffers are filled to the brim with gold. But with all this show of opulence, the colony is at the razor's edge of an economic disaster.

The author had no intention of writing a serious book. He just wanted to write a few pages which could be read without boring the reader.

The Italians have a proverb: *Tanto buono che vale niente.* Coming to the last page of this book, if the reader understands the writer's intentions for writing this book, he might talk about it to the others. That itself would be an accomplishment of the writer's goal.

In the pages of this book there are printing and grammatical errors. I did not correct either of them. It is also possible, there could be many mistakes in the statistics and in the calculations. I did not have time to read the galley proofs when the book was in the printing process. I have neither time nor patience to go into the posthumous examination of this book, which is already out in print. I will say like Pilate: "*Quod scripsi, scripsi*".

But I have to clear up this error: the statistics of import and export that appear on page 65, were taken by mistake from *Anuário do Estado da India*, 1932, p. 518 (the chart that includes the imports of gold and silver and bonds) instead of from the chart on p. 519, which gives statistics of import and export, without the inclusion of the imports of gold, silver and bonds.

26

BEING CONSTRUCTIVE IN THE COMMUNITY

There are many opportunities for any human being with a will to be useful to the community of his country. For example, a person who has the capability to construct ideas of usefulness should do so and then discuss those ideas among his compatriots. Spread among your fellow men the knowledge of science, the arts and religion. If it is not in you to do so, either plant a tree. This too is being useful and constructive to the community in which you live. If you do not want to plant a tree, teach a child to read. This too, is a way of being constructive and useful to the community. Bring the notions of being useful to the illiterate and ignorant and by doing so, you are building the community. One is indeed fortunate to know more than others, but to share learning with the less fortunate is being useful and constructive to the community.

To instil kindness, gentility and Christian brotherhood into the souls of our fellow men is being useful and constructive to the community. So go on building and continue sowing. Seeds will sprout into either plants or trees, and yield accordingly. Likewise, thoughts stimulated by our souls will blossom into the traits that define our characters.

The degree of our society's progress depends upon the intellectual and moral level of all segments of the population. It is not so important to have an intellectual elite nor is it so important to have a cultured class, a large number of literate people. But, what is necessary is among all the segments of our population, irrespective of whether they are educated or ignorant, rich or poor, man or woman, *bhatkar* or *mundkar*, there should be a spiritual link between us, connecting us all together, as one people. That is what is important.

Without being egoists or fanatics we should nurture the soul of our nation. Step by step, without respite, we must go on building. This is a long road and we should not be faint-hearted.

Reader, if you are a *bhatkar*, go and visit your *mundkar* at the end of the day. Talk to him and his family. At your convenience, teach him the basic principles of hygiene and instil in him the advantages of cleanliness in the household. Find ways to lift up his soul!

If you are a Christian and a Catholic at heart, call upon your friends and neighbours who belong to that faith and propose to them the need of a small garden. The garden can be within your compound or the compound of the parish. That way, in the chapel of your ward or in the church of your village, there always will be some roses at the feet of Our Lady.

If indeed you love your village why do you not propose forming a small club. Ask all the villagers to come and help to build such a garden. If you love your village, why do you not propose building a small reading room. If you love your village, why do you not propose building playing fields for the youth. These foundations, laid through the participation of people working together, might seem insignificant in the purpose they serve today. But as time goes by they will grow and be very effective.

All these little things contribute to the progress of a nation. To make these dreams into realities, we need an upsurge of goodwill within each of us. If we have that, we will care less for financial assistance from the State or from the municipalities.

One of the greatest weaknesses in our way of thinking is the inability to depend upon ourselves. We are in the habit of complaining disgracefully about others for not lifting a finger to help us.

We direct all our energies to debating about what the State and the municipalities could have accomplished, should have accomplished and should accomplish. But we never explore our own potential to accomplish our own goals. We have to free ourselves from this mentality. It retards our progress. If we want our communities to succeed, we should ask little from the State or the municipalities, but instead ask ourselves what we can do, that we are not doing, to better our communities.

The rich or the poor, the humble people or the elite, landlords or workers, the gentlemen or the common people, all of us, whatever be our station in life, each of us within the sphere of our actions, must help each other to build a better tomorrow, a nation of the future. If each of us were to take that first step individually and start doing the tasks that we have worked out, we would have laid the foundation for the progress of this land. The builders of a nation are not only statesmen, reformers, scientists, philosophers or creative artists, but all of us, including the unknown old man who teaches religion to the village children in the absence of a priest.

Vasco Dias

(*Portugal e Colonias*, May 19, 1937)

27

GARDENS

Intellectual development without the blossoming of the soul is imperfect education. Men might have their intellectual faculties disciplined to discern various abstract concepts and they might know how to read and write, but that alone is not enough. Equal importance should be given to cultivating the aesthetic values in children and adults, to elevate their souls. Man is both an intellectual and a spiritual being. If a man wants to live to the fullness of life, besides knowledge of the sciences, economics or social sciences, he must be sensitive to the objects that surround him. Being one with the rhythm of the universe, he should learn to cherish nature, its colours, its sounds, its very harmony.

We, who are the tillers of the soil, should know this better than anybody else. The countryside with its trees and flowers should be objects of our love. Though we till the ground and raise crops to produce food for the sustenance of our bodies, we, as a rural people should also come to appreciate agriculture not only because it nourishes our bodies but also because it soothes our souls. To till and fructify the land is an art. It is an occupation which is more poetic and more spiritual than any other occupation. A farmer who tends his fields can reap spiritual benefits too, if he knows how.

In Portuguese India we have many schools, primary schools, secondary schools and higher secondary schools. We have Portuguese schools, English schools, Marathi schools and Gujarati schools. All these institutions of learning are geared towards the development of our intellects. We want our children to become physicians, erudite scholars, scientists and writers and yet, to this very day, we have not any school that would teach our children the aesthetic values, values to enrich our aesthetic sensitivity.

A nation without gardens is like a sky without stars. A man in that environment, unaware of the beauty of flowers, develops an intellect void of imagination, becoming a conceited fellow and a man without kindness.

How can Indo-Portuguese people claim to love agriculture if they are not touched by the beauty of the land that surrounds them? We cultivate our lands without joy in our souls. We cultivate our lands without the flutter of happiness in our hearts.

We cultivate our lands because that is the only way we know how to earn our daily bread. We cultivate our lands because we do not know other alternatives for earning our living. A farmer tills his lands without any joy in his heart. A farmer tills his lands bemoaning his fate and, casting his eyes to the heavens, blasphemes against God for having been made a farmer.

We need gardens and lots of them to awaken the spirits of the Indo-Portuguese people so that they can experience within their souls an aesthetic appreciation for the beauty of things.

Gardens in the schoolyards, gardens in the compounds of churches and chapels and gardens in front of our houses. School children learning to tend gardens and the priests instilling in their congregation the appreciation of the beauty of nature. And then, in our homes at the feet of the crucifix or at the panel of Sacred Heart of Jesus we should have flowerpots blooming.

Each of our villages has a magnificent church and inside each one, there are beautiful artefacts made of gold, silver candlesticks and chandeliers but do we see a flowerpot in bloom at the feet of Our Lady? Or on that small altar where we have enthroned the panel of the Sacred Heart of Jesus in our homes, do we have fresh flowers?

To have gardens is to enhance our culture. To have gardens is to enrich our creativity. In the quietude of a garden one can peacefully contemplate how to accomplish noble deeds and watching the beauty of the flowers, one can fill one's heart with joy. Gardens bring out the best in men. In the attractive environment of flowers, it has been observed, man has a better attitude towards his work, and produces more. Sad thoughts are driven away and joy enters his heart. He dreams uplifting dreams and thoughts of a profound nature waft into his mind. This marvel holds equally true for both the man of solitude as well as all of us, the people.

It has been observed that houses with gardens are often inhabited by people who are happy both intellectually and spiritually, and with strong aspirations. People without gardens, on the other hand, are often depressed and sad people. They are indifferent to and skeptical of, the life around them, trusting no one, doubting everything.

Let us, then, awaken in the hearts of the Indo-Portuguese a love for flowers, stir in the hearts of Indo-Portuguese an appreciation for the beauty of colours, kindle in them the very love of nature. Flowers, flowers, flowers everywhere; flowers in the cities and flowers in the villages; flowers blooming in school gardens and flowers blooming in church gardens; flowers in the living room, flowers on the work desk and flowers on the dining table; flowers for the sick, flowers for the healthy, flowers for the rich, flowers for the poor. Flowers for everybody!

People who love flowers and are enchanted by the beauty of nature have a refined taste for things artistic. Japan is one of those countries, whose people have a natural taste for the aesthetic in their souls, and they can create graceful colour combinations, as if they are born to it. This creative activity is spontaneous and this is what is called the learning of arts.

Vasco Dias

(*Portugal e Colonias*, August 21, 1937)

28

EMANCIPATING WOMEN

The truth is, the people in British India, our neighbours, are indeed making a great deal of progress in various fields of human enterprise. But that is not the case in Portuguese India. In Portuguese India, we are marching backwards in the activities of human life, be it economic, political or social. Portuguese India is not moving upwards but sliding downwards and that is painful.

The Indo-Portuguese population because of the incentives in the field of education and other intellectual areas should have progressed in the various spheres of life. But, that is not happening. They are going downhill. And it is not hard to understand why.

Once, this small country had a sound economy and the people of this land, being conscious of their political rights, fiercely defended them. Great men were born in this small country, who dedicated their lives to the causes of the people. They exemplified honest politics. They were the pride of their people. But today, there is decadence in politics.

The people in the villages, who were once prosperous and happy, have no self-esteem left in them. In their households there is sadness and despondency where once there was joy and comfort. Agriculture, which was their pride and source of their income, is dead. Small industries, which once provided economic security to these people, no longer exist. Professions such as journalism, law, politics, which were once commanded by men of integrity, have fallen into the hands of small-minded people.

Once, in this land, lived a people who passionately upheld their dignity and with zeal, defended their civic rights. But members of today's generation are educated to be servile and phony. They would sell anyone for a pittance. They have shamefully given up the principles of honesty, which were once the honour and pride of this race.

At the moment, however, we are not going to investigate this plight. It is enough to know that it exists. We, who should have been marching towards progress, are regressing instead; whereas our neighbours, many of whom are immersed in superstition and obscurantism, have overtaken us, and boast of being civilised. What lesson can we learn from our regression and our neighbour's march to progress?

If one were to study very carefully the evolution of the present day societies, or the progress of any nation, it will be noticed, definitely, that it came about with the intellectual emancipation of women. If women are kept imprisoned in the environment of submissiveness, and if they are kept from addressing national problems because of our belief that they have to be a symbol of respect and that they have to uphold the future of our race, then, we are doing an injustice to them.

The status that is bequeathed upon women, makes them apathetic to the various ideological movements that are streaming into the bosom of their own society. They lack intellectual curiosity to understand the revolutionary changes that are taking place outside their country. Keeping women away from these ideas is suicidal for the progress of the people.

It is essential to any nation, if that nation wants to march towards progress, that women should participate in the affairs of their government. They should acquaint themselves with various political ideas and philosophical thoughts, the integral elements of the nation. Being cognizant of the changes that are taking place in the world today and adjusting to new concepts, they should take part in bringing in reforms to the different public institutions.

In a country where women are treated either as passive animals and made to toil in the kitchen like slaves or like objects of decoration, hiding their obesity, dressed in silk and velvet, and are not invited to participate in the betterment of society, such attitudes towards women are unrewarding to a nation that has dreams to fulfill.

The political societies, that we call nations, are a body of families. If the wife is not a participant in the process of decision-making within the family, because of mistaken ideas about the respect owed to her, then that family lags behind in its progress. On the other hand, in a family where the wife participates in the decision-making process, running her household and making decisions with respect to the education of her children, that family succeeds. In the same fashion, if women are kept away from national problems, because of the mistaken notion of the amount of respect that should be conferred upon them, the progress that we dream of as a nation, will never materialise. To cut off the intellectual curiosity of women is like isolating them like hermits. Keeping them from participating in parliamentary debates, is to switch off the destiny of the nation. And that is not just.

The world that we live in today is not the same world of fifty years ago. The world has changed, and so have attitudes. We cannot dream of human progress by relegating women to the kitchen, nor can we assign them to a seat before a piano in the parlour. We have given them the role of domestic animals. They are either beasts of burden or objects of decoration, like Chinese vases.

In Portuguese India, women's education is disgustingly behind. No women ever take any interest in the activities of the nation. Their only mission in life is to give birth to sons and if they are poor, they work like black slaves. If they are rich, they doll themselves up, go to church, ballets, cinemas and to other similar amusements.

Women never concern themselves with solving national problems; nor do they participate in any civic activities. They have no opinion on their town's politics. Just as we are unaware of the things that are taking place on the planet Mars, likewise, women know nothing that goes on in their own country. They voice no opinion and they have no vote. Aside from the superficial education they receive, which is there simply to enhance their role as women of noble birth, they are too insufficiently educated to carry any weight in the decision-making process involved in solving the social problems that their country faces.

Bring women out of their closets and ask them to address the responsibilities of the nation. Awaken their interest to the civic issues and ask them to come and debate them before the public; and listening to the people's opinion, let them engage in the decision-making process. In this way, they will be part and parcel of the ideas that tick within the nation's bosom. If we do not want them to be sepulchered, bring women out of their closets, and give them a chance to participate in the economic, intellectual and moral development of this country.

Vasco Dias.

(*Portugal e Colonias*, April 30, 1938)

GLOSSARY

bhatkar: village land (palmgrove) owner
comunidade: village community
Conselho da Fazenda: Treasury Council
confraria: church confraternity
contucares: village servants
Cruzados: a Portuguese coin (originally of gold) in value equal to 400 *réis*
ganvkar: member of the village community
Infante de Sagres: Prince Henry the Navigator of Portugal established a school of navigation at Sagres from which voyages of exploration set out which eventually led to the creation of the Portuguese overseas empire.
khandi: measure equivalent to twenty maunds or 480 lbs. wt.
mão: a measure in use in Goa, lit. "a hand".
mundkar: bonded labourer generally resident in palmgroves
New Conquests: territories in the interior of Goa which were conquered by the Portuguese after the initial conquests known as Old Conquests.
Praças do Norte: Portuguese possessions in north west India (Bassein, Daman and Diu)
Quartel de policia: police barracks
Ranes: feudal lords of Satari who resisted Portuguese rule
real: the lowest denomination of currency in Goa (pl. *réis*)
Terreiro do Paço: the address of the Portuguese Parliament or Cortes
xerafim: a silver coin used in Goa with an equivalence of 5 *tangas* or 300 *réis*

NOTES

1. Vasco Dias and F. de Lemos were pen names used by José Inácio de Loyola.

2. *Estado da India*: Goa, Daman and Diu, as well as pockets of Dadra and Nagar-Haveli, were known as *Estado da India* during the Portuguese colonial period. Goa, which is on the west coast of India in the Konkan region, had a varied history until it was conquered by Governor Afonso de Albuquerque, on November 25, 1510.

   In the *Estado da India*, during the process of colonisation, the Portuguese brought in their religion, Roman Catholicism, the legal system and the concept of westernisation, all of which were introduced by some force within the colony. These changes profoundly influenced some sections of the people giving them a different identity, and they became known as Luso-Indians or Indo-Portuguese. The history of *Estado da India* is thus associated with Portugal and her colonies.

   Though in the *Estado da India* there were some uprisings against Portuguese domination, the spirited political awakening of the Goans came as British India was approaching her independence. On June 18, 1946, Ram Manohar Lohia, who had come to Goa at the invitation of Julião Menezes, launched a movement for civil liberties. Many Goans actively participated in the movement. Some of the important Goan intellectuals and leaders who supported it were Tristão de Bragança Cunha, Rama Krishna Hegde, Purushotam Kakodkar, Laxmikant Bhembre and José Inácio Candido de Loyola. These five were later deported and incarcerated in the Peniche jail in Portugal.

   On December 19, 1961, the government of Prime Minister Jawaharlal Nehru used armed force to liberate the *Estado da India* from Portuguese rule that had lasted for four hundred and fifty-one years.

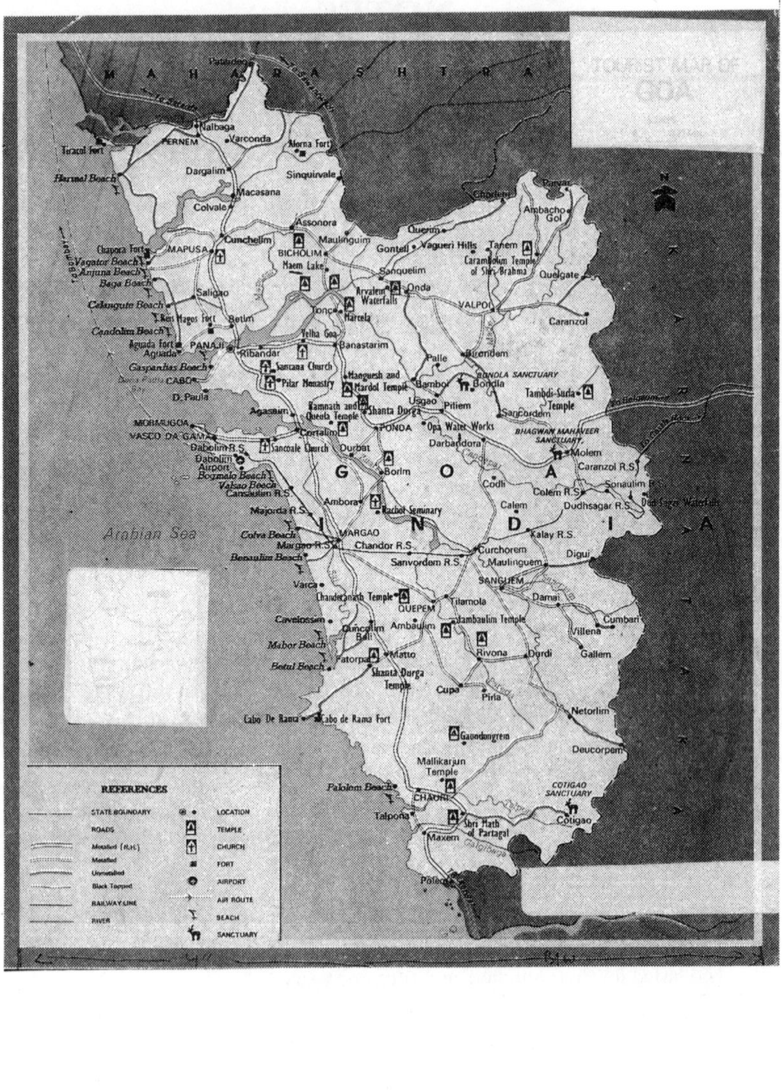
M A H A R A S H T R A
Pernem
Nalbaga
Varconda
Alorna Fort
Teracol Fort
Harmal Beach
Dargalim
Sinquirvale
Macasana
Colvale
Assonora
Chapora Fort
Vagator Beach
Anjuna Beach
Baga Beach
MAPUSA
Cunchelim
Maulinguim
BICHOLIM
Maem Lake
Gontell
Vagueri Hills
Tanem
Querim
Chorlem
Parvar
Ambacho Gol
Sanquelim
Onda
Arvalem Waterfalls
Saligao
Calangute Beach
Reis Magos Fort
Betim
Candolim Beach
Aguada Fort
Aguada
PANAJI
Ribandar
Tonca
Marcela
Velha Goa
Banastarim
VALPOI
Quelgate
Caranzol
Gaspandias Beach
CABO
D. Paula
Santana Church
Pilar Monastry
Manguesh and Mardol Temple
Palle
Birondem
Bambol
Bondla
BONDLA SANCTUARY
Tambdi-Surla Temple
Usgao
Pitiem
Sancordem
Agassaim
Ramnath and Queula Temple
Shanta Durga
PONDA
Opa Water Works
MORMUGOA
VASCO DA GAMA
Dabolim R.S.
Dabolim Airport
Cortalim
Sancoale Church
Durbat
Darbandora
BHAGWAN MAHAVEER SANCTUARY
Molem
Caranzol R.S.
Bogmalo Beach
Velsao Beach
Cansaulim R.S.
G O A
Borim
Codli
Colem R.S.
Sonaulim R.S.
Amborа
Rachol Seminary
Calem
Dudhsagar R.S.
Majorda R.S.
Colva Beach
MARGAO
Margao R.S.
Chandor R.S.
I N D I A
Kalay R.S.
Arabian Sea
Benaulim Beach
Curchorem
Digui
Sanvordem R.S.
Maulinguem
SANGUEM
Varca
Chandrenath Temple
QUEPEM
Tilamola
Damai
Cavelossim
Cuncolim
Bali
Ambaulim
Jambaulim Temple
Cumbari
Villena
Mobor Beach
Betul Beach
Fatorpa
Matto
Rivona
Dordi
Gallem
Shanta Durga Temple
Cupa
Pirla
Netorlim
Cabo De Rama
Cabo de Rama Fort
Gaundongrem
Deucorpem
Mallikarjun Temple
Palolem Beach
CHAURI
COTIGAO SANCTUARY
Talpona
Shri Math of Partagal
Cotigao
Maxem
Poleo
REFERENCES
STATE BOUNDARY
ROADS
Metalled (N.H.)
Metalled
Unmetalled
Black Topped
RAILWAY LINE
RIVER
LOCATION
TEMPLE
CHURCH
FORT
AIRPORT
AIR ROUTE
BEACH
SANCTUARY

INDEX